FOOD AND TRANSFORMATION IN
ANCIENT MEDITERRANEAN LITERATURE

WRITINGS FROM THE GRECO-ROMAN WORLD SUPPLEMENT SERIES

Clare K. Rothschild, General Editor

Number 14

FOOD AND TRANSFORMATION IN ANCIENT MEDITERRANEAN LITERATURE

Meredith J. C. Warren

Atlanta

Copyright © 2019 by Meredith J. C. Warren

All rights reserved. No part of this work may be reproduced or transmitted in any form or by any means, electronic or mechanical, including photocopying and recording, or by means of any information storage or retrieval system, except as may be expressly permitted by the 1976 Copyright Act or in writing from the publisher. Requests for permission should be addressed in writing to the Rights and Permissions Office, SBL Press, 825 Houston Mill Road, Atlanta, GA 30329 USA.

Library of Congress Cataloging-in-Publication Data

Names: Warren, Meredith J. C., author.
Title: Food and transformation in ancient Mediterranean literature / by Meredith J. C. Warren.
Description: Atlanta : SBL Press, 2019. | Series: Writings from the Greco-Roman world Supplement series ; Number 14 | Includes bibliographical references and index.
Identifiers: 2019000484 (print) | LCCN 2019009641 (ebook) | ISBN 9780884143574 (ebk.) | ISBN 9781628372380 (pbk. : alk. paper) | ISBN 9780884143567 (hbk. : alk. paper)
Subjects: Food—Religious aspects. | Classical literature—History and criticism
Classification: LCC BL65.F65 (ebook) | LCC BL65.F65 W37 2019 (print) | DDC 809/.93382—dc23
LC record available at https://lccn.loc.gov/2019000484

Printed on acid-free paper.

Dedicated to my writing group,
Sara Parks and Shayna Sheinfeld,
without whom this book would not have been written.

Contents

Acknowledgments ix
Abbreviations xi

Introduction 1

1. Persephone Traditions 19

2. 4 Ezra 37

3. Revelation 59

4. Joseph and Aseneth 75

5. Apuleius's *Metamorphoses* 101

6. The Passion of Perpetua and Felicitas 129

Conclusion 151

Bibliography 159
Index of Ancient Texts 177
Index of Modern Authors 185
Index of Terms 188

Acknowledgments

I am indebted to a number of people who were instrumental in helping me wrench this idea out of my head and into a book. First is Ellen Bradshaw Aitken, who first pointed out to me that Aseneth's honeycomb might not be unique. Nicolae Roddy also helped me develop hierophagy as the term to describe this literary genre. Sune Auken talked through aspects of genre theory with me. Shayna Sheinfeld suggested I look at 4 Ezra for an example of hierophagy.

I am grateful to the Fonds de recherche du Québec Post-Doctoral Fellowship of the Government of Québec for awarding me the postdoctoral funding that allowed me to begin this project in earnest and for Adele Reinhartz at the University of Ottawa for helping me develop my research.

I probably could have written something approximating a book by myself, but it would not have been fit to read without the critical editing of my writing group, nor would I have had the encouragement and support I needed to keep working on it, little by little. Thank you, Sara Parks and Shayna Sheinfeld. In that light, I would like to thank my Jessop Left comrades and the friendships forged during 2018 USS strike picket lines, whose camaraderie and sharp workplace analysis helped me learn to carve out time for myself, but also to discover what I value in my job.

My family was and is ever supportive. I thank my patient parents, who gamely kept straight faces every time I told them the book still was not finished and whose constant encouragement made me feel like I could do it. Last but not by any means least, I thank my husband, who cheerfully moved continents for me, put up with my bad writing days and celebrated my good ones, and is an all-around catch.

Abbreviations

Primary Sources

1 En.	1 Enoch
2 En.	2 Enoch
2 Bar.	2 Baruch
3 Bar.	3 Baruch
Achill.	Statius, *Achilleid*
Agr.	Cato, *De agricultura*; Columella, *De re agricultura*
Alex.	Nicander, *Alexipharmaca*
Amat. narr.	Plutarch, *Amatoriae narrations*
An.	Tertullian, *De Anima*
An. orig.	Augustine, *De anima et eius origine*
Antr. nymph.	Porphyry, *De antro nymphorum*
Apoc. Ab.	Apocalypse of Abraham
Apoc. Adam	Apocalypse of Adam
Argon.	Apollonius of Rhodes, *Argonautica*
Aug.	Suetonius, Divus Augustus
b.	Babylonian Talmud
Bib.	Apoloodorus, *Bibliotheca*
Bib. hist.	Diodorus Siculus, *Bibliotheca historica*
Contra haer.	Ephrem the Syrian, *Hymnni contra haereses*
Cor.	Tertullian, *De corona militis*
De an.	Aristotle, *De anima*
Descr.	Pausanias, *Description of Greece*
Dion.	Nonnos, *Dionysiaca*
Div. haer.	Filastrius of Brescia, *Diversarum hereseon liber*
Ebr.	Philo, *De ebrietate*
Fast.	Ovid, *Fasti*
Fug.	Philo, *De fuga et invention*
Galb.	Suetonius, *Galba*

Georg.	Vergil, *Georgica*
Haer.	Augustine, *De haeresibus*; Praedestinatus, *Praedestinatorum haeresis*
Hag.	Hagigah
Hel.	Euripides, *Helen*
Hist.	Herodotus, *Histories*
Hist. an.	Aristotle, *Historia animalium*
Hom. Dem.	Homeric Hymn to Demeter
Il.	Homer, *Iliad*
Jos. Asen.	Joseph and Aseneth
Ker.	Kerithot
Leg.	Plato, *Leges*
Marc.	Tertullian, *Adversus Marcionem*
Mat. med.	Dioscorides, *De materia medica*
Med.	Celsus, *De Medicina*
Metam.	Apuleius, *Metamorphoses*; Ovid, *Metamorphoses*
Nat.	Pliny, *Naturalis historia*
Od.	Homer, *Odyssey*
Ol.	Pindar, *Olympian Odes*
Onir.	Artemidorus, *Onirocritica*
Or.	Aelius Aristides, *Orations*
Orest.	Euripides, *Orestes*
Pan.	Epiphanius of Salamis, *Panarion*
Paneg.	Isocrates, *Panegyrikos*
Pass. Perp.	The Passion of Perpetua and Felicitas
Phars.	Lucan, *Pharsalia*
Pud.	Tertullian, *De pudicitia*
Sens.	Aristotle, *De sensu et sensibilibus*
Sifre Num.	Sifre Numbers
Sol.	Plutarch, *Life of Solon*
T. Ab.	Testament of Abraham
Theog.	Hesiod, *Theogony*
Ther.	Nicander, *Theriaca*
Verr.	Cicero, *In Verrem*
Yevam.	Yevamot

Secondary Sources

AB	Anchor Bible

AGJU	Arbeiten zur Geschichte des antiken Judentums und des Urchristentums
AIL	Ancient Israel and Its Literature
AJEC	Ancient Judaism and Early Christianity
ANF	Roberts, Alexander, and James Donaldson, eds. *The Ante-Nicene Fathers: Translations of the Writings of the Fathers Down to A.D. 325*. 10 vols. 1885–1887. Repr, Peabody, MA: Hendrickson, 1994.
ANRW	Temporini, Hildegard, and Wolfgang Haase, eds. *Aufstieg und Niedergang der römischen Welt: Geschichte und Kultur Roms im Spiegel der neueren Forschung*. Part 2, *Principat*. Berlin: de Gruyter, 1972–.
ASSR	*Archives de sciences sociales des religions*
ATANT	Abhandlungen zur Theologie des Alten und Neuen Testaments
B	Burchard, Christoph. *Joseph und Aseneth*. PVTG 5. Leiden: Brill, 2003.
BARIS	BAR International Series
BETL	Bibliotheca ephemeridum theologicarum lovaniensium
BibInt	Biblical Interpretation
BZNW	Beihefte zur Zeitschrift für die neutestamentliche Wissenschaft
CurBR	*Currents in Biblical Research*
DNP	H. Cancik and H. Schneider, eds. *Der Neue Pauly: Enzyklopädie der Antike*. Stuttgart: Calwer, 1996–.
EJL	Early Judaism and Its Literature
FCB	Feminist Companion to the Bible
FRLANT	Forschungen zur Religion und Literatur des Alten und Neuen Testaments
HBM	Hebrew Bible Monographs
HCS	Hellenistic Culture and Society
HSCP	*Harvard Studies in Classical Philology*
Historia	*Historia: Zeitschrift für Alte Geschichte*
HTR	*Harvard Theological Review*
HUCA	*Hebrew Union College Annual*
Int	*Interpretation: A Journal of Bible and Theology*
JBL	*Journal of Biblical Literature*

JJS	*Journal of Jewish Studies*
JRS	*Journal of Roman Studies*
JSJ	*Journal for the Study of Judaism*
JSJSup	Supplements to the Journal for the Study of Judaism
JSNT	*Journal for the Study of the New Testament*
JSP	*Journal for the Study of the Pseudepigrapha*
JSPSup	Journal for the Study of the Pseudepigrapha Supplement Series
LCL	Loeb Classical Library
LS	Liddell, Henry George, and Robert Scott. *An Intermediate Greek-English Lexicon: Founded upon the Seventh Edition of Liddell and Scott's Greek-English Lexicon.* New York: Harper & Brothers, 1889.
LSJ	Liddell, Henry George, Robert Scott, and Henry Stuart Jones. *A Greek-English Lexicon.* 9th ed. with revised supplement. Oxford: Clarendon, 1996.
LTQ	*Lexington Theological Quarterly*
LXX	Septuagint
NETS	Pietersma, Albert, and Benjamin G. Wright. *A New English Translation of the Septuagint.* Oxford: Oxford University Press, 2014.
NewDocs	Horsley, G. H. R., et al., eds. *New Documents Illustrating Early Christianity.* North Ryde, NSW: The Ancient History Documentary Research Centre, Macquarie University, 1981–.
NovT	*Novum Testamentum*
OCD	Hornblower, Simon, and Antony Spawforth, eds. *Oxford Classical Dictionary.* 4th ed. Oxford: Oxford University Press, 2012.
OTP	Charlesworth, James H., ed. *Old Testament Pseudepigrapha.* 2 vols. New York: Doubleday, 1983–1985.
P.Oxy.	Grenfell, Bernard P., et al., eds. *The Oxyrhynchus Papyri.* London: Egypt Exploration Fund, 1898–.
Ph	Philonenko, Marc. *Joseph et Aséneth: Introduction, texte critique, traduction et notes.* SVTP 13. Leiden: Brill, 1968.
PVTG	Pseudepigrapha Veteris Testamenti Graece
Q	Qur'an
RSV	Revised Standard Version

SBLMS	Society of Biblical Literature Monograph Series
SBLTT	Society of Biblical Literature Texts and Translations
SC	Sources chrétiennes
SEG	Supplementum epigraphicum graecum
SR	*Studies in Religion/Sciences Religieuses*
SymS	Symposium Series
WBC	Word Biblical Commentary
WUNT	Wissenschaftliche Untersuchungen zum Neuen Testament

Introduction

Whether we recognize it or not, taste informs our interactions with the world, filtering information through our cultural lenses and signifying all manner of social meanings. Metaphors of flavors garnish our language: melodies are sweet; memories are bitter; we are left with a bad taste in our mouths; when frustrated, we might use salty language. Eating and tasting, and their constructed meanings, are reflected in the literature we produce and consume. Each morsel is a loaded symbol that is ingested and digested according to expectations we may not even know we have. Ancient literature likewise works through assumed symbolic associations that reflect understandings about food, eating, and taste. Sometimes food and its ingestion are ordinary, or part of a well-known meal practice; sometimes it is very peculiar. In certain cases, eating brings about unexpected results, such as the transformation of the eater or the opening of windows into another realm. Such examples in literature are relatively common, but neither the pattern itself, nor the reason for the pattern, have been investigated.

The purpose of this book is to articulate a category of narrative-level transformative eating. I call this category *hierophagy*, a term that has been used, infrequently and uncritically, to point to specialized, sacred eating.[1]

---

1. Apart from my own use of the term (Meredith J. C. Warren, "Tasting the Little Scroll: A Sensory Analysis of Divine Interaction in Revelation 10:8–10," *JSNT* 40 [2017]: 101–19; Warren, "My Heart Poured Forth Understanding: *4 Ezra*'s Fiery Cup as Hierophagic Consumption," *SR* 44 [2015]: 320–33; Warren, "Tastes from Beyond: Persephone's Pomegranate and Otherworldly Consumption in Antiquity," in *Taste and the Ancient Senses*, ed. Kelli C. Rudolph [London: Routledge, 2017]; Warren, "Like Dew from Heaven: Honeycomb, Religious Identity and Transformation in *Joseph and Aseneth*" [MA Thesis, McGill, 2006]) and two conference presentations by Nicolae Roddy ("'Taste and See…': Hierophagy as Religious Experience" [paper presented at the Trends of Ancient Jewish and Christian Mysticism Seminar (TAJCM), University of Dayton, 7 March 2008]; "Fill Your Stomach with It: Hierophagy as Religious Experi-

My use of hierophagy here represents a significant development in definition from these brief previous allusions. This category of transformative eating is a recurring pattern of language that expresses both shared and particular meanings across several ancient texts; this pattern also reflects something of the expectations of the societies that found this pattern expressive.

My narrative-level approach to the primary sources is differentiated from a historical or sociological approach in that I will consider the literary ramifications of transformative eating rather than any links this type of eating may or may not have to historical ritual or sacred meals. Examining texts at the narrative level allows the hierophagic event to be understood as part of the literary toolbox used by ancient authors to transmit a certain understanding of the relationship between God and mortals, heaven and earth.

Definition

My definition of hierophagy emerges from a close reading of the texts examined in the present volume, but also applies to other examples not treated here. In its essence, hierophagy is a mechanism by which characters in narrative cross boundaries from one realm to another. In all cases, and as the term suggests, this is accomplished by the character consuming some otherworldly item.[2] With specific contexts removed, a generic pattern emerges in which a mortal character interacts with another realm.

---

ence" [paper presentenced at the Annual Meeting of the Society of Biblical Literature, San Diego, CA, 20 November 2007]), the term is only used in two other places. Roddy suggested I use the term *hierophagy* to describe the phenomenon I was examining in my research. At the time Roddy understood that he was responsible for the neologism but later found it referred to in Henri Desroche, *Jacob and the Angel* (Amherst: University of Massachusetts Press, 1973), 40 n.18. Desroche gives credit for the term to F. A. Isambert, review of *Religion and Society in Tension*, by Charles Y. Glock and Rodney Stark, *ASSR* 21 (1966): 183–84, but I have not been able to find the term in this citation. I have since also found the term in the work of Oskar Pfister, who simply defines it as a "sacral meal [that] represents the eating of the god or of the holy entity" (*Christianity and Fear: A Study in History and in the Psychology and Hygiene of Religion*, trans. W. H. Johnston [London: Allen & Unwin, 1948], 262).

2. While certain patterns emerge in terms of what kinds of things are consumed, the item is not always food—I merely use the word *food* here and throughout as a general term indicating that something is ingested, whether or not that item is liquid or solid, or even edible in an ordinary context.

The character ingests something from that realm, and the act of eating precipitates a change in the character such that the character is more closely related to the other realm. The eating of this otherworldly food brings about three specific transformations, both physical and ontological:

(1) *Hierophagy binds the person to the place of origin of that food.* All of the incidents of ritual eating to be discussed below result in the eater having some close tie to another world. This is most obvious with the Persephone story and Perpetua's vision. Persephone, having eaten the pomegranate, is bound to remain in Hades, while Perpetua's cheese meal points to her impending access to heaven as a martyr.

(2) *Hierophagy transforms the eater in some way.* While the most extreme case of transformation is Lucius's in *Metamorphoses*, since he transforms from an animal into a human being, the other recipients of this kind of food are also changed in their own ways. Ezra, Ezekiel, and John of Patmos, for example, have new abilities after their hierophagic meals: the prophets are given the ability to speak to their audience and to prophesy truly. Joseph and Aseneth also participates in this phenomenon of transformation: Aseneth becomes physically transformed, so much so that the members of her family scarcely recognize her (Jos. Asen. 18.9), and is described as chosen (like the visitor, the bees, and Joseph himself) after eating the honeycomb (18.11).

(3) *Hierophagy transmits knowledge.* Some eaters of otherworldly food receive knowledge directly related to their heavenly situation. Perpetua is a clear example of this phenomenon since she receives the knowledge of her impending martyrdom. Ezekiel and John eat the scroll in order to gain special divine knowledge of what God wants them to prophesy, while Ezra drinks from the cup in order to re-receive the Torah and hidden books, just like Moses received the Torah before him. Lucius, after he is transformed, becomes initiated into the mysteries of Isis. Aseneth's visitor tells her that the mysteries of the Most High had been revealed to her.

This study is founded on a literary analysis of ancient texts, closely reading and exploring, on the one hand, the role of the hierophagic scene within the overall narrative and, on the other hand, the commonalities among the hierophagic scenes across the variety of texts under examination. These commonalities, however, do not suppose a direct influence among the texts that make use of the genre of hierophagy. In other words, except for Ezekiel and Revelation, the inclusion of hierophagy in these narratives is due to shared cultural expectations within the ancient Mediterranean milieu rather than literary dependence of one text upon another.

These narratives use the consumption of otherworldly food to convey the idea of transformation because of ancient assumptions about how food facilitates the transgression of boundaries.

Approaching texts as representatives of cultural ideas about the relationship between this world and other worlds also means that specific dates for textual production do not play a significant role in my analysis. For the most part, the texts I examine here fall into a range of three hundred years on either side of the zero-mark, although some texts touched upon briefly, such as Ezekiel and the Homeric Hymn to Demeter, are older than this and are analyzed for the purpose of elucidating related narratives that do fall in this range. This is not to say that hierophagy as a narrative phenomenon is contained within this range of dates; on the contrary, much earlier examples (i.e., the story of the fall in Genesis) and much later examples (*Alice in Wonderland* [1865 (film 1951)], *The Matrix* [1999], *Spirited Away* [2001], etc.) exist. Rather, this is the period of time in which a high concentration of texts have made use of hierophagy, and thus my chosen era allows for the most fruitful comparison of such texts.

Genre as Fictional Action[3]

To understand patterns of discourse across a range of texts and cultures, it is necessary to employ a system of analysis that articulates how these patterns emerge and diverge and that explains their resonance internally and in a broader context. Genre as an analytical method allows for such an explanation. Traditional ideas of genre in literary studies are not altogether distinct from form criticism in biblical studies; in broad strokes, these categories of analysis can be useful for understanding the relationship of texts as a whole to each other. However, the pattern of discourse I identify in this book requires more precise tools. Carolyn R. Miller's 1984 work on genre as social action created a more precise way of understanding genre that moved beyond Aristotelian genre categories and their derivatives.[4] She proposes a five-part understanding of genre:

---

3. This heading is taken from Sune Auken, "Genre as Fictional Action: On the Use of Rhetorical Genres in Fiction," *Nordisk Tidsskrift for Informationsvidenskab og Kulturformidling* 2.3 (2013): 19–28.

4. Carolyn R. Miller, "Genre as Social Action," *Quarterly Journal of Speech* 70 (1984): 152.

1. Genre refers to a conventional category of discourse based in large-scale typification of rhetorical action; as action, it acquires meaning from situation and from the social context in which that situation arose.
2. As meaningful action, genre is interpretable by means of rules; genre rules occur at a relatively high level on a hierarchy of rules for symbolic interaction.
3. Genre is distinct from form: form is the more general term used at all levels of the hierarchy. Genre is a form at one particular level that is a fusion of lower-level forms and characteristic substance.
4. Genre serves as the substance of forms at higher levels; as recurrent patterns of language use, genres help constitute the substance of our cultural life.
5. A genre is a rhetorical means for mediating private intentions and social exigence; it motivates by connecting the private with the public, the singular with the recurrent.[5]

Miller's definition allows intercourse between the social realm and the realm of discourse, articulating that genres are culture-bound ways of expressing even the smallest action and ways of creating meaning from those actions. In other words, genres are functional and bring about action in those participating in the discourse.

Miller's theoretical approach to genre resides in the real, social world of human interaction, moving away for the most part from analysis of literature or narrative worlds. Sune Auken has begun to apply Miller's analysis of genre in the social realm to the fictional realm. Auken points out that, because all characters within fiction are creations, rather than real social beings, the only social action that occurs takes place within the narrative realm and has no effect whatsoever on the social relationships of the real world.[6] However, internal to the narrative these generic actions advance the action of the story. Within the fictional frameworks social action takes place and creates meaning that characters react to and understand. The creation of this meaning, just as in the real, social world, is understandable within that created world and its systems.[7] Auken discusses human social ends that characters attempt to achieve according to certain genres; however, the social must include not

---

5. Miller, "Genre as Social Action," 163.
6. Auken, "Genre as Fictional Action," 20.
7. Auken, "Genre as Fictional Action," 22.

just human interactions but also interactions with the divine realm, which likewise take place according to structures of meaning.

I agree with Auken that the analysis of genre as social action can apply to the fictional realm. Indeed, it is this kind of analysis that allows hierophagy to be visible. In other words, as a genre, hierophagy is a symbolic way of expressing meaning within a culture that holds certain expectations around category hierarchy and order, such as the division of heaven and earth, the implications of taste and eating, and the accessibility of the former by way of the latter.

A genre analysis of hierophagy allows me to remain in the world of narrative and discourse, even as I analyze the social, cosmological, and ontological relationships affected by the hierophagic act. Even if these meals were to reflect eating rituals practiced in a historical community—and I make no claim either way—the representation of eating otherworldly food in narrative serves a distinct function within the text.[8] In other words, this study treats the narrative world as worthy of study in its own right, with its own conventions and producing its own realities. As such, hierophagy participates in what might be called a "ritual in ink"—a phrase used by Jorg Rüpke to highlight the importance of the narrative world, especially in its depiction of performance:

> If rituals matter in society, literary rituals must matter in texts. Rituals in ink matter. Ancient texts do not constitute a hermetically sealed realm.

---

8. I must emphasize that hierophagy is not the pharmacological altering of an individual's state through a drug. Part of the reason why this is not the case is that the items consumed in hierophagy are frequently not considered edible, or they would be considered edible but for some small modification (e.g., a cup full of liquid is ordinarily consumable, but a cup full of flames is not). A pharmacological approach to religious eating—as has been attempted, unsuccessfully in my opinion, by John M. Allegro, Carl A. P. Ruck, Blaise D. Staples, and Clark Heinrich, among others—obscures the narrative-level activity that this type of meal brings about. Indeed, given that we know little about the actual activities of ancient mystics around the Mediterranean, we cannot responsibly say anything about whether consumptive practices described in narratives reflect actual practices. My current focus on the use of hierophagic behaviours in the narrative realm respects indigenous categories of thinking as preserved in ancient texts. For examples of what I am not doing, see, e.g., John Marco Allegro, *The Sacred Mushroom and the Cross: A Study of the Nature and Origins of Christianity within the Fertility Cults of the Ancient Near East* (Garden City, NY: Doubleday, 1970); Carl A. P. Ruck, Blaise D. Staples, and Clark Heinrich, *The Apples of Apollo: Pagan and Christian Mysteries of the Eucharist* (Durham, NC: Carolina Academic Press, 2001).

> Texts participate in the wider society in which they were created. In that space texts have a performative dimension regardless of the mimetic or fictitious character of their embedded rituals.[9]

Or, as Auken writes,

> regardless of whether imitation is to make an action mirror real life or simply to make it look real, the genres brought into the story will, one way or the other, be recognizable from the culture surrounding the work, and knowledge of the genres of a given culture may be a prerequisite for understanding its narratives.[10]

The importance of narrative-level performance to the narrative events has been underappreciated; this study participates in the move to prioritize an examination of this kind of event, especially as it reflects not an equivalent historical ritual, but rather a pervasive worldview that has crafted the genre governing the accessibility of other realms.

Indeed, rather than revealing a one-to-one reflection of historical meal rites in antiquity, the examples of hierophagy investigated here reflect a cultural understanding of how otherworldly food works to transform. This understanding is part of a "genre of social action,"[11] preserved in fiction. Our understanding of patterns of engagement with our surroundings, which is to say our ability to anticipate generic elements in our everyday lives,[12] is the same mechanism by which we communicate and interpret meaning in literature. It is also the reason we recognize "utterances"[13] that play with genre: "the anticipation, however, need not necessarily be fulfilled. It can instead be the subject of counter-play, modification, or parody, thus activating the viewers' pre-existing knowledge in the course

---

9. Jörg Rüpke, Introduction to *Rituals in Ink: A Conference on Religion and Literary Production in Ancient Rome Held at Stanford University in February 2002*, ed. Alessandro Barchiesi, Jörg Rüpke, and Susan A. Stephens, Postdamer altertumswissenschaftliche beiträge 10 (Stuttgart: Steiner, 2004), vii–viii.

10. Auken, "Genre as Fictional Action," 22.

11. Miller, "Genre as Social Action," 151–67.

12. Auken, "Genre and Interpretation," 163.

13. Utterances in the context of hierophagy refer to the food given to the eater: the honeycomb, the roses, the cheese, the scroll, the pomegranate, and the cup. Each of these utterances participates in the genre, contributing to its overall form, while also diverging from it in ways that are meaningful to the individual narrative.

of meaning-making of this specific utterance."[14] This preexisting knowledge is crucial for hierophagy: it is this knowledge, shared among the ancient communities that produced texts, that allows authors and readers to create meaning out of the hierophagic experience. That is, the presence in literature of so many examples of this kind of transformational eating suggests that this literary genre represents real-world expectations of the ramifications of consuming heavenly food, with or without a hypothetical practice behind it. "Genre manifests existing cultural norms."[15] Genres cannot exist without shared cultural knowledge. The present book leaves aside any investigation of historical ritual(s) behind these examples, since (1) the purpose of this work is to trace the genre and its function and (2) such reconstructions from narrative are notoriously difficult, as previous studies of many of the texts examined here have proven.[16]

Two important features of many of the narratives examined in the present volume warrant particular attention. First, many biblical examples of hierophagy are preserved in apocalyptic or protoapocalyptic texts; many of those Jewish or Christian noncanonical texts that could not be properly termed apocalypses also embed their hierophagic events in apocalyptic scenes. The non-Jewish and non-Christian examples of hierophagy, on the other hand, do not participate in the apocalyptic genre, even though the Hellenistic world "provided the matrix for apocalyptic literature."[17] Thus, while Christian and Jewish examples of hierophagy use apocalyptic imagery to convey the transformation that occurs as a result of eating otherworldly food, non-Jewish/non-Christian examples do not. Perhaps this is because Jews and Christians used apocalypses to talk about the heavenly realm—after all, one of the features by which apocalypses are defined is a dualistic "spatial axis" of the earthly and the heavenly realms.[18]

Second, and perhaps relatedly, many of the examples examined in this study depict the hierophagic event as part of a vision or a dream. The

---

14. Auken, "Genre and Interpretation," 163.

15. Sune Auken, "Genre and Interpretation," in *Genre and ...* , ed. Sune Auken, Palle Schantz Lauridsen, and Anders Juhl Rasmussen, Copenhagen Studies in Genre 2 (Copenhagen: Ekbatana, 2015), 155 n. 1.

16. For a discussion of previous interpretations of the texts relevant to this study, see the dedicated chapter for each text.

17. John J. Collins, *The Apocalyptic Imagination: An Introduction to Jewish Apocalyptic Literature* (Grand Rapids: Eerdmans, 1998), 37.

18. John J. Collins, "Introduction: Towards the Morphology of a Genre," *Semeia* 14 (1979): 7.

fact that the events under discussion here frequently take place in dreams does not take away from their narrative reality. As Frances Flannery-Dailey points out, "whereas we tend to view dreams as unreal, interior, subjective phenomena, ancient peoples believed that some dreams were genuine visits from deities or their divine representatives."[19] Thus, the distinction that we moderns maintain between "dream" and "vision," where one is imaginary and the other true, is not enforceable in ancient modes of thought. Whether while sleeping or while awake, interaction with the divine sphere was taken as a reasonable, if infrequent, occurrence—one which is represented also in literature which deals with how human beings envision their relationship to the other realms.

Other Worlds, Other Foods

In reviewing the history of scholarship on otherworldly journeys and access to divine realms, I articulate the importance of the porous-but-present boundary between worlds in the cultural expectation of the ancient Mediterranean cultures, and as such, the significance that mechanisms for breaching those boundaries held. Many ancient texts demonstrate a preoccupation with regard to the difference between angelic/otherworldly food and mortal/earthly food, even in texts that do not contain hierophagic events. The anxiety displayed by angelic characters in mortal disguise at the prospect of eating human food, for instance, suggests that divine/mortal geographical boundaries are also reflected in the distinction between heavenly and mortal foods, as the texts under examination in this volume also illustrate.

One example of this porous boundary is the Testament of Abraham, a first-century CE text that does not include a hierophagic scene but that nonetheless expresses angelic apprehension at the prospect of consuming earthly food. In the Testament of Abraham, the angel Michael visits Abraham to give him the news of his impending death. While there, Abraham observes culturally expected hospitality rites and presents the angel with a table of food for the two to share. Michael returns to heaven to ask God for advice, since, as an angel, he cannot eat human food.[20] Michael argues, "Lord, all the heavenly spirits are incorporeal, and they neither drink

---

19. Frances Flannery-Dailey, *Dreamers, Scribes, and Priests: Jewish Dreams in the Hellenistic and Roman Eras*, JSJSup 90 (Leiden: Brill, 2004), 1.
20. See also, David Goodman, "Do Angels Eat?," *JJS* 37 (1986): 160–75.

nor eat, and he has set a table with an abundance of good things that are earthly and corruptible" (T. Ab. 4 [Recension A]).[21] Michael is incapable or unwilling to eat the same food as Abraham—it is corruptible, just as Abraham is susceptible to the death Michael is about to pronounce upon him.[22] This division between heavenly and mortal creatures seems to be articulated in what each category of being consumes.[23]

This culturally understood division between human and divine food can also be observed in certain accounts of how human beings prepare for contact with the divine. So, for instance, Moses does not eat during his encounter with God on the mountain (Exod 34:28); Daniel does not eat food or drink wine for three weeks prior to his vision (Dan 10:2–3); Ezra fasts prior to his second and third revelatory episodes (4 Ezra 5.20; 6.35); and Baruch fasts before his encounters with the divine (2 Bar. 5.7; 9.1; 12.5; 20.5–21.1; 43.3; 47.1; 86.1). In fasting, humans separate themselves from ordinary life, creating space for the divine realm to punctuate the earthly realm.[24] Hierophagy, however, involves eating the food of another realm,

---

21. E. P. Sanders, trans. "Testaments of Abraham," *OTP* 1:871–902.

22. The issue is resolved by God, who sends with Michael a "devouring spirit," invisible to Abraham, which will consume all the food that Michael brings to his mouth while making it appear that Michael himself is sharing in Abraham's table.

23. Of note in this discussion are two passages in the Qur'an which discuss the difficulties in sharing table fellowship with angels. Quran Hud 11:69–70 discusses the visit of the angels to Abraham at Mamre (cf. Gen 18:1–8, where the three visitors Abraham receives do eat): "Our messengers came to Abraham with good news. They said: 'Peace!'; he said: 'Peace!', and immediately set about bringing in a roast calf. When he saw their hands did not reach out towards it, he felt uneasy with them and started to be afraid of them. They said: 'Do not act afraid; we have been sent to Lot's folk'" (trans. Irving, Ahmad, and Ahsan). Here Abraham serves the messengers according to ordinary hospitality customs, but the angelic visitors do not eat, which makes Abraham uneasy. There is no explanation given as to why these divine messengers do not eat; rather, it is expected within the text that the assumed readers would understand the reason behind this break with hospitality customs. In Q Adh-Dhariyat 51:24–37, we read a similar version of the same account: "Has the report of Abraham's honored guests ever come to you, when they entered his home and said: 'Peace [be upon you]!'? He said: '[On you be] peace!' [even though] they were people he did not know. So he slipped off to his family and fetched a fattened calf, and brought it up to them. He said: 'Will you not eat?' He felt a fear concerning them. They said: 'Don't be afraid,' and gave him the news of a clever lad" (trans. Irving, Ahmad, and Ahsan).

24. Carla Sulzbach, "When Going on a Heavenly Journey, Travel Light and Dress Appropriately," *JSP* 19 (2010): 163–93, esp. 183–84. See also Thomas B. Dozeman, *God on the Mountain*, SBLMS 37 (Atlanta: Scholars Press, 1989), 34.

which only those beings residing there are able to consume. Otherworldly food yields different results than the simple absence of human food can bring about.

Just as humans might avoid earthly food in order to gain proximity to the divine realm, so too might divine beings avoid mortal food, lest they compromise their divinity. Many ancient texts indicate that heavenly food is eaten by the gods instead of earthly food. That is, the prohibition on angels eating earthly food is matched by a tendency of gods to eat only heavenly food. In the Septuagint, the Wisdom of Solomon describes manna, food from heaven, as ἀμβροσίας τροφῆς (19:21), and the History of the Rechabites recounts how the inhabitants of the Isles of the Blessed consume water that comes from the ground tasting like honey, that is, nectar (7.2; 11.4; 12.5). In the Protoevangelium of James, Mary is fed heavenly food by an angel (8.2), which Lily C. Vuong briefly notes points to Mary's special status.[25] Vuong likewise draws connections to certain narratives in early Judaism and Christianity where manna as divine food plays a role, but she neglects to include almost all of the texts that depict hierophagy. Nonetheless, this example, as with the others, signals how prevalent the same cultural expectations around heavenly food are that undergird hierophagy.

Comparisons between this biblical heavenly food and the ambrosia of the Homeric gods are therefore warranted.[26] Ambrosia and nectar are the food of the gods in Greek traditions.[27] This divine food is reserved for the gods and seems to be the source of immortality.[28] This food is ordinarily

---

25. Lily C. Vuong, *Gender and Purity in the Protevangelium of James* (Tübingen: Mohr Siebeck, 2013), 102–3.

26. Tobias Nicklas, "Food of Angels (Wis 16:20)," in *Studies in the Book of Wisdom*, ed. Géza G. Xeravits and József Zsengellér, JSJSup 142 (Leiden: Brill, 2010), 95; cf. Fritz Graf, "Ambrosia," *DNP* 1:581–82; K. Wernicke, "Ambrosia," in *Paulys Real-Encyclopädie der Classischen Altertums-wissenschaft* (Stuttgart: Calwer 1894): 1:1809–11.

27. See Emily Gowers on ambrosia as a metaphor for sweet kisses, and Sarah Hitch on wine so tasty that it is compared to this divine food. Emily Gowers, "Tasting the Roman World," in Rudolph, *Taste and the Ancient Senses*, 90–103; Sarah Hitch, "Tastes of Greek Poetry: From Homer to Aristophanes," in Rudolph, *Taste and the Ancient Senses*, 22–44. Hitch also addresses the dining event between Calypso and Odysseus in *Od.* 5.194–199. There, Hitch observes, the divine and mortal share space, allowing human proximity to the divine, but not food, marking their distinct natures.

28. Ambrosia literally means immortality. On the gods' consumption of ambrosia and nectar as opposed to mortal food, see *Il.* 5.342; in *Od.* 5.135, Calypso indicates

kept away from mortal people; for instance, when the goddess Calypso dines with Odysseus, we read that "the goddess gave him human food and drink. She sat and faced godlike Odysseus while slave girls brought her nectar and ambrosia" (Homer, *Od.* 5.197–199 [Wilson]). When human beings do interact with ambrosia or nectar, they do not eat it,[29] but rather it is poured on or into their bodies in order to prevent, for example, the corruption of a corpse (e.g., Patroclus [*Il.* 19.37–39], Sarpedon [*Il.* 16.670, 680]) or the experience of hunger (e.g., Achilles [*Il.* 19.352–354]).[30] It seems that ambrosia must be consumed through the mouth to have its full effect.[31] Above all, ambrosia as divine food is always contrasted with mortal food.[32]

It is notable that otherworldly food in the texts under examination here is frequently described as sweet. Perpetua awakes from her vision with a sweet taste in her mouth; the scrolls in Ezekiel and Revelation are described as sweet; and Aseneth eats honey itself.[33] The food of the gods in the Greek tradition is also associated with honey. In the Homeric Hymn to Hermes this is made explicit (559–562), and Porphyry, writing much later, also associates the food of the gods with honey (*Antr. nymph.* 15–19).[34] This sweetness finds echoes in the various traditions examined here—in

---

that she would have made Odysseus immortal (had he eaten ambrosia?) but for Zeus's command through Hermes.

29. Tantalus, a son of Zeus (and therefore half divine), was invited to share the gods' table and their immortal food, but squandered his opportunity when he stole ambrosia to bring back to his drinking companions (Euripides, *Orest.* 10; Pindar, *Ol.* 1.95).

30. See also Mark Bradley, "Introduction: Smell and the Ancient Senses," in *Smell and the Ancient Senses*, ed. Mark Bradley (London: Routledge, 2015), 4.

31. Apollonius, *Argon.* 4.869–872 implies that had Thetis been successful in completely anointing Achilles with ambrosia, he would have become immortal and ageless, which contradicts this idea. Later tradition (e.g., Statius, *Achill.* 1.122–223; 269–270; 480–481) replaces ambrosia as the mechanism of Achilles's potential immortality with the river Styx.

32. Ashley Clements, "Divine Scents and Presence," in Bradley, *Smell and the Ancient Senses*, 50.

33. The pomegranate that Persephone ingests and the roses eaten by Lucius are not explicitly depicted as sweet in the text, but are also not described as bitter.

34. Susan Scheinberg, "The Bee Maidens of the Homeric *Hymn to Hermes*," *HSCP* 83 (1979): 5; see also W. H. Roshcer, *Nektar und Ambrosia* (Leipzig: Teubner, 1883), 25 et passim. See also Ross Shepard Kraemer, *When Aseneth Met Joseph: A Late Antique Tale of the Biblical Patriarch and His Egyptian Wife, Reconsidered* (New York: Oxford

almost every case, the eater is left with the impression of having consumed something sweet, tasting like honey, even when the consumable would not naturally have that flavor, for example, a scroll. This sweet taste operates as a symbol by which the eater interprets his or her experience. Sweetness is representative[35] and participates in culturally governed expectations of meaning. Our interpretation of taste is bounded by intellectual and cultural categories—the perception of a right or wrong eating experience depends on whether the eater perceives the item ingested as belonging to an accepted edible category first and then on whether the experience of eating the item corresponds to one's expectations of that category. Carolyn Korsmeyer gives the example of a "fluffy yellow mound swallowed under the expectation that it is lemon sherbet"[36] when in fact it is butter. The surprise of expecting one taste and experiencing another is a familiar one and one which depends on a reorientation of categories in order to be reinterpreted as enjoyable or appropriate to eat. This kind of recognition through categorization also informs our understanding of hierophagy, since categories of taste are also at work here. Perpetua, for example, awakes from her vision with a sweet taste in her mouth and correctly interprets it; John of Patmos is forced to reinterpret his taste experience with the scroll, whose sweetness turns bitter once ingested. In the texts under examination here, ingestion creates meaning for the consumer.

Other Approaches to Eating

I have already said that interpreting how hierophagy works as a genre depends on the culturally held expectations. Representational foods and eating abound in ancient literature, and the culturally bound expectations of taste in general and sweetness in particular are part of their interpretation. Culturally held expectations about food and taste are one factor in understanding how hierophagy functions the way it does. Although I will give an overview of previous approaches to specific food items in individual chapters, there is one feature of ancient taste that potentially affects all the texts examined here and therefore undergirds hierophagy as

---

University Press, 1998), 169–71, which will be discussed in greater detail in the chapter on Aseneth.

35. Carolyn Korsmeyer, *Making Sense of Taste: Food and Philosophy* (Ithaca, NY: Cornell University Press, 1999), 115–18.

36. Korsmeyer, *Making Sense of Taste*, 90–91.

a genre. As I discussed above, ambrosia and nectar are associated with the divine realm in Greek, Roman, and early Jewish contexts; however, there are also several more specific associations with sweetness in biblical and early Jewish texts that point toward God's wisdom. In other words, while one factor of sweetness supports the element of hierophagy that binds the eater to the other realm, another factor highlights the knowledge-giving function of transformational eating of this genre. In their 2017 article, "Edible Media: The Confluence of Food and Learning in the Ancient Mediterranean," Steven Muir and Frederick Tappenden trace the prominent association between food and eating and learning in biblical texts.[37] From the tree in Gen 2:16–18 and 3:1–7 to the Psalms (19:10; 34:9) to the gospels (Matt 4:4) and to Paul (1 Cor 2:6–3:3), metaphors of tasting and eating are consistently used to point to the ingestion of information in ancient texts. As a metaphor, this is distinct from the genre of hierophagy, in which a literary character performs certain actions within a narrative. However, metaphors function to express meaning that is intended to be interpreted by readers; in that way, metaphors reflect the world that created them and its expectations. Food is a vehicle[38] by which ancient peoples understood acquiring knowledge. As such, while not identical with what happens in a hierophagic experience, food as metaphor for knowledge works to support hierophagy as a genre, since it articulates the societal association between food and eating and knowledge, whether divine or mortal.

Taste as a Sense

Since taste was considered one of the baser senses by some ancient philosophers,[39] the question of how it came to represent access to divine realms is key to this project. It is clear that for many philosophers, vision and hearing were at the top of the sensory hierarchy, since they were considered the means of acquiring knowledge, as opposed to touch and taste,

---

37. Steven Muir and Frederick S. Tappenden, "Edible Media: The Confluence of Food and Learning in the Ancient Mediterranean," *LTQ* 47 (2017): 123–47.

38. See Ivor A. Richards, *The Philosophy of Rhetoric* (Oxford: Oxford University Press, 1936), esp. 95–100.

39. Korsmeyer, *Making Sense of Taste*, 26–29, 35. For an overview of the human senses, including and beyond the five "classical senses," see John M. Henshaw, *A Tour of the Senses: How Your Brain Interprets the World* (Baltimore, MD: Johns Hopkins University Press, 2012).

whose close association with the body sullied their usefulness in terms of pure information. Aristotle states that "among the senses, vision is the most important, both in itself and for the necessities of life; on the other hand, for the uses of reason, and accidentally, hearing is the most important" (*Sens.* 437a9–10),[40] while touch is the lowest of the senses (*De an.* 421a25). For Aristotle, taste is the type of touch that mediates nutrition (*Sens.* 438b21).[41] That Aristotle is rather dismissive of taste in its relation to digestion of food for sustaining life highlights a tension in antiquity: while taste as a sense is considered less frequently than sight, food and its pleasures is the subject of constant discussion. The ancient philosophers appear to be uncomfortable engaging with taste as philosophically important because of its relation to the body.[42] It is more closely tied to the body even than touch, since the body is actually penetrated by the sense-object and in the end, absorbs it.

Since with taste the sense-object is actually internalized by the eater, this kind of interaction with the divine realm has more profound ontological repercussions on the eater than, for example, divinely sent dream visions or oral discourse with a being from another realm; in effect, the consuming of otherworldly foods serves to embed the eater in the realm to which the consumed food belongs. This is one of the cultural expectations that hierophagy as a genre exploits in its construction of meaning.

Taste is therefore the most intimate of the traditional senses in the sense that the object of taste is taken into the body, removing it from public accessibility.[43] Taste's intimacy with relation to the eater may indicate this sense's popularity in apocalyptic texts, where a certain intimacy with the divine facilitates the acquisition of specialized, hidden, privileged knowledge. This is clear especially in 4 Ezra, where an escalating progression of the senses, from hearing, to seeing, to tasting, leads to the final revelatory experience and yields the revelation of the new Torah. Further, the

---

40. This bias toward vision and hearing continues in modern and even postmodern philosophy, as Korsmeyer illustrates (*Making Sense of Taste*, 26–37).

41. Korsmeyer, *Making Sense of Taste*, 20.

42. The significance of the body in relation to hierophagy and taste will be dealt with more fully in the chapter dedicated to the Passion of Perpetua and Felicitas.

43. Korsmeyer, *Making Sense of Taste*, 35; Andrea Beth Lieber, "Jewish and Christian Heavenly Meal Traditions," in *Paradise Now: Essays on Early Jewish and Christian Mysticism*, ed. April D. DeConick, SymS 11 (Atlanta: Society of Biblical Literature, 2006), 316 n. 8

intimacy inherent in taste is what "betokens the community that eating together promises."[44] That sharing a meal is a significant part of community formation in ancient communities is well established. What I propose is that in hierophagic eating, the bond created is between the eater of the food and the otherworldly giver of the food, who in some cases also shares the meal. This type of bonding through eating participates in accepted ways of building relationships in antiquity but offers a different way of belonging for the privileged eater; he or she belongs to the community of the other realm.

Chapter Outline

This introduction lays the groundwork for approaching texts that employ hierophagy. I have defined the generic category under discussion and provided methodological approaches of taste and genre analysis to facilitate specific discussion of texts throughout the remaining chapters.

Chapter 1, "Persephone Traditions," begins with a preliminary example of hierophagy from classical Greek and first-century Roman myth. It explores two texts from outside the realm of Jewish and Christian literature that both describe the same hierophagic story, which is that of Persephone or Proserpina. The fact that characters in the myth take for granted the effects of the pomegranate supports my argument that hierophagy is a culturally accepted expectation and that otherworldly food consumption effects significant and often irrevocable change upon the eater, since in both Ovid's *Metamorphoses* and the Homeric Hymn to Demeter, Persephone is required to reside in Hades after having consumed pomegranate seeds in that realm.

Chapter 2, "4 Ezra," examines the development of apocalyptic hierophagy in the form of the fiery cup in 4 Ezra. I propose that Ezra's seven revelatory experiences reach their pinnacle in the seventh, hierophagic experience, since it is only with this final episode that Ezra is able to understand and transmit the divine knowledge shown to him by Uriel and God. My examination of Ezra's experiences highlight the sensory aspect of hierophagy, since at first he only receives revelation through discourse, then through sight, and finally, with the seventh episode, through taste. Ezra also gains new abilities, namely, the ability to

---

44. Korsmeyer, *Making Sense of Taste*, 187.

transmit his heavenly knowledge to the people; but further, Ezra is taken up into heaven at the end of his revelation. His heavenly assumption reflects the translocational aspects of hierophagy, as seen also in Perpetua's and Persephone's experiences.

Chapter 3, "Revelation," analyzes Revelation's hierophagic scene, Rev 10:8–10, where the sweetness of the scroll turns to bitterness. The mechanism of transformation is not elaborated upon. This is in contrast to the Persephone traditions' legalistic explanation, suggesting that the consequences of otherworldly consumption were part of the accepted understanding of the relationship of this world to the other, heavenly realm, whereby the eater not only gains access to the other world, but also receives heavenly knowledge. John is directed by a voice from heaven to consume the scroll, which tastes sweet; it is only when the scroll is in John's stomach that it turns bitter, signaling both judgement and authority.

Chapter 4, "Joseph and Aseneth," explores the curious honeycomb scene in Jos. Asen. 16–18. I argue that neither initiatory meals nor eucharistic practices are useful comparators in this case; rather, Aseneth's transformation is best understood as hierophagy. When Aseneth is fed the heavenly honeycomb by her angelic visitor, she attains eternal life (16.14), she understands divine wisdom (17.1–2), and she is physically transformed such that she is unrecognizable (18.8–10). While this scene has typically been understood as a conversion, certain elements, such as the fact that Aseneth retains her name and status as an Egyptian, speak against such a conclusion; rather, her affiliation to the divine is characterized in terms that participate in the genre of hierophagic transformation.

In chapter 5, "Apuleius's *Metamorphoses*," we find another instance of hierophagic eating—one that emphasizes the significance of consuming food from a different ontological category. While the texts examined so far portray the two categories as heavenly and mortal, in the *Metamorphoses* the categories are human and animal. Lucius, the main character, experiences a transformation through hierophagy that alters his physical appearance: having been transformed into an ass by a curse, Lucius's floral meal returns him to his human form. Lucius's transformation is facilitated by direct instructions from his patron deity, Isis (11.5–6). Lucius follows through on these instructions, eating the roses given to him by a priest of Isis; the priest is someone who is also of a different, more elevated, species compared with Lucius the donkey. The potential for physical transformation through hierophagy is emphasized in this text.

Chapter 6, "The Passion of Perpetua and Felicitas," examines Perpetua's heavenly vision in Pass. Perp. 4.8–10, which describes how Perpetua enters heaven and is fed a mouthful of cheese. Perpetua's vision gives her knowledge about her impending martyrdom through a very special mechanism, which is the hierophagic meal facilitated by the heavenly shepherd. Previous discussions of this event have assumed it to be some form of eucharistic or baptismal meal, but I propose that it participates in the genre of hierophagy, since Perpetua has already been baptized earlier in the narrative. As in Joseph and Aseneth and Revelation, Perpetua's hierophagic experience involves sweet-tasting food; Perpetua returns from her vision with that sweet taste in her mouth. The knowledge that she will be presently martyred comes from the ritual knowledge that eating food belonging to a world of a different category binds the eater to that other world, a ramification we also saw in Persephone's pomegranate meal. It seems clear that both Perpetua and her "brother" in 4.10 are familiar with the implications of eating otherworldly food and understand the consequences. The food presented to and eaten by Perpetua narratively transforms her from an earthly being to one of the heavenly people. Perpetua's meal exemplifies the translocational aspects of hierophagic meals, in that Perpetua symbolically becomes a member of the heavenly realm in advance of her actual death.

The conclusion examines the ramifications of the identification of this genre, common across religious boundaries and in a variety of geographical locations. Rather than pointing to direct literary influence, except in a few cases, the prevalence of hierophagy in the literature of the ancient Mediterranean suggests a cultural and literary proximity among the various religious communities that inhabited that world. I return to the question of genre analysis and propose that hierophagy as a genre might find use in other fields beyond the study of antiquity. In a broader sense, then, this study of hierophagy promotes increased study of the literary interactions, which in turn may reflect the lived realities of ancient people.

1
Persephone Traditions

As I will argue throughout this volume, one specific way that taste works in literature is by allowing characters to access other realms by consuming some article of food from that foreign realm.[1] This process is what I am calling hierophagy. In some cases hierophagy allows mortal humans to breach the boundary between earth and heaven, and sometimes the boundaries are crossed by divine beings themselves. The latter is the case in the three texts examined here that detail the story of the so-called Rape of Persephone: the anonymous Homeric Hymn to Demeter, as well as Ovid's *Fasti* and *Metamorphoses*. The Homeric Hymn to Demeter is an anonymous text probably composed between 650 and 550 BCE. Ovid lived and wrote *Metamorphoses* and *Fasti* (among other texts) in and around Rome in the first century CE under the reign of Augustus.[2] These three texts all narrate the

---

An earlier version of this chapter appeared as "Tastes from Beyond: Persephone's Pomegranate and Otherworldly Consumption in Antiquity," in *Taste and the Ancient Senses*, ed. Kelli C. Rudolph (London: Routledge, 2017). I am grateful to the publishers for granting permission to republish an edited version here.

1. On the senses generally in antiquity, see Mark Smith, *Sensing the Past: Seeing, Hearing, Smelling, Tasting, and Touching in History* (Berkeley: University of California Press, 2007); Jerry Toner, *A Cultural History of the Senses in Antiquity*, vol. 1 (London: Bloomsbury, 2014); on angelic foods, see Nicklas, "*Food of Angels*," 83–100; Goodman, "Do Angels Eat?," 160–75; on other worlds and travel to them in antique literature, see Nicklas et al., *Other Worlds and Their Relation to This World: Early Jewish and Christian Traditions*, JSJSup 143 (Leiden: Brill, 2010); Carla Sulzbach, "When Going on a Heavenly Journey," 163–93.

2. Ovid spent some time in exile and wrote a portion of the *Fasti* outside of Rome proper. See Ovid, *Metamorphoses V–VIII*, ed. and trans. D. E. Hill (Warminster, UK: Aris & Philips, 1992), 1–2. For further discussion of the Homeric Hymn to Demeter, see Nicholas J. Richardson, *The Homeric Hymn to Demeter* (Oxford: Clarendon, 1974), 5–12; and Helene P. Foley, *The Homeric Hymn to Demeter: Translation, Commentary,*

myth of the abduction of Persephone, also called Proserpina, by the god of the underworld; while in Hades, the goddess ingests some pomegranate, rendering her sojourn in the underworld semi-permanent. Tasting the pomegranate results in a change of identity for Persephone; whereas before she belonged wholly to the cohort of Olympian deities, afterwards she is required to spend a portion of her year as Hades's consort. The ramifications of eating food from another realm are simply assumed by the authors. I suggest that the Hymn to Demeter, *Fasti*, and *Metamorphoses* illustrate how taste works to transport the taster across boundaries between realms, a ramification of taste that is shared across ancient cultures and the texts they have produced.[3] This argument represents a departure from, though not an opposition to, the vast body of scholarship that analyzes Persephone's pomegranate event as a sexual experience. Numerous scholars view the seed as either a symbol of fertility or as a metaphor for sexual intercourse, or both. The analysis presented here views the pomegranate as participating in the cross-cultural genre of hierophagy. As I outlined in the introduction, the basic event of hierophagy involves the eating of something otherworldly, which then associates the eater with another world; in antiquity this is often the divine realm. A hierophagic analysis does not exclude the sexual element of the seed's ingestion but rather seeks

---

and Interpretive Essays (Princeton: Princeton University Press, 1994), 28–31, 79–83; for further discussion of Ovid's historical, political, and social context, see Hill's comments in Ovid, *Metamorphoses V–VIII*, 1–4.

3. Another example from Roman antiquity, in Apuleius's *Metamorphoses*, will be discussed in chapter 5. Regarding the Persephone narrative, A. Suter discusses the Hymn to Demeter from a psychoanalytical perspective as well as from an anthropological one. A. Suter, *The Narcissus and the Pomegranate: An Archaeology of the Homeric Hymn to Demeter* (Ann Arbor: University of Michigan Press, 2002). She rejects that the pomegranate episode represents a marriage (94–95) and instead favors an understanding of the pomegranate as inherently sexual (22, 83, 90, 97). J. L. Myers concludes that the pomegranate acts as a love charm in that Hades, in rubbing it on himself in some kind of magical act, binds Persephone to himself. J. L. Myres, "Persephone and the Pomegranate (H. Dem 372–74)," *Classical Review* 52.2 (1938): 51–52; C. Bonner, responding to Myres, views the seed as a fertility charm (esp. p. 4) encapsulated in the seed by Hades's action of moving the seed around himself (as opposed to rubbing it on himself) C. Bonner, "Hades and the Pomegranate Seed (Hymn to Demeter 372–74)," *Classical Review* 53.3 (1939): 3–4. Faraone outlines the use of sweet fruits in popular love charms (although at least half of the examples given involve throwing rather than ingesting the fruit; see esp. p. 238; C. Faraone, "Aphrodite's ΚΕΣΤΟΣ and Apples for Atlanta: Aphrodisiacs in Early Greek Myth and Ritual," *Phoenix* 44 (1990): 219–43.

to explain why eating, and particularly tasting, would be used in this way so consistently. In other words, even if we accept that Hades's actions with the seed enable him to bind Persephone to the underworld, the question why she must ingest the seed in order for the magic to work is left unanswered by evaluations that simply take for granted the sexual metaphor of the act. Rather, the changes undergone by Persephone are illuminated by other examples of this kind of tasting from antiquity.

The significance of hierophagy in antiquity hinges on the porous-but-present boundary between worlds in the cultural expectation of the ancient Mediterranean.[4] Although the most prominent boundary is between the human and divine realms, in some stories involving hierophagy other boundaries are breached. For instance, both Ovid and the author of the Hymn to Demeter treat the Chthonic and Olympian realms as distinct;[5] Hades rules one realm while Zeus rules another. Tasting food from another realm is one way in which such boundaries can be crossed.

Tasting the Pomegranate

The myth of Persephone's capture by Hades illustrates how pervasive hierophagic tasting and its implications were in the culture and literature of the antique world. The Homeric Hymn to Demeter is the earliest of the Persephone stories discussed here.[6] It is likely that the later *Metamorphoses*

---

4. By *cultural expectation* I mean knowledge passed down as part of the cultural heritage of ancient communities, knowledge that would have been commonly accepted among culturally literate participants in the ancient world. Here, I follow Richard Horsley's use of the term *cultural repertoire*. Richard A. Horsley, *Scribes, Visionaries, and the Politics of Second Temple Judea* (Louisville KY: Westminster John Knox, 2007), esp. 128–29; and David Carr's discussion of how cultural-religious traditions are communicated in antiquity. David M. Carr, *Writing on the Tablet of the Heart: Origins of Scripture and Literature* (Oxford: Oxford University Press, 2005), esp. 3–14.

5. For a discussion of the use of these terms in cult practice, see S. Scullion, "Olympian and Chthonian," *Classical Antiquity* 13 (1994): 75–119.

6. See Richardson, *Homeric Hymn to Demeter*, 74–86 for a full discussion of other literary versions of the myth. The myth of Persephone's capture is briefly mentioned in Hesiod, *Theog.* 9.14, and also appears in Pamphos, *Hymn to Demeter* (preserved in Pausanias, *Descr.* 1.38.3; 8.37.9; 9.31.9); Argonautica Orphica 1191–1996; the Orphic Hymn to Pluto, the Orphic Hymn to Proserpine, the Orphic Hymn to the Ceralian Mother, and the Orphic Hymn to the Seasons; Euripides, *Hel.* 1301–1368; Isocrates, *Paneg.* 28–29; Callimachos, *Hymn to Ceres*; Nicander, *Ther.* 483–487, *Alex.* 129–132; Apollodorus, *Bib.* 1.5.1–3; Diodorus Siculus, *Bib. Hist.* 5.3–5; Cicero, *Verr.* 2.4; Vergil,

and *Fasti* were composed at least partly in response to the hymn.[7] In the Homeric Hymn to Demeter, we see Demeter mourning her daughter's kidnapping.[8] Those familiar with the story will recall how she allows nothing to grow on earth, no crops of any kind, in her grief and rage (Hom. Dem. 302–313). Each of the gods entreats Demeter to allow the earth to be fertile again, but she refuses. Demeter is determined not to allow any crops to grow on the earth until her daughter is returned to her.

Zeus, complicit in his own daughter's abduction by his brother Hades (78–79), is held hostage by Demeter's actions and eventually has to send Hermes to negotiate with Hades (334–349). Hades seems to obey and tells Persephone to return to her mother (360–369), but before she leaves, Hades "stealthily gave her a honey-sweet[9] pomegranate seed to eat, looking around, so that she might not stay there for all time with the venerable dark-robed Demeter" (my trans.).[10] The phrasing of this excerpt, which emphasizes in two places the intentional secrecy employed by Hades, suggests that Persephone's eating is not accidental; rather, it is Hades who, *knowing what the end result would be*, slips Persephone some seeds to eat in order to keep her as his wife in the underworld.[11] Indeed, the phrase "looking around" (ἀμφὶ ἓ νωμήσας, 373) may emphasize the furtiveness of

---

Georg. 1.39; Lucan, *Phars.* 6.698–700, 739–742; Lactantius Placidus on Statius *Thebaid* 5.347; Claudian, *On the Rape of Proserpina*; Nonnos, *Dion.* 6.1–168; Second Vatican Mythographer 94–100. Of these, Apollodorus mentions the pomegranate, stating that Pluto gave the seed to the maid and she, "not foreseeing the consequences," ate it.

7. Stephen Hinds, *The Metamorphosis of Persephone: Ovid and the Self-Conscious Muse* (Cambridge: Cambridge University Press, 1987), 51–98.

8. Persephone falls to the underworld when reaching for a fragrant narcissus flower (Hom. Dem. 5–14). The sensory implications of this event of relocation are no doubt significant, but beyond the scope of this project.

9. As I will discuss further throughout the other chapters, the sweet taste is also a feature of other examples of hierophagy, such as in Passion of Perpetua and Felicitas, Joseph and Aseneth, and the book of Revelation.

10. αὐτὰρ ὅ γ' αὐτὸς / ῥοιῆς κόκκον ἔδωκε φαγεῖν μελιηδέα λάθρῃ, / ἀμφὶ ἓ νωμήσας, ἵνα μὴ μένοι ἤματα πάντα / αὖθι παρ' αἰδοίῃ Δημήτερι κυανοπέπλῳ.

11. For a discussion of the potential relationship between the pomegranate meal in the Hymn to Demeter and actual Athenian marriage, see Foley, *Homeric Hymn to Demeter*, 107–9. She notes that "the bride's acceptance of food was a form of acknowledging the groom's authority over her" (108) and that the ingestion of some ritual food (quince in Plutarch, *Sol.*, 89C or wedding cake in Aristophanes, *Pax*, 869) was part of the marriage rite. As has been noted by other scholars (see note 3 above), sexual experiences follow; see also Suter, *Narcissus and the Pomegranate*, and R. Sutton, "The

Hades's behavior,[12] describing how he looks around himself, hoping that he is not observed as he tricks his stolen bride into consuming the fruit.

That Persephone consumes pomegranate at all is peculiar. Greeks and Romans understood a division between divine and mortal foods—a division that reflects "the wider symbolic economy" that distinguishes gods from human beings in culinary terms.[13] When gods appear to consume human foods in literature, it is usually in the context of hospitality, the gods enjoying a rich banquet, having taken on mortal disguises (see Homer, *Od.* 1.105–149; Ovid, *Metam.* 8.616–724).[14] However, this is not the case in the Persephone myth. Persephone is not in human guise, and she does not enjoy a banquet. These two aspects—the lack of ambrosia and the lack of hospitality—serve to highlight the potential for transformation that the tiny pomegranate seed will bring about. Persephone's food is marked;[15] the

---

Interaction between Men and Women Portrayed on Attic Red-Figure Pottery" (PhD diss.; University of North Carolina, Chapel Hill, 1981), 153–54.

12. Richardson, *Homeric Hymn to Demeter*, 277. Foley opts to interpret the phrase as referring to a magical rite by which Hades binds Persephone to himself through the movement of the pomegranate seed around his captive (*Homeric Hymn to Demeter*, 56); this interpretation is unnecessary in light of my analysis, which proposes that the eating of otherworldly food is binding in and of itself, and does not require additional magical actions. See also Myres, "Persephone and the Pomegranate," and Bonner, "Hades and the Pomegranate Seed."

13. Clements, "Divine Scents and Presence," 52. The banquet of the Phaeacians (Homer, *Od.* 8), the banquet served by Tantalus (Pindar, *Ol.* 1.26–27), and the meal hosted by Baucis and Philemon (Ovid, *Metam.* 8.621–96) might seem like exceptions, where gods do consume human food. Tantalus attempts to serve a monstrous human sacrifice to the gods who attend his banquet; aside from human flesh being out of the realm of normal mortal food, only Demeter eats at the banquet, and she does so only because she is distracted by her grief at Persephone's absence. Baucis and Philemon do set out a table for their divine guests, and items of food, including eggs and cheese, are described, but the only reference to ingestion is to the wine jug, which mysteriously refills itself each time Baucis refills the cups. Indeed, the gods actually prevent the host couple from serving them meat by revealing their divine identities. As for the banquet of the Phaeacians, the gods are lauded in song but do not attend the meal.

14. The cultic practice of *theoxenia* is a separate matter; see Gunnel Ekroth, "Meat for the Gods," in *Nourrir les dieux? Sacrifice et représentation du divin*, ed. Vinciane Pirenne Delforge and Francesca Rescendi, Kernos supplement 26 (Liège: Centre International d'Étude de la Religion Grecque Antique, 2011), 15–41.

15. I use the term *marked* to refer to the cultural encoding of certain terms, items, and/or behaviors as unusual and therefore informative in the context of the familiar or ordinary ("unmarked") categories of meaning accepted by a culture. In this use I

pomegranate is out of place here, foreshadowing that this ingestion—and its ramifications—are out of the ordinary.

The sweet taste that the seeds have is likewise marked. Even present-day pomegranates, bred for their sweetness, are still better described as tart; in contrast, wild pomegranates are described as "extremely acidic."[16] The food of the gods in the Greek tradition is also associated with honey and sweet tastes.[17] The fact that these pomegranate seeds are explicitly described as "honey sweet" (μελιηδής) may highlight the special nature of this food as opposed to an ordinary, often sour, pomegranate seed.

When Demeter finally sees her daughter and embraces her, her first emotion is not relief but anxiety, as if Demeter can tell that Persephone is changed in some way:

> [While holding her dear child in her arms], her [heart
> suddenly sensed a trick. Fearful she] drew back
> from [her embrace and at once inquired:]
> "My child, tell me, you [did not taste] food [while below?]
> Speak out [and hide nothing, so we both may know.]
> [For if not], ascending [from miserable Hades],
> you will dwell with me and your father, the
> dark-clouded [son of Kronos], honoured by all the gods.
> But if [you tasted food], returning beneath [the earth,]
> you will stay a third part of the seasons [each year,]
> but two parts with myself and the other immortals." (Hom. Dem. 390–400 [Foley])

Demeter is concerned with whether Persephone has "tasted" food while she was in Hades—the verb πατέομαι (398) connotes not just the ingestion

---

follow, for example, Edwin L. Battistella, *Markedness: The Evaluative Superstructure of Language* (Albany, NY: State University of New York Press, 1990); Battistella, *The Logic of Markedness* (New York: Oxford University Press, 1996); and L. R. Waugh, "Marked and Unmarked: A Choice between Unequals in Semiotic Structure," *Semiotica* 38 (1982): 299–318.

16. Ed Stover and Eric W. Mercure, "The Pomegranate: A New Look at the Fruit of Paradise," *HortScience* 42 (2007): 1088; the chart found on p. 1091 outlines the range of sweetness and acidity expected in the variety of modern cultivars.

17. See Hitch, "Tastes of Greek Poetry" for the poetics of sweetness in Greek literature, and Laurence Totelin, "Tastes in Botany, Medicine and Science in Antiquity: Bitter Herbs and Sweet Honey," in Rudolph, *Taste and the Ancient Senses*, 60–71 for sweetness in medical and scientific texts.

of food but also the tasting of it.[18] The implications of this verb are important, given the usual silence in Greek literature about how food tastes. As Sarah Hitch argues, abundance is usually emphasized over aesthetic quality, and when taste is an operative descriptor, it is usually used metaphorically.[19] Using this verb, as opposed to an unmarked verb of eating such as ἐσθίω, especially when the object consumed also has the aesthetic descriptor "sweet," implies that taste is a significant factor in Persephone's experience.

When pressed, Persephone admits that Hades forced her to eat something sweet: "but he stealthily put in my mouth a food honey-sweet, a pomegranate seed, and compelled me against my will and by force to taste it" (411–413).[20] Persephone's words here are almost identical to those in 371–374 when the narrator describes Hades giving her the seed. In this section, Persephone is emphatic that she has *tasted* (πατέομαι) the honey-sweet pomegranate.[21] The implications of this experience are clear to Demeter, who, like Hades, is fully aware of the rules: Persephone is bound to the underworld if she has tasted food there.[22] The potential danger of tasting food was acknowledged in the ancient world; "once food is consumed, it cannot return to its previous state, and by extension, in Greek thought the irreversible change brought about by ingestion can affect the eater too."[23] Zeus, too, is cognizant of the law governing otherworldly tasting, for he proclaims that Persephone, as Demeter feared and Hades hoped, "would spend one-third of the revolving year in the misty dark and two-thirds with her mother and the other immortals" (446–448). The

---

18. LSJ, s.v. "πατέομαι"; cf. *Il.* 24.642.

19. Sarah Hitch, "Tastes of Greek Poetry," 22–44.

20. αὐτὰρ ὁ λάθρῃ / ἔμβαλέ μοι ῥοιῆς κόκκον, μελιηδέ ἐδωδήν, / ἄκουσαν δὲ βίῃ με προσηνάγκασσε πάσασθαι. Suter argues that Persephone willingly ingested the pomegranate and here lies to her mother in order to prevent Demeter's anger (*Narcissus and the Pomegranate*, 58). I rather prefer to believe the survivor's own account and posit an unreliable narrator. I am grateful to Megan Goodwin for her input.

21. This verb is also used in line 50: "In her grief [Demeter] did not once **taste** ambrosia or nectar sweet-to-drink, nor bathed her skin." Οὐδέ ποτ' ἀμβροσίης καὶ νέκταρος ἡδυπότοιο **πάσσατ'** ἀκηχεμένη, οὐδὲ χρόα βάλλετο λουτροῖς. Trans. and text from Foley, *Homeric Hymn to Demeter*.

22. Suter convincingly problematizes the assumption that a marriage takes place in Hades (*Narcissus and the Pomegranate*, 90–97); thus the binding that occurs through the pomegranate event is more complex than a simple marriage ritual.

23. Hitch, "Tastes of Greek Poetry," 29.

seasonality of the pomegranate may also be significant; while other fruit is harvested at the end of summer, pomegranates become ripe during the winter months, precisely when Persephone resides in Hades, corresponding with the bleak mourning period observed by Demeter. The type of fruit ingested by the goddess therefore seems to indicate the temporal restrictions imposed on her; a winter fruit points to a winter in Hades. Here (and again in 463–466) Zeus uses the same phrasing that Demeter does in 390–400; the repetition drives home the ramifications of eating the pomegranate. The Homeric Hymn to Demeter expresses not only the significance of tasting food from another realm but also the idea that this kind of tasting is governed by cosmic law.

A significant reinterpretation of the Persephone myth is found in Latin, in a poem composed by Ovid under the reign of Augustus, some half a millennium after the Homeric Hymn to Demeter. In Ovid's version of the myth, Proserpina, as she is called in the Latin tradition, unintentionally binds herself to Hades when she happens to pluck a pomegranate. Proserpina is transformed by the pomegranate, in keeping with the series of other transformations detailed by Ovid throughout the *Metamorphoses*.[24] In contrast to the Homeric Hymn to Demeter, Ovid does not describe Pluto, the Latin equivalent of Hades, as having a direct role in feeding Proserpina the food. We read that by the time she is returned to her mother,

> the maiden had broken
> her fast and, while wandering innocently in the well-kept gardens,
> had plucked a crimson fruit from a bending tree
> and taken seven seeds from its pale rind
> and pressed them to her mouth. (Ovid, *Metam.* 5.534–537 [Hill])[25]

---

24. See Hill's comments in Ovid, *Metamorphoses V–VIII*, 2.

25. The number seven is significant in antiquity, occurring in important foundational contexts, such as the seven hills of Rome, the seven kings of Rome, the seven wonders of the ancient world, and in literature, such as *Seven against Thebes*. The significance in Ovid is, however, contested. Persephone ingests seven pomegranate seeds, a departure from the single seed in the Homeric Hymn to Demeter and the three seeds in *Fasti* (4.607–608), where, as E. Fantham observes, the number of seeds is equivalent to the months spent in Hades. See E. Fantham, "The Growth of Literature and Criticism at Rome," in *The Cambridge History of Literary Criticism*, ed. George A. Kennedy (Cambridge: Cambridge University Press, 1989), 207. Cf. Hinds, who suggests the three seeds in *Fasti* represent the "twice three months" Proserpina spends out of the

In the *Metamorphoses*, Proserpina takes the food of her own accord,[26] perhaps not aware of the ramifications. When she is discovered, and as the gods determine the right course of action, Jupiter as judge invokes a certain cosmic law pertaining to this issue, namely, that Proserpina may leave the underworld only if she has not eaten any food from that place: "Proserpina will return to heaven, / but on this clear condition, that she has not touched any food / there with her mouth; for so it was decided by the compact of the Fates" (5.530–533 [Hill]). Both Jupiter, and Ascalaphus, the underworld's gardener, in describing what he saw, use a curious phrase to describe Proserpina's interaction with the pomegranate. Ascalaphus says that she "pressed them to her mouth" while Jupiter's condition is that she has not "touched any food there with her mouth." Thus, as in Homeric Hymn to Demeter, the language used to describe Proserpina's ingestion of the seeds is unusual. Given the close relationship between the texts, it would not be surprising if Ovid used this curious phrase to evoke the "tasting" made explicit in the hymn, especially since lips, as much as tongues, were considered organs of taste in antiquity.[27]

In the end, Jupiter compromises; Ceres, the Latin equivalent of Demeter, must share custody of Proserpina with her daughter's abductor-turned-husband as a result of her tasting of the fruit.

> But, mediating between his brother and his grieving sister,
> Jupiter, divided the revolving year equally:
> now the goddess, a deity common to the two realms,
> is with her mother for as many months as the months she is with her
> husband. (Ovid, *Metam.* 5.564–567 [Hill])

The division between realms—that of the upper realm and that of the lower—is explicitly negotiated in the *Metamorphoses* through the inges-

---

underworld (4.614) (Hinds, *Metamorphosis of Persephone*, 89 n. 39). See also Richardson, *Homeric Hymn to Demeter*, 276–77, 285. Seven seeds in the *Metamorphoses* may be a generally powerful (potentially magical) symbol, rather than a specific one.

26. It is possible, and would be in line with Ovid's characterization of women, that Persephone's agency in plucking the fruit participates in what some scholars have suggested is an overarching metaphor of sex and sexuality in the myth of Persephone.

27. As Gowers points out, particularly as regards potentially dangerous ingestion ("Tasting the Roman World," 95). The absence of explicit language in Ovid, aside from the general absence of tasting language in ancient literature, can also result from the fact that in neither case is Proserpina's point of view made apparent.

tion of pomegranate. This underworld meal redefines Proserpina's relationship with her original realm where the other Olympian deities dwell and associates her instead with the gods of the underworld. She is, in effect, transformed by her experience, from a goddess of the upper realm to one who straddles the two. This metamorphosis is brought about by those seven seeds and confirmed by Jupiter when he hears what she has done. Jupiter's pronouncement does not bring about this change—Proserpina's reaction to his decree, the brightening of her disposition recounted in 5.568–571, rather reflects her relief at being returned at least part time to her mother.[28] The identity change Proserpina undergoes has already taken place by the time Jupiter makes his judgement, since it is dependent, as he articulates in 5.530–532, on her having consumed underworldly food.

Ovid gives a similar version of the myth in the *Fasti*. As in other renditions, in this account, when Proserpina is abducted to Dis's (another name for Pluto) own realm (4.445–446), Ceres searches the entire realm to which she has access. Here, the normally strict division between worlds is made explicit in the emphasis placed on Ceres searching the *entire* upper world for her daughter:

> For at one time she looks down on incense-gathering Arabs, at another on Indians; next Libya is below, next Meroe and the parched land. Now she approaches the Hesperians—the Rhine, the Rhone, the Po, and you, Thybris, destined to be the parent of a powerful water. Where am I being carried? It's a huge task to tell the lands she roamed. No place in the world is omitted by Ceres. She roams in heaven too, and speaks to the constellations nearest to the icy pole, which are immune from the watery ocean. (Ovid, *Fasti* 4.569–576 [Wiseman and Wiseman])

Ceres is only capable of searching the upper realm, including the earth and sky, and must eventually be told where Proserpina is. Ceres's quest is also found in *Metam*. 5.438–459; the goddess searches for her daughter on land and in the sea (5.434; cf. 5.462–463; Hom. Dem. 43–44). As in the Homeric Hymn to Demeter and the *Metamorphoses*, the *Fasti* emphasizes the breadth and depth of Ceres's search. Proserpina remains hidden not for lack of trying—her mother has searched in every possible location available to her, while the underworld exists on a different plane, inacces-

---

28. Ceres likewise appears relieved in Ovid, *Metam*. 5.572.

sible to the gods of the upper realm. Ceres's limited search thus illustrates that Proserpina, Ceres, and Jupiter exist in one realm, while the king of the Underworld exists in another.

Eventually Ceres discovers that her daughter has been taken to the "third kingdom" (*tertia regna*)—the underworld (*Fast.* 4.584). This same location is singled out by the *Metamorphoses* as well as the Hymn to Demeter as distinct from the upper realms of the earth and the heavens. In the Hymn to Demeter (398–400), Demeter warns her daughter that remaining in the depths of the earth is the consequence of breaking her fast. In the *Metamorphoses*, Ovid likewise depicts the underworld as a foreign realm, ordinarily inaccessible to the gods of the upper realm (5.492; 501–508). Ceres then begs Jupiter to annul the marriage-by-capture; he is willing, but he sets certain, by now familiar, conditions. "If it happens that your heart cannot be moved, and is set to break the bonds of a marriage once joined, then let us try to do just that," Jupiter tells Ceres, "if only she has remained fasting. If not she will be the wife of an underworld husband" (4.601–604 [Wiseman and Wiseman]). To Ceres's dismay, in this version as well, her daughter has broken her fast on some pomegranate seeds (4.607–608). As in the *Metamorphoses*, Ceres immediately understands the ramifications of this tiny taste and further explains her grief by declaring that just as Proserpina no longer calls heaven home, neither will Ceres (4.610–614). This statement, though hyperbolic on the part of Ceres, highlights the very real change that Proserpina has undergone: just as Ceres was unable to access the underworld by her nature as a goddess of the upper realm, now Proserpina properly belongs to the "third kingdom." Proserpina's hierophagy therefore amounts to more than a simple marriage-by-capture, where the bride now resides in her husband's home; that is, the abduction would have been ineffective by itself to bring about Proserpina's bond to the underworld. Tasting the pomegranate effects a change that renders her association with the underworld semi-permanent, even if she does return to her mother for half the year. She is now a goddess of that third kingdom and can only visit her former home.

Proserpina/Persephone's experience with these seeds hardly constitutes a meal—no one in antiquity would recognize it as such, since it lacks the two major components of wine and bread. Further, in viewing it in contrast to other examples of deities-in-disguise eating nonambrosial foods, the seeds seem even more insignificant—the plentiful banquet depicted in *Metam.* 8.616–724 contains multiple courses of rich and abundant food.[29] That Persephone consumes such a small unit of food signals the event as distinct from ordinary ingestion.

Two things are made apparent through this analysis of the Persephone stories: first, Ovid and the author of the Homeric Hymn to Demeter share ideas about food-transformation both with each other and with other texts from the ancient Mediterranean, as I will illustrate. Whether Hades or Heaven, the same cultural rules apply: food from another world, when eaten, binds the eater to that place. Second, in the *Metamorphoses*, the *Fasti*, and the Homeric Hymn to Demeter, the gods, at the very least, know that these gustatory regulations exist. Jupiter is bound by this rule in Ovid's versions and is unable to completely return Persephone to her mother; in the Homeric Hymn to Demeter, Hades takes advantage of this restriction and purposely feeds Persephone the food which binds her to himself and his world.

Sensory Intimacy, Social Intimacy

One of the reasons why taste brings about Persephone's identity transformation is because sharing tastes with others establishes a bond among the eaters. Thus, the binding effect of the pomegranate's taste can be elucidated by looking at the sociology of taste. A bond is accomplished through the intimacy of taste when compared with other senses.[30] If smells evoke the presence of the gods in public,[31] then taste, in the mouth and on the lips and tongue, represents interaction with another realm in a very private way. As I explored in the introduction, ramifications of eating and tasting arise because the sense-object is actually internalized by the eater. For this reason, this form of interaction with another world has more profound repercussions than, for example, a conversation with a being from another realm, or in the case of Persephone, even being in the physical location of that other realm: tasting otherworldly foods brings about a bond between the eater and the realm to which the ingested food belongs.

---

29. See Hitch for a discussion of descriptions of banquets; ancient texts tend to emphasize the quantity of food and its surplus rather than specific taste experiences at feasts ("Tastes of Greek Poetry," 24).

30. See Kelli C. Rudolph, "Introduction: On the Tip of the Tongue; Making Sense of Ancient Taste," in Rudolph, *Taste and the Ancient Senses*, 1–21.

31. Clements, "Divine Scents and Presence," 46–59.

Taste accomplishes this transformation because of its intimacy.[32] The privacy of the sense of taste (as opposed to the shared, "objective" senses of sight or hearing) suggests that hierophagy exploits the intimacy of taste to express its meaning.

The social implications of sharing this intimate sense in antiquity supports the idea that tasting food from another realm metamorphoses the eater.[33] A key social aspect of the sense of taste resides in how it signifies and effects community formation—common meals promote group formation and cohesion and are frequently used in initiatory contexts to establish or renew community membership (e.g., Apuleius, *Metam.* 11.24).[34] While community is not an explicit concern of the myths, the social implications of taste illuminate the literary role of the pomegranate; in the social world, sharing a meal creates a bond not just between coeaters of a meal, but also between the provider of the food and the consumer of it, as in the case of Hades and Persephone.[35] While host and guest bond through shared tasting of a meal, as Hitch points out, providing food to guests also established the power of the host; thus by accepting the host's food, the guest concomitantly accepts his power.[36] So Hades, in providing

---

32. David Potter, "The Social Life of the Senses: Feasts and Funerals," in *A Cultural History of the Senses in Antiquity*, ed. Jerry Toner (London: Bloomsbury 2014), 24.

33. The important role of meals in community formation in ancient communities is well established. Dennis E. Smith goes so far as to declare that "the idea that sharing a meal together creates a sense of social bonding appears to be a universal symbol" (*From Symposium to Eucharist: The Banquet in the Early Christian World* [Minneapolis: Fortress, 2003], 14). It is not just sharing a meal at the same table that produces this community, but also *sharing tastes with a community even at a great distance*. See M. P. Lalonde, "Deciphering a Meal Again, or the Anthropology of Taste," *Social Science Information* 31 (1992): 82–83.

34. Korsmeyer, *Making Sense of Taste*, 187; Smith, *From Symposium to Eucharist*, 14, 80.

35. Hierophagic eating creates a bond between the eater of the food and the giver of the food, even when the provider of the food resides in a different world. It is important to remember that hosts and guests (providers and receivers) might not eat the same food even when dining together (Smith, *From Symposium to Eucharist*, 11, 45). Thus, the fact that Hades does not share the pomegranate does not negate the binding effects of Persephone's taste experience. Of course, the bond created between Hades and Persephone through this small taste of underworldly food can be, and has been, viewed as representative of the relationship between husband and wife (see above, note 11) and/or of a sexual bond formed between two lovers (see above, note 3).

36. See further Hitch, "Tastes of Greek Poetry," 23.

the few seeds, might be seen as asserting his authority over Persephone. Meals were shared among members of a group that was already established, for example, a family or a guild, but they could also create new associations. Ancient writers, like modern scholars, were conscious of how meals established and reinforced social bonds. Plutarch considers the common meal a place where friendship is forged. He remarks upon this quality most memorably when he writes, "A guest comes to share not only meat, wine and dessert, but conversation, fun and the amiability that leads to friendship" (Plutarch, *Table-Talk* 660b [Clement]).[37] Sharing a meal does more than fill the stomach; it also forges relationships among diners. Modern anthropologists argue that food also creates a bond between the eater and the provider of food through its incorporation into the consumer.[38] In eating food, the eater brings into him or herself the qualities imbued in the food, including the social (or other) stratification implied in the meal, the culturally loaded symbolism of the food itself, and the memory of previous meals consumed in similar or different ways. The fact that Persephone tastes food that, for her, is out of the ordinary creates tension within the existing Olympian-Chthonic narrative structure.[39] In tasting the honey-sweet pomegranate, Persephone gains privileged access to the other realm—Hades—which necessitates her participation in it.

Excursus: Hierophagy in Genesis?

In the next few chapters I will be examining other sources of hierophagy from around the same era as the *Metamorphoses* and the *Fasti*. How-

---

37. Paul likewise recognizes this quality of sharing food. As he explains in 1 Cor 10:17, "Because there is one bread, we who are many are one body, for we all partake of the one bread" (RSV). Paul also believes that a bond can be created not only between people but also between divine forces and those who share ritually marked food. He famously warns the Corinthians that they might find themselves "partners with demons" (1 Cor 10:20) if they share in food offered to gods whom Jews do not worship.

38. G. Weichart and P. van Eeuwijk, "Preface," *Anthropology of Food* S3 (2007): 3; Mary Douglas, "Deciphering a Meal," *Daedalus* 101 (1972): 61–81; Peter Farb and George J. Armelagos, *Consuming Passions: The Anthropology of Eating* (Boston: Houghton Mifflin, 1980), 4. The penetration of the eater by the food also has implications for understanding Persephone and the pomegranate as a sexual metaphor.

39. While pomegranates might grow abundantly in the underworld, they are not normal food for Olympian deities, as I have established above.

ever, before moving on, it might be useful to briefly look at a potential comparator from the era in which the Homeric Hymn to Demeter was composed: the book of Genesis. That Genesis does not emerge from the geographical areas that produced the Homeric Hymn to Demeter serves to illustrate the pervasiveness of the use of taste to depict boundary crossing in literature, whether poetry or narrative. It is possible that Genesis participates, like the Homeric Hymn to Demeter, the *Fasti*, and the *Metamorphoses*, in a common cultural imagination of the ancient Mediterranean and therefore sheds light on the societal expectations about how distinct realms interact. The common use of hierophagy as a means by which foreign realms are entered into rather reflects a shared ancient expectation about the ramifications of ingesting otherworldly food. Genesis 3 depicts the expulsion of Adam and Eve from the garden of Eden after they disobey God and consume fruit from the tree of knowledge of Good and Evil. This story has been interpreted as a "simple metaphor for intercourse" whereby ancient authors euphemistically describe the first sexual contact and the subsequent "carnal knowledge."[40] However, I propose that the use of ingestion as a metaphor for knowledge functions precisely because of taste's role in hierophagy: that it transmits knowledge from one realm to another.

It is in this capacity that I analyze the fruit here. Genesis 3 represents a worldview roughly contemporaneous with that preserved in the Homeric Hymn to Demeter.[41] The Genesis story narrates Adam and Eve's eviction from Eden. Eden contains two named trees: the tree of the knowledge of good and evil and the tree of life. Adam and Eve's removal from paradise occurs as a direct result of their ingestion of the fruit of the former tree.

Eve examines the fruit and determines that it is "good for food," among other things:

---

40. Ronald A. Veenker, "Forbidden Fruit: Ancient Near Eastern Sexual Metaphors," *HUCA* 70–71 (1999–2000): 57–73; E. A. Speiser, *Genesis*, AB (Garden City, NY: Doubleday, 1964), 26.

41. David Carr writes that most Pentateuchal scholars are now skeptical of a preexilic Yahwist source. David Carr, *The Formation of the Hebrew Bible: A New Reconstruction* (New York: Oxford University Press, 2011), 358–59; see also Thomas B. Dozeman and Konrad Schmid, eds., *A Farewell to the Yahwist? The Composition of the Pentateuch in Recent European Interpretation*, SymS 34 (Atlanta: Society of Biblical Literature, 2006). On the date of the Homeric Hymns, see Richardson, *Homeric Hymn to Demeter*, 5–11.

> So when the woman saw that the tree was good for food, and that it was a delight to the eyes, and that the tree was to be desired to make one wise, she took of its fruit and ate; and she also gave some to her husband, and he ate. Then the eyes of both were opened, and they knew that they were naked; and they sewed fig leaves together and made themselves aprons. (Gen 3:6–7)[42]

In other words, Eve experiences the fruit synaesthetically and understands through seeing the fruit that it will taste good.[43] She eats some and gives some to Adam to eat. The couple then experiences an awakening of sorts in that they become "wise," as the text puts it, and realize that they are naked. However, God's experience of their hierophagic experience is different; Adam and Eve have not just seized knowledge, but have brought about a transformation: "Behold, the man has become like one of us, knowing good and evil" (3:22). In tasting this fruit, Eve and Adam have become closer to the divine realm. God fears that ingesting the fruit of the tree of life (3:22) would render Adam and Eve fully divine and so ejects them from the garden "lest he put forth his hand and take also of the tree of life, and eat, and live for ever—therefore the LORD God sent him forth from the garden of Eden" (3:22–23).[44] As in the Homeric Hymn to Demeter, then, the god of Genesis also understands the ramifications of consuming food from another realm. The curses that God imposes on the humans and their subsequent expulsion from Eden in Gen 3:22–24 are the results of tasting the "good to eat" fruit of the tree of knowledge. Thus, the Eden narrative reflects the tension typical of hierophagic events, wherein the boundaries between realms are breached.

The ramifications of Persephone's taste of underworldly fruit participate in the expectations held in antiquity about eating and drinking food from other realms.[45] That tasting food is transformative is clearly seen in

---

42. All translations of the Bible are from the RSV.

43. Hitch notes that "if any sense provides pleasure associated with food, it is vision" ("Tastes of Greek Poetry," 25).

44. The serpent suggests this in Gen 3:5; it is also supported by various commentaries on the expulsion narrative.

45. Richardson notes a few places where the belief that eating the food of the dead requires the eater to reside with the dead (*Homeric Hymn to Demeter*, 276); cf. T. W. Allen, W. R. Halliday, and E. E. Sikes, *The Homeric Hymns* (Oxford: Clarendon, 1936). Richardson also confirms my argument above that shared meals solidify bonds among community members.

the anxiety displayed by the divine being in Genesis, as it is in depictions of ambrosia in ancient literature.

Conclusions

Tasting food from another world allows the eater to cross the semi-permeable boundary between heaven and earth, or in the case of Persephone, between the Chthonic and Olympian realms. Not only are these boundaries breached, they are irrevocably so. Calypso, for example, sets her table with two distinct meals: one of sweet ambrosia for herself, and one of ordinary mortal food for Odysseus (Homer, *Od.* 5.195–199). This division between the members of each realm is articulated in what each category of beings consumes. Even though Persephone and Hades are both deities—and are even related—they initially belong to different realms; Hades belongs to the Chthonic realm and Persephone to the Olympian. Tasting food from another realm, however, creates a bridge to the underworld and brings about the metamorphosis of a deity from a being of one realm to another, as Ovid and the author of the *Hymn* are both aware. When Persephone consumes the pomegranate seeds, she is bound to Hades; likewise Adam and Eve are also expelled from paradise lest they become divine like God. The various renditions of the Persephone story also illustrate the extent to which the ancient world takes for granted the ramifications of consuming other-worldly food. In both the Homeric Hymn to Demeter and the works of Ovid, the gods are fully aware of the cosmic requirements to which they are bound, just as they are in Genesis. The mechanism by which the first humans are rendered (partially) divine is not explained to the reader; rules governing hierophagy are simply assumed to be common knowledge among characters and the audience alike. In other words, the genre is assumed to be understood widely. It is accepted without question in each of these texts that boundaries between different realms are permeable.

When Persephone tastes the pomegranate seeds,[46] her abduction to Hades is rendered semi-permanent. The discussion held by the gods indicates that her visit to the underworld might have been temporary but for her ingestion of some food from that realm. The intent of Hades himself

---

46. The pomegranate's centrality to Persephone's story of abduction is also illustrated by its prominent use as a symbol of Persephone and Hades in art (Richardson, *Homeric Hymn to Demeter*, 276).

does not alter the fact that Persephone is bound to his realm by this meal; whether he stealthily feeds her the seeds as in the Hymn to Demeter or whether their ingestion is unintentional as in the *Fasti* and the *Metamorphoses*, the outcome is the same.

The effectiveness of hierophagy in narrative corresponds to the role of taste in historical antiquity; hierophagy participates in accepted conventions governing the social and sensory intimacy of shared tasting. Even though Hades does not share in the meal, as host and provider of food, he participates in the binding of the eater by means of taste, just as historical meals are understood to create a social bond among mortal and/or divine diners. Likewise, although Persephone is physically already in Hades, the permanence of her visit is only realized when she internalizes some element of that realm, namely the seeds. The intimacy of the sweet taste, marked as extraordinary in the text, effects Persephone's metamorphosis. Persephone's bond with the underworld (Hades) and with its god (Hades) is transformed when she tastes the pomegranate: the intimacy and power of the sense of taste forever associates her with that realm. This is also the case in our next text, 4 Ezra, whose protagonist likewise is assumed into heaven after his experience with hierophagy.

2

4 Ezra

This chapter focuses on a text that expresses all of the major features I identify as part of hierophagy: transformation of eater, relocation of eater, and the receipt of new knowledge. While Persephone's pomegranate brought about relocation in a very explicit way, other elements were not as obviously represented. Fourth Ezra includes a hierophagic scene wherein the protagonist, Ezra, is offered a cup in the course of his final revelatory episode. This cup, containing a fiery liquid, comes from heaven and is given to Ezra by God, who in turn speaks directly to Ezra. Consuming the heavenly cup enables Ezra for the first time to both receive and understand heavenly wisdom; further, it precipitates Ezra communicating this knowledge to others, something he has not done up until this point. The seventh episode of 4 Ezra represents the climax of Ezra's revelatory experiences.

Fourth Ezra was most likely composed in Hebrew and then translated into Greek, though it is now preserved only in fragments of Greek and Coptic and in Latin, Syriac, Ethiopic, Georgian, Arabic, and Armenian.[1] Most scholars, present company included, rely on the group of witnesses categorized as Group 1, made up of the Latin and Syriac versions.[2] In terms of genre, 4 Ezra fits the definition of apocalypse: it consists of a series of revelatory episodes facilitated by an angel as a divine mediator.[3]

An earlier version of this paper was published as "My Heart Poured Forth Understanding: *4 Ezra*'s Fiery Cup as Hierophagic Consumption," *SR* 44 (2015): 320–33. I am grateful to *SR* for agreeing to let me republish this edited version.

1. Karina Hogan, *Theologies in Conflict: Wisdom Debate and Apocalyptic Solution*, JSJSup 130 (Leiden: Brill, 2008); Michael Stone, *Fourth Ezra: A Commentary on the Book of Fourth Ezra* (Minneapolis: Fortress, 1990), 1–2.

2. Stone, *Fourth Ezra*, 3.

3. An apocalypse, as outlined briefly above, is "a genre of revelatory literature with a narrative framework, in which a revelation is mediated by an otherworldly

As Michael Stone, among others, has pointed out, "the apocalypse is a highly traditional genre.... Most apocalypses ... describe ecstatic states in very similar terms ... drawn from biblical prophecy, particularly from Ezekiel and Zechariah."[4] In other words, certain conventions utilized in 4 Ezra to describe the revelatory episodes experienced by Ezra—the use of an other-worldly mediator, the prominence of revelatory episodes, et cetera[5]—are shared by other works of the same genre. However, I would argue that the literary genre of hierophagy, found also in Ezekiel and in the Revelation of John, as I demonstrate in chapter 3, is a convention not unique to either biblical prophecy or the apocalyptic genre, but rather one that represents a shared cultural understanding or expectation of the ramifications of consuming other-worldly food. In this way, 4 Ezra indeed utilizes the traditional language of ecstatic experience as also preserved in biblical prophetic sources, as Stone suggests is typical of apocalypses, but it further engages hierophagy, which appears throughout a wider range of genres and religious traditions. Ezra's hierophagic experience in the seventh episode (4 Ezra 14) conveys its significance both because of the similarities it shares with a similar scenario in Ezekiel, but also because of its intersection with ancient Mediterranean expectations about what interaction with divine beings and their food might entail. This chapter outlines the ways in which hierophagy is demonstrated in 4 Ezra 14 specifically and how hierophagy functions to create meaning within the text as a whole.

While many current and previous scholars have attempted to reconstruct the sociohistorical situation out of which 4 Ezra arose or to identify the psychological or theological mindframe of the author through the characters of Ezra and/or Uriel,[6] the present project rather limits its examination of 4 Ezra to the narrative level, insofar as its literary tropes function

---

being to a human recipient, disclosing a transcendent reality which is temporal, insofar as it envisages eschatological salvation, and spatial insofar as it involves another supernatural world" (Collins, "Introduction: Towards the Morphology," 9–10; Collins, *Apocalyptic Imagination*, 4–5).

4. Stone, "A Reconsideration of Apocalyptic Visions," *HTR* 96 (2003): 170.

5. Collins, *Apocalyptic Imagination*, 4–5.

6. E.g., Hogan, *Theologies in Conflict in 4 Ezra*; Stone, *Fourth Ezra*; E. Brandenburger, *Die Verborgenheit Gottes im Weltgeschehen*, ATANT 68 (Zurich: Theologischer Verlag, 1981); Wolfgang Harnisch, *Verhängnis und Verheissung der Geschichte: Untersuchungen zum Zeit- und Geschichtsverständnis im 4.Buch Esra und in der syr. Baruchapokalypse* (Göttingen: Vandenhoeck & Ruprecht, 1969).

within a given plot and genre. This narrative-level analysis necessarily engages with 4 Ezra primarily as a story that uses plot devices, generically defined patterns, allusions, and symbols to communicate meaning. In order for them to communicate their meaning, these tools must be comprehensible within the culture that produced them; in other words, 4 Ezra's use of literary devices participates in the culturally accepted norms of the ancient literary realm at the same time as it deviates from them, as all texts within a genre necessarily do.[7] By engaging directly with one narrative-level example of hierophagy, I illustrate how 4 Ezra's use of this particular element both emerges out of an ancient expectation concerning the (narrative) consumption of other-worldly food and also develops the genre to its own ends.[8]

Fourth Ezra is a text that describes one way that the boundary between this world and the other world can be transgressed. In 4 Ezra, the eschatological expectation does not reside in a rebuilt Jerusalem temple, nor in the earthly realm at all.[9] Rather, in this text, the hope is always in another, heavenly world.[10] At the same time, however, 4 Ezra is accurately described as an historical apocalypse—all of the revelations imparted to Ezra take place on earth.[11] At the outset, then, this text establishes itself as navigating between two separate worlds, human and divine. Ezra receives divine instruction and wisdom, eventually communicating God's will to both ordinary and extraordinary mortals. This divine instruction is mediated

---

7. Thomas O. Beebee, *The Ideology of Genre: A Comparative Study of Generic Instability* (University Park: Pennsylvania State University Press, 2004), 19.

8. It is necessary to reiterate that I am not making claims about historical or otherwise "real world" rituals, which may or may not have been understood to involve food from other worlds. As Carla Sulzbach underscores in her article, we do not and cannot know about the "actual preparatory practices of early mystics" and therefore we are limited in our discussion of meals in texts to the narrative function or literary pattern of such meals; "the significance lies in the fact that an important ritual is described prior to the activation of the visionary experience" ("When Going on a Heavenly Journey," 177).

9. In contrast, see, for example, Ezek 40–48; 1 En. 90.20–37; the Temple Scroll; and the New Jerusalem Text.

10. Hindy Najman, "Between Heaven and Earth: Liminal Visions in *4Ezra*," in *Other Worlds and Their Relation to This World: Early Jewish and Ancient Christian Traditions*, ed. Tobias Nicklas et al., JSJSup 143 (Leiden: Brill, 2010), 152–53.

11. Collins, *Apocalyptic Imagination*, 6. 4 Ezra reviews the history of Israel in 3.5–27.

by the angel Uriel, who answers for God when Ezra addresses questions to the divine. Uriel acts as the interpreter of Ezra's episodes—Ezra is not able to comprehend the meaning of the things God tells and shows him on his own until the seventh episode and thus requires an *angelus interpres* in the first six episodes. Benjamin Reynolds observes that, in some instances, it is difficult to discern whether God or Uriel responds to Ezra's questions, since Ezra frequently addresses himself to God directly, although Uriel is present in the narrative.[12] He concludes, however, that the use of third-person terminology to describe God in the divine responses suggests that Uriel (and not God) is the speaker, despite certain uses of the first-person. Significant for the present study is Reynolds's acknowledgement that the only time God directly speaks to Ezra is in 4 Ezra 14.[13] I maintain that the only clear instance of God speaking directly to Ezra without a mediator is in the final episode; in each other instance, Uriel dictates the words of the Most High.[14] In other words, the only time that Uriel does not mediate the divine response is in the seventh episode—when Ezra ingests the heavenly cup. The significance of this shift should not be overlooked: the fourth episode (to be discussed below) marks a turning point in both the narrative and in the character of Ezra, but the seventh episode equally indicates a fundamental alteration of the relationship between Ezra and the divine, and, I argue, of the relationship between Ezra and the earthly realm.

Two recent studies engage with 4 Ezra's food imagery and its significance to the text's structure,[15] but both studies, surprisingly, neglect to comment on the role of the fiery cup in 14.39–40. Jonathan A. Moo

---

12. Benjamin E. Reynolds, "The Otherworldly Mediators in *4 Ezra* and *2 Baruch*: A Comparison with Angelic Mediators in Ascent Apocalypses and in Daniel, Ezekiel, and Zechariah," in *Fourth Ezra and Second Baruch: Reconstruction after the Fall*, ed. Matthias Henze and Gabriele Boccaccini (Leiden: Brill, 2013), 180.

13. Reynolds, "Otherworldly Mediators," 180; Loren Stuckenbruck disagrees, proposing that Ezra interacts "more directly" with God after the fourth episode. Loren T. Stuckenbruck, "Ezra's Vision of the Lady: Form and Function of a Turning Point," in Henze and Boccaccini, *Fourth Ezra and Second Baruch*, 147. So does Jacob M. Myers, *I and II Esdras*, AB (Garden City, NY: Doubleday, 1974), 201, 252, who interprets those speaking to Ezra as continually shifting between God and Uriel throughout the narrative.

14. Reynolds, "Otherworldly Mediators," 180; for example, 5.38; 7.17, 45; 12.7–9; 13.14 all use the third-person to talk about God, while 5.42; 6.6; 7.1, 11; 9.10–11; and 13.32, 37 use the first-person to express God's words.

15. Jonathan A. Moo, *Creation, Nature and Hope in 4 Ezra* (Göttingen: Vanden-

recognizes the importance of Ezra's floral meals, especially after fasting, but suggests the possibility that the text reflects the practices of actual seers consuming opium-poppies, while admitting that the evidence for such practices in antiquity is scant.[16] He further proposes that Ezra's consumption of the flowers in the field in the fourth episode represents his participation in the heavenly world to come, since flowers "can often be associated with Eden and paradise (cf. *1 En.* 24:4; *2 En.* [J] 8:2; *3 Bar.* 4:10; *Apoc. Adam* 7:21; *Jos. Asen.* 16:14–16)."[17] Moo's analysis, and his connection of the flowers with the heavenly realm, is not incorrect, but he misses the fact that Ezra's connection to that other realm is still incomplete. Ezra still requires explanation of his revelations from Uriel. It is not until the final episode that Ezra's association with the heavenly realm is made complete, through the fiery cup. In fact, according to his index, Moo does not mention the final, and I argue climactic, cup episode.

Peter-Ben Smit, for his part, is primarily interested in the metaphorical use of food imagery. He rightly recognizes that the progression of 4 Ezra literarily is related to the progression of Ezra's relationship to food, and I agree with his conclusions, which I also argue here, that Ezra's ability to speak wisdom is related to his consumption of foodstuffs.[18] However, while he recognizes these structural-consumptive elements, Smit neglects to recognize the role of Ezra's senses in this progression, as I outline in the present study, and further, neglects to discuss the function of the cup except to trace the metaphor of "drinking wisdom" in other Jewish texts.[19] Smit's otherwise excellent and thorough study, then, likewise misses the significance of Ezra's experiences as sensory revelations that culminate in the ingestion of heavenly food. As I argue here, examining the final cup episode alongside other examples of this kind of consumptive behavior in

---

hoeck & Ruprecht, 2011); Peter-Ben Smit, "Reaching for the Tree of Life: The Role of Eating, Drinking, Fasting, and Symbolic Foodstuffs in *4 Ezra*," *JSJ* 45 (2014): 1–22.

16. Brent Landau makes a similar suggestion about hallucinogens with reference to what he calls the "star food" in the *Revelation of the Magi*, where he also correctly notices the affinity that text has with 4 Ezra, Joseph and Aseneth, Ezekiel, and Revelation. Brent Landau, "The Star-Child and His Star-Food: Fragments of Visionary Experience in the Syriac *Revelation of the Magi*" (paper presented at the Second Century Seminar at Texas Christian University, Fort Worth, Texas, November 7, 2013), 12–13.

17. Moo, *Creation, Nature and Hope*, 147.
18. Smit, "Reaching for the Tree of Life," 8, 12.
19. Smit, "Reaching for the Tree of Life," 2–21.

narrative elucidates the importance of this episode to the narrative structure of 4 Ezra.

Structure of Episodes

Fourth Ezra is structured around seven revelatory episodes. Four of these episodes involve visions that communicate divine meaning to Ezra concerning God's role in the world. The episodes vary in terms of location, content, and what activity on Ezra's part facilitates the revelation. Table 1 outlines the locations and contexts of the seven revelatory episodes. Ezra fasts before receiving the second and third revelation and consumes flowers before the fourth and sixth. Although Flannery-Dailey maintains that all of the first six episodes are dreams and that only episode seven occurs while Ezra is awake, and Smit states that Ezra receives visions (rather than auditory revelation) after fasting and dreams after consuming flowers, most scholars agree that the fifth and sixth visions come to him like dreams, while the others take place while Ezra is awake.[20] The seventh episode takes place in the same location as the fourth, fifth, and sixth visions, but instead of consuming flowers, Ezra consumes a heavenly liquid.

Episode	Revelatory Trigger	Interlocutor
First Episode: 3.1–5.20	meditation/lying in bed	Uriel
Second Episode: 5.21–6.34	seven days of fasting	Uriel
Third Episode: 6.35–9.25	seven days of fasting	Uriel
Fourth Episode: 9.26–10.59	eating flowers from a field	Uriel
Fifth Episode: 11.1–12.51	sleeping in the field	Uriel
Sixth Episode: 13.1–13.58	eating flowers;[21] sleep	Uriel
Seventh Episode: 14.1–14.48	call narrative; fiery cup	God

Since five of Ezra's seven revelatory experiences hinge on his relationship to consumption—he either eats peculiar things or eats nothing at all—it

---

20. Flannery-Dailey, *Dreamers, Scribes, and Priests*, 212–20; Smit, "Reaching for the Tree of Life," 12. For the majority opinion, see, for example, Hogan, *Theologies in Conflict in 4 Ezra*; Stone, *Fourth Ezra*.

21. Stone remarks that there is an "absence of any fasting or food discipline in Visions 5 and 6" ("Reconsideration of Apocalyptic Visions," 172), but 4 Ezra 12.51 clearly indicates that Ezra consumes the flowers of the field prior to the sixth episode.

is clear that consumption plays a role in how we should understand the progression of Ezra's interaction with the divine.

First through Third Episodes

The first episode begins with Ezra resting in his bed, musing over the state of Jerusalem, which at this point in the narrative, has just been destroyed by Babylon. Ezra, unable to reconcile Jerusalem's fall with the chosenness of God's people, begins to address God, tracing God's involvement with human beings and their disobedient actions from Adam through Noah, Moses, and David. Ezra wonders how God allows such wickedness to prevail, and relatedly, whether Babylon's victory over Jerusalem really reflects the Babylonians' higher moral character. God sends Uriel to answer Ezra's questions about human behavior and divine theodicy. The angelic mediator challenges Ezra, if he would understand divine will, to explain earthly phenomena—the weight of fire, the volume of wind; Ezra, he purports, cannot possibly understand God's ways (4.1–2) if he cannot even know anything of earthly matters (4.9–12). Testing Ezra's ability to judge right from wrong, it is revealed that Ezra has no interest in understanding the workings of the heavenly realm, but rather only in understanding *at the same level as the divine* the workings of the earthly realm (4.23). Uriel, using figurative examples, explains to Ezra the end of the age and tells him about the signs that will indicate that time, while Ezra continues to ask questions about wickedness and righteousness. At the conclusion of the episode, Uriel instructs Ezra to fast for seven days in preparation for the next revelation (5.13); Ezra emerges from the episode feeling faint and shaken and proceeds with the angel's instructions (5.20–21). This episode establishes the pattern of revelation for 4 Ezra, where Ezra's questions, directed to God, are answered by the divine mediator, who at the same time points out Ezra's inability to fully comprehend God's plan for the world. In this episode, the revelation is brought on by ordinary contemplation and prayer rather than by any particularly performative action on the part of Ezra, save his speaking to God.

The second episode commences once Ezra has completed the seven days of fasting[22] and once more addresses God, wanting to understand

---

22. Hindy Najman understands that Ezra eats the "little bread" offered to him by Phaltiel in 5.18 ("Between Heaven and Earth," 160), but I view Ezra's response to him in 5.19 as proof that Ezra refuses to break his fast.

why God is seemingly unjust in punishing those who are supposed to be his chosen people (5.21–30). Note that although Ezra speaks his complaint to God directly, God again does not respond directly, choosing instead to send Uriel in his place. The angel once more points out the impossibility of Ezra coming to know divine equity by using examples of earthly things beyond Ezra's comprehension, before he explains the division of earthly time and how to tell its conclusion. At the end of the episode, Uriel promises that if Ezra fasts and prays for another seven days, he will be made party to even more information (6.30–31). Ezra's continued fasting, while it does yield heavenly information about the earthly realm and how God has chosen to organize it, nevertheless does not contribute to Ezra's understanding of these things; Ezra persists in asking questions of Uriel and of God and continues not to understand the examples Uriel uses to illustrate the logic of God's plan unless Uriel explains the examples in detail (e.g., 5.46–55).

After Ezra again fasts for seven days, the third episode occurs. As in the previous two episodes, it is Ezra's direct address to God which initiates the dialogue between Ezra and the angelic mediator, Uriel (6.38–9.25). Referencing creation, Ezra again questions the chosenness of God's people, since they alone seem singled out for destruction by Babylon. Ezra demands to know why nations that mean nothing to God have dominated while his favorite people have languished (6.55–59). Once more, Uriel speaks figuratively in order to prod Ezra toward divine understanding (7.1–9), and once more, Ezra fails to comprehend directly (7.10), and Uriel must explain more explicitly how the divine plan for Israel functions (7.11–8.3).

Fourth Episode

It is in the fourth episode where Ezra's mode of revelation shifts from just auditory to both auditory and visual. At the end of the third episode, Uriel gives Ezra a series of instructions:

> Go into a field of flowers where no house has been built, and eat only the flowers of the field, and taste no meat and drink no wine, but eat only flowers, and pray to the Most High continually—then I will come and talk with you. (4 Ezra 9.25)[23]

---

23. Translations follow M. Metzger, "The Fourth Book of Ezra," *OTP* 1:517–59.

As instructed, Ezra consumes the flowers of the field and again contemplates how it is possible for the law of God to be eternal while those who observe it perish. Having addressed God "in his heart," Ezra looks up and sees a vision of a woman mourning for her dead son (9.38–10.4). Unsympathetically, Ezra admonishes the woman for publicly displaying her private sorrows at a time when such a great public calamity has the very earth in mourning. In 10.25–28 the woman suddenly transforms into the heavenly city of Jerusalem, flashing with light. Ezra is astounded and confused and calls for Uriel to come explain his vision (10.28). Uriel urges Ezra to appreciate the vision of Jerusalem, "as far as it is possible for [his] eyes to see it … [and] as much as your ears can hear it" and tells him not to be afraid (10.55); Ezra is still unable to comprehend the meaning of the vision on his own and can only see the glory of Jerusalem in part, and not as it truly is.[24]

This fourth revelatory episode marks a turning point in both the plot and in Ezra's experience.[25] While Stone's analysis of the structure of 4 Ezra exemplifies the major arguments in this position, recently his conclusions about the structure of the episodes have come under scholarly criticism. Stone notes that the pattern of the first three episodes is maintained in the fourth and that "highly significant differences" point to the fourth episode as a pivotal event in the book. However, scholars such as Hindy Najman and Karina Hogan deemphasize the fourth episode as central to Ezra's transformation, seeing this transformation instead as a gradual shift throughout the narrative.[26] This trend is heartening, since in my view the seventh episode represents the climax of Ezra's alteration from uncomprehending mortal to a being of divine understanding. Nevertheless, certain differences signal the importance of the fourth episode in Ezra's development. First, while the preceding three episodes took place in Ezra's bedroom, in this one he is in a field. Second, while the second and third episodes required fasting, for the

---

24. Stone interprets the phrases concerning the capabilities of Ezra's eyes and ears as an indication that Ezra is sensing more than ordinary human abilities ("Reconsideration of Apocalyptic Visions," 176), but I understand these phrases to mean that even with Ezra's floral meal, he is still limited at this point in the narrative to sensing human-level experiences.

25. Stone, *Fourth Ezra*, 17; Stone, "Reconsideration of Apocalyptic Visions," 171, 177; Hogan, *Theologies in Conflict in 4 Ezra*, 4; Stuckenbruck, "Ezra's Vision of the Lady," 139.

26. Najman, "Between Heaven and Earth," 164–65; Hogan, *Theologies in Conflict in 4 Ezra*, 205–206, although Hogan still views this episode as "pivotal" (160).

fourth episode Ezra is to eat flowers (9.24).[27] Further, Stone observes that the fourth episode diverges from the previous three in that Ezra experiences not a dream, but a waking vision.[28] Stone notes that the structural elements of the fourth episode also share aspects in common with the subsequent visions, five and six, in that Ezra consumes flowers (12.51) and stays in the same field (10.58; 12.51). In this way, Stone sees the fourth episode as the hinge on which the surrounding episodes turn. I agree that the fourth episode represents a change in how Ezra receives divine knowledge. The sensory imagery employed in 4 Ezra points to the fourth episode as demarcating a shift in how Ezra experiences revelation. Indeed, Ezra's revelations escalate throughout the text, from hearing, to seeing, and finally to tasting. The first three episodes are only auditory—Ezra and Uriel converse with words alone. In the fourth episode, Ezra at last *sees* a vision of a woman, with whom he also converses; Uriel describes how Ezra experiences the revelation of the transformed woman/city "as far as it is possible for [his] eyes to see, and … as much as [his] ears can hear" (10.55–56). The fourth episode thus represents the point at which Ezra's ordinary human senses are expanded—hearing is supplemented with seeing, a pattern of growth that continues throughout the narrative. But tasting, as opposed to seeing or hearing, represents a more direct interaction with the sense-subject, that is, with the divine realm.[29]

The import of Ezra's augmented sensory abilities is reflected in how he reacts to the vision of the woman. Ezra is finally able to put aside his own problems and focuses instead on the woman (9.39; 10.5)—for Stone, this suggests that "what is abandoned is not only the train of thought expressed in the address but the whole set of questions that have preoccupied the seer from the start of the book."[30] Several scholars have suggested that Ezra is changed in this vision from one who needed comforting to one who is able to comfort others, namely, the personification of Jerusalem.[31] How-

---

27. Stone, *Fourth Ezra*, 29.

28. Stone, *Fourth Ezra*, 29; Flannery-Dailey argues that all of the first six episodes are dreams and that only episode seven occurs while Ezra is awake (*Dreamers, Scribes and Priests*, 212–20); for a discussion of Flannery-Dailey's argument, see Hogan, *Theologies in Conflict in 4 Ezra*, 160 n. 1.

29. Lieber, "Jewish and Christian Heavenly Meal Traditions," 316.

30. Stone, *Fourth Ezra*, 311.

31. For example, Stone, *Fourth Ezra*, 318; Brandenburger, *Die Verborgenheit Gottes im Weltgeschehen*, 81.

ever, it is questionable whether one can, as Stone does, call Ezra's behavior to the woman "comforting"—his harsh and unsympathetic tone hardly exudes consolation. Ezra is described as having anger towards the woman, not sympathy (10.5–6). Hogan notes that Ezra seems to be taking out his own frustration on the woman in his vision and that this scene indicates how Ezra is far from being consoled himself.[32] Stone proposes that Ezra takes on traits that were, in previous episodes, characteristic of Uriel—just as Uriel pointed out to Ezra that his mourning for Jerusalem was narrow and short-sighted, so here Ezra suggests to the woman that her grief for her son is misplaced given the larger events.[33] Ezra, having questioned God's justice in previous episodes, in this episode brings up the reality of God's righteousness; in other words, he appears to have taken on the role of Uriel in relation to this woman.[34] As such, Stone argues that this episode represents Ezra's complete acceptance of Uriel's message to this point.[35] However, as Hogan points out, Ezra at this stage is still grieving for the destruction of Jerusalem[36] and thus has not fully accepted Uriel's words. In my view, the fact that Ezra behaves towards the woman in a similar manner to how Uriel has behaved to him ironically underscores how little Ezra has understood up until this point. As the woman whom he has scolded transforms into Jerusalem, Ezra's words likewise transform in meaning from powerful to foolish.

The force with which Ezra experiences the transformation of the woman into the city of heavenly Jerusalem indicates that this scene is a turning point in 4 Ezra. For Stone, this experience represents some kind of conversion—the blinding light, the fainting, and the crying out for guidance resemble "the major sort of reorientation of personality usually associated with religious 'intensification,' a powerful and sudden integrating internalization of religious beliefs previously assented to intellectually.

---

32. Hogan, *Theologies in Conflict in 4 Ezra*, 163, 166.
33. Stone, *Fourth Ezra*, 319; Stone points out the parallels between the rhetorical techniques used by Uriel and then Ezra, respectively: 10.12–14 // 5.51–53; 10.15–17 // 5.54–55.
34. Stone, *Fourth Ezra*, 319; Stone further observes a page later that this conflation of roles is not absolute—where Uriel has consistently shown patience to Ezra, Ezra lashes out in anger at the woman (320).
35. Stone, "Reconsideration of Apocalyptic Visions," 172–74.
36. Hogan, *Theologies in Conflict in 4 Ezra*, 166.

This may be called, not quite accurately, conversion."[37] In other words, for Stone, Ezra has "assented ... intellectually" to Uriel's statements about God's role in Jerusalem's past, present, and future, but it is with his physical experience that this acceptance becomes realized and internalized.[38] However, throughout the subsequent episodes, Ezra is still unable to internalize the message that God sends him through Uriel. This suggests that Ezra is not fully transformed at this point but has at least made a move in the right direction. Hogan views this episode as the event that transforms Ezra into a "willing recipient" of revelation.[39] She disagrees with Stone that this episode marks Ezra's complete acceptance of Uriel's point of view but admits that "Ezra's resistance to Uriel's revelations has finally broken down, which is the first step in his gradual transformation."[40] This is a perspective which I support: after this experience, Ezra's behavior changes: he blames himself rather than God or Uriel for his weakness, for his inability to comprehend (12.4–5) and prays to God for strength (12.6).[41] Since Ezra is still incapable of true understanding in the subsequent visions, I am inclined to the opinion that although this fourth episode is an important step in Ezra's eventual transformation, that transformation is not yet complete.

Thus, while I agree that the fourth episode represents a shift in the previous vision pattern, and, as Stone suggests, that from this point "Ezra ceases to mourn and becomes the recipient of eschatological visions,"[42] I suggest that this shift is one step in the continuous escalation of Ezra's experiences, with the seventh episode actually representing the climax of received divine knowledge. The fourth episode still requires explication by Uriel; in this sense, Ezra has not internalized the divine message. In other words, Ezra does not have the heavenly wisdom he requires to make sense of his experience and needs an explanation:

> I lay there like a corpse and I was deprived of my understanding. Then he [the angel] grasped my right hand and strengthened me and set me on my feet, and said to me, "What is the matter with you? And why are you troubled? And why are your understanding and the thoughts of your

---

37. Stone, "Reconsideration of Apocalyptic Visions," 173. For an in-depth discussion of the issues around conversion in hierophagic texts, see chapter 5.
38. Stone, "Reconsideration of Apocalyptic Visions," 173–74.
39. Hogan, *Theologies in Conflict in 4 Ezra*, 4.
40. Hogan, *Theologies in Conflict in 4 Ezra*, 167.
41. Hogan, *Theologies in Conflict in 4 Ezra*, 169.
42. Stone, *Fourth Ezra*, 336.

mind troubled?" I said, "Because you have forsaken me! I did as you directed, and went out into the field, and behold, I saw, and still see, what I am unable to explain." He said to me, "Stand up like a man, and I will instruct you." I said, "Speak, my lord; only do not forsake me, lest I die before my time. For I have seen what I did not know, and I have heard what I do not understand. Or is my mind deceived, and my soul dreaming? Now therefore I entreat you to give your servant an explanation of this bewildering vision." (10.30–37)

Loren Stuckenbruck agrees that "the shift [the fourth episode] represents in the narrative *does not translate into any real or new understanding or insight on his part.*"[43] In other words, the vision of the heavenly Jerusalem alters Ezra's attitude so that he is a more willing recipient of revelation, but it does not transform his ability to understand.

Ezra's lack of comprehension makes sense in light of the hierophagic pattern—heavenly food given by a heavenly being yields heavenly understanding. But the flowers that Ezra eats in 9.26, though unusual for a person to eat, did not grow in heaven but rather in a field on earth, albeit one set apart by its lack of previous human interference. The food that Ezra consumes prior to the fourth episode, while it triggers revelation, is not heavenly in origin; it is therefore insufficient to grant the eater true understanding. As I will demonstrate below, only in the seventh (hierophagic) episode does Ezra at last commune directly with God, without Uriel as mediator. Far from being an afterthought or a literary epilogue,[44] it is this final episode which marks the climax of Ezra's revelatory experiences.

Fifth and Sixth Episodes

At the end of the fourth vision, Uriel commands Ezra to stay in the field and spend the night there, which he does. At the start of the fifth episode, there is no indication that Ezra consumes flowers, as he did prior to the fourth episode; Ezra merely sleeps two nights in the field and receives a dream about an eagle. It is significant that the revelation occurs in a

---

43. Stuckenbruck, "Ezra's Vision of the Lady," 145, emphasis original.
44. Stone, *4 Ezra*, 171; Hogan, *Theologies in Conflict in 4 Ezra*, 23; e.g., Stone describes it as merely a conclusion even while he admits that the episode provides "a climax of revelation before Ezra's assumption to heaven" (*4 Ezra*, 428). Nonetheless, most scholars, including Stone, spend a disproportionately small amount of time examining the seventh episode.

dream. This is a new development for Ezra, since while previous episodes occurred at night, these were "waking visions."[45] This new variation, the revelation within a dream, is indicative of the escalation of the series of episodes, an escalation that culminates in the seventh and final episode. The fourth episode, as discussed above, represents a turning point after which Ezra and the divine become more closely linked, though Ezra is still unable to comprehend God's message without an *angelus interpres*. To this end, the function of dreams in narrative is often to indicate direct or at least intimate interaction between a seer and the divine.[46] Thus, while the fourth episode does represent an explicit and pronounced shift in the series of episodes, it seems to me that the escalation of the mechanism of revelation in the fifth episode (and, as I will demonstrate, the sixth), suggests that the seventh episode holds more significance than has previously been acknowledged in scholarship on 4 Ezra. The parallels between the first and fifth episodes noted by Stone[47] certainly suggest a new section of the book beginning at the fifth episode, one which, like the first section, culminates in a transformative episode for Ezra. While the first three episodes culminate in the fourth transformative episode, the fourth through sixth episodes, and indeed, the entire narrative, reach their zenith in the seventh.

The content of the fifth episode, which is commonly called "The Eagle Vision," resembles in some aspects the visions recounted in Dan 7 and Rev 13: a great eagle appears, with "supernumerary heads and appendages," symbolic, according to Uriel in 12.1–39, of the various reigns leading up to the eschaton.[48] A lion, who appears in 11.37, represents a messiah who delivers God's people from the reign of the unrighteous rulers (12.34). Despite the fact that Ezra has been deemed worthy to receive this heavenly vision (12.7–9), he nonetheless cannot interpret what he sees in the dream without Uriel's assistance:

> Then I awoke in great perplexity of mind and great fear, and I said to my spirit, "Behold, you have brought this upon me, because you search

---

45. Stone, *Fourth Ezra*, 341–42.
46. Stone, *Fourth Ezra*, 347–48; e.g., Gen 37; 41; Dan 2; 2 Bar 36.1. See also Flannery-Dailey, *Dreamers, Scribes, and Priests*, esp. 6.
47. Stone, *Fourth Ezra*, 355.
48. See Stone, *Fourth Ezra*, 348. For the quotation, see Hogan, *Theologies in Conflict in 4 Ezra*, 179.

out the ways of the Most High. Behold, I am still weary in mind and am very weak in my spirit, and not even a little strength is left in me, because of the great fear with which I have been terrified this night.... O sovereign Lord, if I have found favour in thy sight and if I have been favoured before thee beyond others, and if my prayer has indeed come up before thy face, strengthen me and show thy servant the interpretation and meaning of this terrifying vision, that thou mayest fully comfort my soul. For thou has judged me worth to be shown the end of the times and the last events of the times." (12.3b–9)

Ezra's long, fearful speech to Uriel after the vision repeatedly emphasizes how little Ezra is able to understand, even after his transformative experience in the fourth episode.[49] Indeed, the interpretation that Ezra receives from Uriel suggests that Ezra is still incapable of communicating directly with the Most High, or of understanding divine wisdom on his own. Ezra's apparent "conversion" in the fourth episode has not increased his ability to comprehend divine revelation. The use of the third-person to describe the Most High several times during the interpretation (e.g., 12.23, 30, 32, 37) confirms Uriel remains the interlocutor; God has yet to make an appearance. At the conclusion of the fifth episode, Ezra speaks to his people to reassure them about his absence but does not communicate to them any of what he has learned—this is something that Ezra is only able to do after he ingests the fiery cup at the end of the seventh episode (14.45–48).

Like the fifth episode, the sixth revelation received by Ezra occurs in a dream. Prior to the sixth episode, in 12.51, Ezra follows the instructions of the angel and sits in a field for seven days, eating only the plants and flowers growing there, although the narrative is not explicit about Uriel uttering these instructions. Then Ezra receives the vision of the Man from the Sea, but again, Ezra cannot understand the meaning of it. He asks again for the angel to "show [him] also the interpretation of this dream" (13.15) since his consumption of the flowers might have facilitated the episode but could not provide Ezra with the means of proper understanding of the divine message. Ezra continues to ask clarifying questions of the angel while Uriel interprets this vision (13.51) until finally the angel puts an end to his explanation with the offer of further understanding in the coming days.

---

49. Stone, *Fourth Ezra*, 354.

Thus, as a result of his peculiar floral meals, Ezra has certain experiences: in the fourth episode he is first visited by a woman who transforms into Jerusalem (9.38–10.28); then in the sixth episode Ezra has a dream of the Man from the Sea (13.1–58). In both cases, Ezra has these experiences after eating the flowers and subsequently has them interpreted by a divine being because he does not understand their meaning (10.32; 13.14–15). These meals do not follow the hierophagic pattern: first, the flowers are not divine, having grown in a field on earth; second, Ezra is not physically or spiritually changed by the meals, and the experiences he has are still not readily understandable by him—an other-worldly mediator, Uriel, must explain their meaning.

As in the fourth episode, the fifth and sixth revelatory scenes make use of Ezra's sense of sight: these episodes extend the visual qualities introduced in the fourth episode by using language that emphasizes the visuality of these experiences: "and I looked, and behold …" (11.2, 3, 5, 7, 10; 13.3, 5, 8, etc.). The emphasis in these sections on visuality, in contrast to the auditory revelations of the previous sections, contributes to the gradual increase in Ezra's ability to receive divine wisdom. Although in both the fourth and sixth episodes Ezra consumes flowers from the field, Ezra still maintains his ordinary human senses: he has visions and hears Uriel speak to him but has no divinely-given understanding—he is still unable to ingest God's message. Indeed, in including these other instances of eating in the previous visions, 4 Ezra highlights the important differences between hierophagy and other types of eating.

Seventh Episode

When Ezra first consumes the flowers of the field prior to the fourth episode, we read that Ezra's "mouth was opened" (9.28)—this same phrase is used in the seventh episode, in 14.41. In this way, it appears that the fourth and the hierophagic seventh episode are parallel, but the significant differences between the two indicate that the fourth episode does not represent a hierophagic event. The flowers, like the fasting before, initiate a revelatory episode, but they do not facilitate understanding, something only hierophagic consumption brings about. The use of parallel language in the seventh episode suggests that, just as the fourth episode marked a turning point for Ezra, so too the seventh represents a shift in Ezra's relationship to the divine realm.

The seventh episode is structured differently from previous episodes: the call narrative that precedes the actual revelation signals the major difference between this section and the others, which is that, for the first time, God and Ezra interact directly. The call echoes those of Moses (Exod 3:4), Abraham (Gen 22:11), and Samuel (1 Sam 3:10). Given Ezra's responsibility with regard to torah[50] and the direct reference to Moses in 4 Ezra 14.3, this scene most strongly brings to mind Moses's call. If Ezra's preoccupation with torah is central to 4 Ezra's message,[51] then surely Ezra's receiving of scripture in the seventh episode, especially when viewed in conjunction with the introductory call narrative at the start of the episode, marks the culmination of the entire revelatory sequence. Further, in contrast with the previous episodes, here Ezra displays neither anxiety nor mourning. His emotional state signals how different this experience will be from the previous ones.[52]

God instructs Ezra to prepare himself to write things that God will tell him, some to be made public and some to be kept secret (14.24–26). God tells Ezra that God will illuminate his heart (14.25); when Ezra returns from reproving his people, Ezra has the hierophagic experience that at last grants him understanding:

> And on the next day, behold, a voice called me, saying, "Ezra, open your mouth and drink what I give you to drink." Then I opened my mouth and behold, a full cup was offered to me; it was full of something like water, but its colour was like fire. And I took it and drank; and when I had drunk it, my heart poured forth understanding, and wisdom increased in my breast, for my spirit retained its memory; and my mouth was opened, and was no longer closed. (4 Ezra 14.38–41)

At this point, Ezra is able to dictate to his five scribes the contents of ninety-four books over a period of forty days. The scribes have also been

---

50. According to Karina Martin Hogan, in 4 Ezra "*tôrâ* is a highly abstract concept associated with wisdom, the natural order, and 'the way of the Most High.' Understanding the term *tôrâ* broadly as divine 'instruction,' the author of 4 Ezra extends it to all of Scripture and by implication to the seventy additional books revealed to Ezra in the epilogue" (Karina Martin Hogan, "The Meanings of '*tôrâ*' in '4 Ezra,'" *JSJ* 38 [2007]: 530). For further discussion of the flexibility of the meaning of torah in early Judaism, see Shayna Sheinfeld, "From Nomos to Logos: Torah Observance in First Century Judaism," in *Paul within Judaism: New Perspectives*, ed. Mgr. František Ábel (Lexington Books/Fortress Academic, forthcoming).

51. Hogan, "Meanings of '*tôrâ*,'" 548; Stone, "Reconsideration of Apocalyptic Visions," 172.

52. Stone, *Fourth Ezra*, 412.

given understanding (14.42), though we are not privy to how their inspiration is delivered, and as a result they are able to write in strange characters. Some of the books, presumably the twenty-four of the Hebrew Bible,[53] are to be made public, but the seventy remaining are only for the wise of Ezra's people. The episode culminates in Ezra's assumption to heaven in 14.50: "at that time Ezra was caught up, and taken to the place of those who are like him, after he had written all these things."[54]

No satisfactory analysis of the cup motif has been carried out to date. Stone's commentary on 4 Ezra 14.38–41 describes the cup as filled with a holy spirit, which communicates wisdom. He rightly emphasizes the importance of this scene and even links it to Ezekiel and the book of Revelation, where, as we will see in the next chapter, revelatory experiences are also mediated through consumptive—and as I argue, hierophagic—imagery.[55] But Stone primarily associates Ezra drinking from the cup with the "Hellenistic theme of 'divine drunkenness' as a way of describing inspiration.[56] Certain elements of the "divine drunkenness" trope match up with 4 Ezra, in that Ezra consumes a divine liquid, like water, but fire-colored, and as a result gains wisdom—but Ezra is not intoxicated by this cup. That is, the text itself does not describe his experience in terms of ecstatic possession. Rather, Ezra is, for the first time, able to *retain memory* (14.41) in a way that is incongruous with drunkenness. Smit, more recently, examines the cup language in the context of "drinking wisdom" (cf. 4 Ezra 8.4), but the function of the cup in the narrative is not Smit's primary concern—he is more interested in the metaphori-

---

53. Stone, *Fourth Ezra*, 439 n. 5 notes, "the alternative tradition of 22 books, according to the letters of the Hebrew alphabet, first occurs in Josephus, *Contra Apionem* 1.38." He also remarks that this is the earliest reference we have to a twenty-four-book canon (441). Lee M. McDonald reminds us that although it is likely that the twenty-four books indicated in 4 Ezra are those of the Bible, the text does not specify which texts were part of this collection Lee M. McDonald, *The Formation of the Christian Biblical Canon* (Peabody, MA: Hendrickson, 1995), 60.

54. Although verses 49–50 do not occur in the Latin version of 4 Ezra, in the opinion of most scholars today, the verses are original and were lost with the addition of 6 Ezra to the text. Stone, *Fourth Ezra*, 442; Jason Zurawski, "Ezra Begins: *4 Ezra* as Prequel and the Making of a Superhero," in *Old Testament Pseudepigrapha and the Scriptures*, ed. Eibert Tigchelaar, BETL (Leuven: Peeters, 2014), 12 and n.40.

55. Stone, *Fourth Ezra*, 119–20.

56. Stone, *Fourth Ezra*, 120; cf. Philo, *Ebr.* 146–148.

cal imagery.[57] Najman likewise only discusses the consumption of the fiery liquid in passing, in the context of textual resonance with previous apocalyptic texts.[58] Even Stone's most recent contribution to the subject only briefly discusses the cup as a "symbolic cup of inspiration."[59] In light of the progression from auditory to visual sensory revelation already articulated, the gustatory aspect of Ezra's cup should not be overlooked. In this final revelatory experience, Ezra is able not just to hear, as in the first three episodes, or to see, as in the next three, but also to taste. It is this sense that is the most intimate of the five natural senses; hearing and sight put distance between the sensor and the sense-object, whereas with taste, the sense object is made internal to the sensor.[60] Thus, Ezra's ingestion of the contents of the heavenly cup indicates the pinnacle of his sensory revelations that began in the previous episodes. Hogan, like Stone, correctly associates the cup scenario with Ezekiel's similar experience and concludes that Ezra's mouth "will not be his own, but … will only be able to speak God's words, like Ezekiel."[61] In linking this pattern of consumption to other similar scenes in ancient literature, the significance of Ezra's cup is increased, lending strength to the idea that the seventh episode represents the climax rather than the epilogue of Ezra's revelations. But Hogan does not go far enough: Ezra's cup scenario is not linked only to Ezekiel's similar experience, but also with a whole wealth of other literary examples of the consumption of heavenly foods, such as Revelation, the Passion of Perpetua and Felicitas, Joseph and Aseneth, and others discussed in further chapters. In these examples, as in 4 Ezra, the mortal consumer of the divine item is changed. Like other characters who undergo such experiences, Ezra gains new knowledge and new abilities: he is finally able understand and to communicate God's word to his people through the books he transcribes.

---

57. Smit, "Reaching for the Tree of Life," 13, 21.

58. Najman, "Between Heaven and Earth," 2–3, 29, 63.

59. Michael Stone, "Seeing and Understanding in *4 Ezra*," in *Revealed Wisdom: Studies in Apocalyptic in Honour of Christopher Rowland*, ed. John Ashton, AJEC 88 (Leiden: Brill, 2014), 136–37.

60. For a fuller discussion of the sensory intimacy of taste, please see the introduction. Cf. Lieber, "Jewish and Christian Heavenly Meal Traditions," 316 n. 8; and especially Korsmeyer, *Making Sense of Taste*.

61. Hogan, *Theologies in Conflict in 4 Ezra*, 215.

In confirmation of Ezra's new divine association, he is even "caught up" into heaven, physically leaving the earthly realm. This translocation is also, I argue, a hallmark of hierophagic experience. We read in verse 50 that Ezra is taken up: "At that time Ezra was caught up, and taken to the place of those who are like him, after he had written all these things. And he was called the Scribe of the knowledge of the Most High forever." This assumption was predicted in 14.9, when God tells Ezra that he "shall be taken up from among men, and henceforth [he] shall be with my servant and with those who are like [him], until the times are ended."[62] It is clear from the text that through his consumption of the fiery cup, Ezra is now closely associated with the divine realm, an association that represents a marked feature of the literary genre of hierophagy.

Thus, I propose that this final revelatory scene in 4 Ezra participates in the hierophagic pattern, in contrast with the fourth and sixth episodes; indeed, the presence of these earlier nonhierophagic meals highlights the importance of recognizing this special category. The full cup from heaven that Ezra drinks allows him, for the first time, to understand the heavenly revelations and to transmit this knowledge to others. In contrast, while eating the plants facilitated his apocalyptic experiences in the fourth and sixth episodes, this earthly food did not grant him knowledge, only visions. In drinking the fiery liquid, Ezra not only gains heavenly wisdom but is at last capable of understanding it and also of communicating it with the larger community in the form of books. Further, whereas previously the angel Uriel was the interlocutor between Ezra and the divine, during the episode with the cup, it is God who speaks with Ezra directly. The cup rests at the center of this more intimate interaction between the mortal and heavenly realms and allows Ezra, at last, direct access to divine wisdom.

---

62. Jason Zurawski, in his article proposing that 4 Ezra is a "prequel" to the biblical Ezra narrative, argues that this assumption into heaven takes place only after Ezra delivers the books to the Jerusalem temple and therefore that 4 Ezra 14.50 alludes to Ezra's narrative future rather than his narrative present. While Zurawski's thesis is compelling, I am inclined to a less complicated chronology for Ezra's experiences. However, regardless of when Ezra's assumption to heaven takes place in the literary-historical time frame, narratively, the text is clear that this final experience is concretely associated with Ezra's being taken up into heaven. In other words, even if Zurawski is right and there is a forty-seven-year gap between when Ezra receives the books and when he goes up to heaven, the narrative structure of 4 Ezra 14 demonstrates that the end result of consuming otherworldly food is that Ezra now belongs in the heavenly realm (Zurawski, "Ezra Begins," 12–15, esp. 15).

Conclusion

Fourth Ezra 14 participates in the hierophagic pattern in each of the genre's three major features: as a result of his heavenly meal, (1) Ezra is finally able to understand the received divine knowledge that he has been transmitted; (2) he gains new abilities, such as the ability to retain memory and to recite and therefore communicate what he has learned from God; and (3) Ezra is translocated to another realm. Fourth Ezra's structure of seven revelatory episodes depicts the gradual escalation of Ezra's revealed knowledge until its pinnacle at the point of consumption of the cup. The first episode occurs under ordinary circumstances, the second and third episodes are brought about through fasting, and the fourth and sixth episodes occur after the consumption of flowers. The fifth vision occurs in a dream, in similar circumstances to the first episode but intensified, as dreams were understood to be a more direct means of contact with the divine. The initial episodes depict auditory revelation while the fourth, fifth, and sixth are marked by the addition of visions. The seventh vision represents a dramatic shift in Ezra's experiences: his consumption there is not ordinary ritual behavior (such as fasting) or earthly edible material (such as the flowers), which previously allowed revelation using two of the more distant human senses. Ezra's revelations escalate throughout the text, from hearing, to seeing, and finally to tasting. In 4 Ezra 14, the sensory intimacy of taste allows Ezra to transcend human understanding and cosmic boundaries. This heavenly consumption in the form of his ingestion of the fiery cup enables Ezra not only to commune directly with God for the first time, but also, and again for the first time, to understand the revelations he is given and communicate them fully to the community. It is only when Ezra consumes heavenly material, given to him directly from the heavenly realm, that he is able to transcend his mortal understanding. This final example of food discipline participates in the genre of hierophagy—food given by an immortal to a mortal that transforms the eater in some way. In this case, Ezra receives the full transmission of heavenly knowledge. The seventh Episode participates in the aspect of hierophagy where otherwordly knowledge is conferred upon the eater. The identification of this scene with hierophagy also aligns with some scholars' suggestion that the character of Ezra, in this episode, becomes heavenly and enters a mythical liminal sphere, as in 4 Ezra 14.50.[63] This liminality and shifting of Ezra's

---

63. Najman, "Between Heaven and Earth," 159.

identity from mortal to heavenly is only possible because of the assumed narrative ramifications of consuming other-worldly food: in short, Ezra's visions are only fully understandable in light of their participation in hierophagy as a genre.

3
Revelation

The hierophagic example in Revelation occurs part way through the revelatory experiences of its seer, John of Patmos.[1] In a scene towards the middle of the text, an angel presents John with an unrolled scroll and directs him to eat it: "It will be bitter to your stomach, but sweet as honey in your mouth" (10:9). This example of hierophagy makes explicit use of taste imagery in order to communicate its message. In a text rich with somatic imagery, the language of taste in this episode is a rhetorical tool that expresses a specific meaning. Viewing John's experience as hierophagic not only allows for the little scroll to be read alongside other examples of this genre, but it also illuminates how generic differences are used by the seer to communicate his divinely granted authority. I argue that the author uses the image of ingesting a scroll to communicate the legitimacy of John's revelatory experiences and, indeed, the authority of the book of Revelation as a whole. This analysis will shed light on how hierophagy functions to transmit divine knowledge as well as the specific ramifications of ingesting sweet- and bitter-tasting substances.

An earlier version of this chapter appeared as "Tasting the Little Scroll: A Sensory Analysis of Divine Interaction in Revelation 10:8–10," *JSNT* 40.1 (2017): 101–19. I am grateful to *JSNT* for allowing it to be reprinted here.

1. I agree with the general consensus that the author of Revelation was not John the apostle but rather a late first-century CE writer familiar with a variety of Christian modes of expression but not particularly with the Johannine epistles or gospel. The author of the text calls himself John, and I see no reason to attribute a different name to that author. See the discussion in Craig R. Koester, *Revelation: A New Translation with Introduction and Commentary*, AB (New Haven: Yale University Press, 2014), 65–68 and Adela Yarbro Collins, *Crisis and Catharsis: The Power of the Apocalypse* (Philadelphia: Westminster, 1984), 27–44.

This short episode in Rev 10:8–10 has received less scholarly attention than many other aspects of this complex apocalypse. Scholars seem not to have considered how strange it is for John to eat a heavenly scroll. Comparing Revelation with the texts discussed in the previous two chapters in which similar ingestion takes place, I argue that Rev 10:8–10 makes use of hierophagy: the eater undergoes a change that renders him uniquely capable of understanding divine knowledge as a result of the eating. Just as the examples in 4 Ezra and in the Persephone myths emphasized the relocation of the eater vis-à-vis the divine realm, this example in Revelation expresses how access to divine knowledge is brought about by ingesting divine food.

The item that is ingested in Revelation is peculiar in that it is not an ordinarily edible object, such as Persephone's pomegranate or Ezra's cup of liquid. These previous examples of hierophagy involve items edible under ordinary circumstances, but the book of Revelation portrays its protagonist ingesting a scroll, an ingredient that does not figure prominently—or at all—in the recipe books of antiquity. Indeed, Revelation's use of a nonfood item highlights that it is the *act of ingesting* the otherworldly item, and not the nature of the item itself, that is a core element of hierophagy in general.

The act of eating a divine substance precipitates a change in John that brings him closer to the heavenly realm. In some comparable cases—such as Joseph and Aseneth and Apuleius's *Metamorphoses*, both of which will be explored in subsequent chapters—one function of eating otherworldly food is the transformation of the consumer's physical appearance: Aseneth emerges from her meal with a radiant beauty that renders her unrecognizable to her foster-father, and Lucius is no longer an ass but a human. Hierophagy can also function to translocate the eater to another realm, as we saw when Ezra is taken up into heaven in 4 Ezra and when Persephone is unable to return from the underworld in Ovid. In Revelation, however, the emphasis is placed on how hierophagy transmits divine knowledge from the one who provides the heavenly substance—the angel—to the one who eats the substance—John.

An important tool for analyzing the theme of hierophagy in Rev 10 is sensory analysis. Sensory analysis has become an increasingly prominent methodological tool, especially in fields such as anthropology, where scholars such as David Howes have recognized the importance of nonvisual, nonaural sensory experience in Western and non-Western cultures alike.[2] In antiquity

---

2. David Howes, *Sensual Relations: Engaging the Senses in Culture and Social Theory* (Ann Arbor: University of Michigan Press, 2003).

studies, sensory analysis is still in the process of gaining more mainstream scholarly attention, although there have been several recent publications.[3] Examining Revelation with the senses in focus showcases the literary techniques by which the author expresses meaning. Sensory and somatic imagery is woven into Revelation's message in a way that makes it impossible to understand the text without investigating the historical and rhetorical meaning behind the imagery. This approach to Revelation also exposes how the audiences of texts like Revelation, as opposed to ancient philosophers from whom we often gather information about the senses, hold different expectations about the bodily ways in which God can be experienced.

To reiterate, in contrast with visual or auditory experiences, the sense of taste is experienced privately. The translation of John's taste experience of the scroll in 10:8–10 into his visions, written down to be heard by an audience, allows a community to partake collectively in the sharing of this intimacy with the divine. I suggest that the special way that John accesses these divine revelations—through consuming the little scroll—shows that he is granted privileged access to God's knowledge, which, when translated into visions, allows others to participate in this intimacy. To establish a hierophagic pattern in Revelation, I will first analyze the text itself and outline Rev 10:8–10's relationship to other parts of the book of Revelation and in light of Revelation's use of sensory imagery. Second, I will explore how the consumption of otherworldly food works to dissolve the boundaries between this world and the heavenly realm. Finally, I will examine how the sense of taste functions in antiquity in order to shed light on how it is used hierophagically in Revelation.

The Scroll in Revelation 5

My argument about the consumption of the little scroll in chapter 10 supports the current consensus that the recommissioning in 10:11, where

---

3. Susan Ashbrook Harvey, *Scenting Salvation: Ancient Christianity and the Olfactory Imagination* (Berkeley: University of California Press, 2006); Deborah A. Green, *The Aroma of Righteousness: Scent and Seduction in Rabbinic Life and Literature* (University Park: Pennsylvania State University Press, 2011); Rudolph, *Taste and the Ancient Senses*; Yael Avrahami, *The Senses of Scripture: Sensory Perception in the Hebrew Bible* (New York: T&T Clark, 2012); Nicole L. Tilford, *Sensing World, Sensing Wisdom: The Cognitive Foundation of Biblical Metaphors*, AIL 31 (Atlanta: SBL Press, 2017).

John is told to prophesy again, demarcates a new section of the entire book of Revelation.[4] Many scholars agree that this recommissioning hinges on this episode of the little scroll. The ingestion of the little scroll marks a shift in the content of the book as a whole.

The rhetorical force of John consuming the scroll in chapter 10 is highlighted by the inclusion of a scroll earlier in the text. The scroll in Rev 5 does not express the same somatic connotations that the scroll in Rev 10 does, which emphasizes the significance of ingesting the scroll, as opposed to simply viewing it. In Rev 5:2–3 we read,

> And I saw in the right hand of him who was seated on the throne a scroll written within and on the back, sealed with seven seals; and I saw a strong angel proclaiming with a loud voice, "Who is worthy to open the scroll and break its seals?" And no one in heaven or on earth or under the earth was able to open the scroll or to look into it, and I wept much that no one was found worthy to open the scroll or to look into it.

The scroll is opened by the Lamb, Jesus, and the opening of each of the seven seals sets off a series of visions of calamity for earth. Scholars debate whether the scroll in Rev 5:1 is the same as that in chapter 10.[5] For my present argument, whether or not the scrolls are identical has little impact. If they are different scrolls, comparing them still emphasizes the significance of eating as opposed to merely viewing a scroll. If they are the same scroll, which is how I treat them here, the escalation of God's message is clearly visible in the progression from vision to consumption. In either

---

4. Collins, *Crisis and Catharsis*, 28; Christopher R. Smith, "The Structure of the Book of Revelation in Light of Apocalyptic Literary Conventions," *NovT* 36 (1994): 373–93; Mark Seaborn Hall, "The Hook Interlocking Structure of Revelation: The Most Important Verses in the Book and How They May Unify Its Structure," *NovT* 44 (2002): 277–96.

5. Koester, *Revelation*, 372–73; Richard Bauckham, *The Climax of Prophecy: Studies in the Book of Revelation* (Edinburgh: Clark, 1993), 243–66. See also Leslie Baynes, "Revelation 5:1 and 10:2a, 8–10 in the Earliest Greek Tradition: A Response to Richard Bauckham," *JBL* 129 (2010): 801–16; and Baynes, *The Heavenly Book Motif in Judeo-Christian Apocalypses 200 B.C.E.–200 C.E.*, JSJSup 152 (Leiden: Brill, 2014), 149–62. I am unconvinced that the difference between *biblion* (5:1) and the diminutive *biblaridion* (10:8–10) is significant enough to identify the scrolls as distinct from one another, nor that the intertexuality with Ezek 2:8–3:4 precludes the "little scroll" being a continued reference to the sealed scroll in chapter 5.

case, the scroll in Rev 5 provides information about how to interpret the scroll in chapter 10.

The scroll in chapter 5 is sealed with seven seals, which are opened one by one, but the contents of the scroll are apparently not revealed to the audience: the opening of the seals prepares readers for what the scroll contains, but the text says that no one is able to open the scroll or to look into it (5:3).[6] Its message is not thus made explicit until it is given to John to consume in chapter 10, after which he reveals the message of the scroll in the prophecies that follow the eating; 11:1–13 are a summary of these contents, but the full message is laid out in the second half of the book.[7] This is observable through a few thematic shifts that the consumption of the scroll precipitates, namely, the specificity with which the chronology of the end times is described and the shift in concern from the sealing of God's chosen to the marking of God's enemies. These shifts indicate significant differences in the functions of the scroll in chapter 5 versus in chapter 10.

First, prior to chapter 10, questions of "when" are answered vaguely. In 6:10, after the opening of the sealed scroll, the martyrs ask, "How long, Sovereign Lord, holy and true, until you judge the inhabitants of the earth and avenge our blood?" The answer is nonspecific: "a little longer, until the number of their fellow servants and brothers who were to be killed as they had been was completed" (6:11). After John eats the scroll, however, specific time units are used, such as "time, times, and half a time" (12:14); forty-two months (13:5); or 1260 days (12:6), each adding up to about three and a half years. These specific time units are used seven times after 10:8.[8] These three and a half years refer to the time it will take from Satan's removal from heaven and Christ's ascension to when Christ will return at the end of the age for the final victory.[9] Indeed, the mighty angel suggests that an understanding of time is part of what John will receive in the little scroll, when he says in 10:6–7 that "the time of waiting will end when the seventh angel blows his trumpet. That is when the mysterious purpose of God will be complete."[10] This shift, from vague language to specific language, illustrates

---

6. Koester, *Revelation*, 405.
7. Koester, *Revelation*, 405; Bauckham, *Climax of Prophecy*, 243–57.
8. Smith, "Structure of the Book of Revelation," 388; Koester, *Revelation*, 486–87, 498; Collins, *Crisis and Catharsis*, 67–68; Harry O. Maier, *Apocalypse Recalled: The Book of Revelation after Christendom* (Minneapolis: Fortress, 2002), 157.
9. Koester, *Revelation*, 498.
10. Koester, *Revelation*, 490.

that consuming the scroll results in a deeper, more thorough understanding of the divine plan. The sealed scroll of chapter 5 does not yield the particular knowledge conveyed by the ingested scroll in chapter 10.

Second, the scrolls in chapter 5 and chapter 10 play different roles in identifying those who are with God and those who are against God. Before John consumes the scroll in Rev 10, the text repeatedly refers to those whom God has sealed on their foreheads: "Do not harm the earth or the sea or the trees, till we have sealed the servants of our God upon their foreheads" (7:3).[11] This sealing represents the protection of these servants but also their belonging to the people of God.[12] This is in contrast to those who are signified as enemies of God with the mark of the beast; people who have the mark of the beast are mentioned only after John consumes the scroll.[13] Just as those who are set apart by the seal of God belong to God, so too those who are marked with the sign of the beast belong to the beast. There is a shift, then, in the focus of identifying groups of people before and after the little scroll. Before chapter 10, those who are marked are exclusively marked positively, with the seal of the divine. After chapter 10, those who are marked are overwhelmingly marked negatively, with the mark of the beast—this symbol only occurs after the little scroll turns John's stomach "bitter."[14]

Thus, the scroll John is shown in chapter 5 certainly provides him with visions as the seals are opened; however, it is only when John consumes the open scroll in chapter 10 that its contents are revealed. In eating the scroll, John literally internalizes its contents, which he can then visualize for his

---

11. In Rev 9:4, the phrase is used similarly.

12. Koester, *Revelation*, 416, 458, 425–27. See Ezek 9:4 for a biblical example of sealing used as protection. Those who are marked with God's sign are also mentioned after the ingestion of the scroll in chapter 10, but the terminology of the "seal" is not used in those examples (e.g., 14:1; 22:4).

13. For example, 13:16–17: "it causes all … to be marked … so that no one can buy or sell unless he has the mark, that is the name of the beast or the number of its name"; 14:9: "If any one worships the beast and its image, and receives a mark on his forehead or on his hand, he also shall drink the wine of God's wrath, poured unmixed into the cup of his anger"; 16:2: "So the first angel went and poured his bowl on the earth, and foul and evil sores came upon the men who bore the mark of the beast and worshipped its image." Perhaps the inversion of tastes that John experiences in 10:10, when the flavor of the scroll changes from sweet to bitter, is paralleled in the inversion of focus from the positive/sealed people to the negative/marked.

14. Smith, "Structure of the Book of Revelation," 388.

readers. The scroll with the seven seals is rendered open but still incomprehensible until John consumes it.[15] Investigating how the scroll in Rev 5 is used in the text to yield information makes it clear that the scroll in Rev 10 works in a different way, not because it is a heavenly scroll, since the scroll in Rev 5 is also from heaven, but because the scroll in Rev 10 is consumed. That is, it is the act of ingesting the heavenly substance that allows it to operate in this special way. Hierophagy is not simply the reception of divine materials, but it is the incorporation of them into the recipient in a way that simply viewing a scroll's contents does not accomplish.

Sensory Imagery in Revelation

John's use of sensory rhetoric in chapter 10 participates in the somatic imagery used in the text as a whole. As several scholars have observed, the poetics of John's experiences include the consistent use of verbs of seeing and hearing.[16] The use of verbs of seeing punctuates the overall narrative in a way that creates episodic units of divine experience.[17] Auditory episodes are sometimes attached to these visual experiences, such as when John *sees* a scroll and then *hears* a divine pronouncement (e.g., 6:1–4) or when he *hears* a trumpet and then *sees* a star (e.g., 9:1). Studies on visions in apocalypses are right to focus on this important connection between vision and auditory experience in divine-human communication, but they have neglected to analyze the rhetorical force of sensory imagery, including visions, on the audience.

Indeed, the apocalypse is replete, in almost every line, with imagery that evokes a sensory response, from thunderous angelic voices to dazzling visions of heavenly beings to the painful woes visited on the people of earth by God. For instance, the one who sits on the throne in Rev 4:2 is described as having "the appearance of jasper and carnelian," and the throne as encircled by a rainbow that looks like an emerald. Emerging from

---

15. The chain of possession of the scroll, from heaven to Jesus to angel to John, may reflect the same chain of command articulated in Rev 1:1: "The revelation of **Jesus Christ**, which **God** gave him to show his servants what must soon take place. He made it known by sending his **angel** to his servant **John**"—i.e., God → Jesus → angel → John.

16. E.g., Ralph Korner, "'And I Saw …': An Apocalyptic Literary Convention for Structural Identification in the Apocalypse," *NovT* 42 (2000): 160–83.

17. See discussion in Korner, "And I Saw …," 171–75 for a list and analysis of linguistic structural markers based on verbs of seeing.

around the throne are "flashes of lightning, and voices and peals of thunder, and before the throne burn seven torches of fire, which are the seven spirits of God." This opening scene represents just one of many examples of the overwhelming descriptive use of heat, light, noise, and other sensory elements. Persistent use of the color white occurs in numerous places in the apocalypse. At times the sun, moon, and stars are made dark, and at one point even the sky itself is rolled away (6:11–14). In terms of auditory imagery, John often includes angelic or other voices calling out or singing. Singing is particularly prominent. The living creatures that surround the throne of God continually sing praise (4:8), and a thunderous multitude of angels sings while surrounding the throne (5:12); they are joined by every creature in heaven and on earth and on the sea. The noise created by such a chorus is palpable. Countless other instances of bodily and sensory imagery permeate the text, including earthquakes, incense, and broken bodies.

Revelation 8 is particularly rich in its use of this kind of rhetoric. The opening of the seventh seal first yields silence. But soon the episode is crowded with sensory language. Seven angels are given trumpets (8:2), and another angel takes a censer of incense to the altar (8:3). We read how the smoke of the incense rises up along with prayers to God. When the angel takes the censer, fills it with fire from the altar, and throws it down onto the earth, there are lightning, voices, thunder, and an earthquake (8:5). The array of smells, sounds, visions, and even the bodily sensation of being shaken by the earthquake creates an overwhelming sensory cacophony, juxtaposed with the silence with which the scene commences. The author uses this rhetorical language to lend force to his argument; he uses the body not only to create the sensation of reality to his audience, but also to legitimate his account of God's message, as I will demonstrate in the next section.

Otherworldly Food

At the start of chapter 10, John witnesses the descent of "another mighty angel" (ἄλλον ἄγγελον ἰσχυρὸν) from heaven. The angel is enveloped in cloud and surrounded by elements of radiant light, including a rainbow over his head, a face like the sun, and legs like pillars of fire. The visual language used to describe the angel make it clear that the angel is associated directly with the divine realm.[18]

---

18. The angel's might links him to other angels described as ἰσχυρόν in 5:2 and 18:21.

This angel holds a little scroll (βιβλαρίδιον) in his hand, which, unlike the sealed scroll in 5:1, is open. This angel stands in a way that bridges three cosmological-geographical zones: his right foot is on the sea, his left foot is on the land, and his right hand is lifted up to heaven (10:2, 5). A voice from heaven tells John to take the scroll (here βιβλίον) from the hand of the angel; when the seer obeys, the angel tells him to eat the scroll (βιβλαρίδιον again) and warns that even though it will taste sweet, it will be bitter in his stomach (10:9). This warning is borne out in the following verse. John then receives the commission to prophesy "again" against/about[19] "many peoples and nations and tongues and kings."

Commentators on this short episode have generally read the consumption of the scroll symbolically. Adela Yarbro Collins, for example, describes the eating of the scroll as "a symbolic action which expresses in a concrete way the idea that the message communicated by the prophet does not originate with himself but has a divine origin."[20] This much is clear from the text: John receives the scroll from an angelic being, one whose presence crosses earthly and heavenly boundaries and as such, represents a bridge by which God-to-mortal communication can take place directly. However, previous symbolic readings have not been able to explain how or why the consumption of something heavenly might express such an idea. I suggest that examining this episode in light of hierophagy illuminates certain features that make clear how Revelation uses this genre to its own ends. I have defined hierophagy as a type of transformative eating in which a being from a more elevated cosmic category feeds otherworldly food to a being of a lower category; the act of eating associates the eater with the other realm—in John's case, the heavenly realm. Hierophagy brings about certain changes in the eater, especially, and most prominently for Revelation, the direct transmission of divine knowledge to the eater.

The significance of hierophagy hinges on the porous-but-present boundary between worlds in the cultural expectation of the ancient Mediterranean cultures. Other examples from antiquity, outlined in the introduction, demonstrate how human beings create space for divine contact by fasting or how angels are concerned about potentially having to eat

---

19. The preposition ἐπί with the dative can be translated either as "about" or "against" (David Aune, *Revelation 6–16* [Dallas: Word, 1997], 573–74).

20. Adela Yarbro Collins, *The Combat Myth in the Book of Revelation* (Missoula: Scholars Press, 1976), 20.

mortal food.[21] Hierophagy, however, involves eating the food of heaven, which only the gods or angels are able to consume. Consuming heavenly food yields different results than abstaining from human food, and in a literary context, the eating of food from a different realm is depicted as dangerous, precisely because it is an effective way of permeating the boundary between worlds. This division between heavenly and earthly realms helps to explain the role of the ingested scroll in Rev 10. In consuming the scroll, John, a mere mortal, is partaking of heavenly food and, in doing so, crosses the boundary between heaven and earth.

Two relevant examples illuminate the significance of hierophagy for understanding the ramifications of the scroll's ingestion in Revelation. The first example is found in Ezekiel. There is no doubt that Ezek 2:8–3:4 is reflected in Rev 10:8–10; most, if not all, scholars who have written on the scroll in Rev 10 have made the connection between the two scenes of scroll ingestion.[22] The passage in Ezekiel has striking similarities with our passage in Revelation. At the start of a vision, Ezekiel hears a voice that tells him,

> "Open your mouth, and eat what I give you." And when I looked, behold, a hand was stretched out to me, and, lo, a written scroll was in it; and he spread it before me; and it had writing on the front and on the back, and there were written on it words of lamentation and mourning and woe. And he said to me, "Son of man, eat what is offered to you; eat this scroll, and go, speak to the house of Israel.'" So I opened my mouth, and he gave me the scroll to eat. And he said to me, "Son of man, eat this scroll that I give you and fill your stomach with it." Then I ate it; and it was in my mouth as sweet as honey. And he said to me, "Son of man, go, get you to the house of Israel, and speak with my words to them." (Ezek 2:8–3:4)

Several commonalities between Ezekiel and Revelation are immediately visible; most obvious is the fact that both figures consume scrolls handed down from heaven. Ezekiel also receives a prophetic commission to "go ... and speak with my words to [the house of Israel]," which is echoed by John having to prophesy "again" in Rev 10:11. In the case of Ezekiel, it is clear that the hierophagic pattern of ingestion is followed: a heavenly

---

21. See the introduction above; Sulzbach, "When Going on a Heavenly Journey," 183–84; Dozeman, *God on the Mountain*, 34. Cultic systems also display anxiety about what food belongs to the gods and what to the mortals who make the offerings.
22. Koester, *Revelation*, 482; Aune, *Revelation*, 558; Collins, *Combat Myth*, 20.

item is given to a special mortal to consume. By consuming the scroll, the eater gains new abilities (to prophesy, or in the case of John, to prophesy again) and new knowledge (the contents of that prophecy). However, although Ezekiel is clearly reflected in structure and theme in Revelation's scroll meal, it is not the only relevant hierophagic event for interpreting Rev 10:8–10.

The second example is from 4 Ezra, discussed in detail in the previous chapter. It is the cup that Ezra receives in chapter 14 that finally allows him to receive direct revelation from God. Through ingesting the heavenly food, he is granted understanding since he has at last literally internalized God's message. In reproducing this quotation here, the parallels to Revelation are even more apparent:

> A voice called me, saying, "Ezra, open your mouth and drink what I give you to drink." Then I opened my mouth and behold, a full cup was offered to me; it was full of something like water, but its colour was like fire. And I took it and drank; and when I had drunk it, my heart poured forth understanding, and wisdom increased in my breast, for my spirit retained its memory; and my mouth was opened, and was no longer closed. (4 Ezra 14.38–41)

Again, there is a voice and a command for the character to open his mouth. Ezra's cup has enabled him to fully access the divine realm, both in being able to dictate the heavenly books and in having spatial access to the heaven. Like John, he is now able to transmit the divine content of that revelation, in Ezra's case, as books. Examining 4 Ezra and Revelation together, along with the example from Ezekiel, highlights some core elements and effects of hierophagy and helps us delineate hierophagy as a genre.

The core event of hierophagic eating is now clearly visible; we can discern a pattern that helps in understanding Revelation's scroll scene. By consuming the scroll, John gains new abilities (to prophesy again) and new knowledge (the contents of that prophecy). The core event of the hierophagic eating in Revelation fits the generic pattern I identify: (1) a heavenly being offers (2) something heavenly (3) for a mortal (4) to eat, (5) which brings about the transformation of the eater in some way.

Revelation makes use of earlier and contemporary narrative events of heavenly ingestion, but at the same time it transforms them in describing the scroll in Rev 10 as both sweet and bitter. Other scholars have understood the scroll and its flavors simply as metaphors pointing to the tone of the revelation John reveals,[23] but I propose that the flavors are more evocative of the efficacy of his message rather than simply the scroll's contents. There are two components of this analysis: first is the fact that the intimacy of the sense of taste has ramifications for creating bonds between those who share tastes with the divine realm; second is the cultural expectations around sweet and bitter foods.

As in the examples involving Persephone, social aspects of eating are foundational for understanding the ramifications of ingesting heavenly food in Revelation. Sharing food and tastes with coeaters brings about community formation and shared cultural meaning.[24] Just as humans might create alliances through commensality, the ingesting of common foods across cosmological realms brings about bonding between humans and divine beings. It is not just sharing a meal at the same table that produces this community, but also *sharing tastes with a community even at a great distance*.[25] Thus, even the distance between heaven and earth can be bridged through the shared tasting of common foods, which is why angels become anxious when invited for dinner and why offering divine food to humans brings about such profound transformations. Another first-century author CE from Asia Minor, Paul, likewise recognizes this quality of sharing food. As he explains to the Corinthians, "because there is one bread, we who are many are one body, for we all partake of the one bread" (1 Cor 10:17). Paul also believes that a bond can be created not only between people but also between divine forces and those who share ritually marked food. He famously warns the Corinthians that they might find themselves "partners with demons" (1 Cor 10:20) if they share in food offered to Roman gods. It seems that ingesting food entails taking on some of what is signified in that food, both the symbolic import of its flavors and its cultural implications.[26] In other words, even though the angel in Revelation does not share John's scroll meal, the fact that John consumes

---

23. Aune, *Revelation*, 572–73; Koester, *Revelation*, 482–83; David E. Holwerda, "The Church and the Little Scroll (Revelation 10, 11)," *Calvin Theological Journal* 34 (1999): 154–55.

24. Korsmeyer, *Making Sense of Taste*, 187; Smith, *From Symposium to Eucharist*, 14.

25. M. P. Lalonde, "Deciphering a Meal Again, or the Anthropology of Taste," *Social Science Information* 31 (1992): 69–86.

26. Weichart and van Eeuwijk, "Preface"; Douglas, "Deciphering a Meal," 61–81; Farb and Armelagos, *Consuming Passions*, 4.

the heavenly item means that he is participating in a meal of divine food; he thereby associates himself with that divine community of eaters even when they do not share that specific meal. The special status granted to the eater does not necessarily make him or her a deity, but it does grant special access to the divine realm, access that is out of reach for ordinary mortals.

The intimacy of the sense of taste, compared with other senses, plays a role in the bonding function of heavenly ingestion in Revelation. The sense-object is internalized by the eater when it is tasted, making taste a more profound interaction with the divine realm than auditory discourse or visual interactions with a heavenly being. The eater of heavenly food is therefore closely associated with the origin world of the consumed item. While visions and auditory revelations might be equally viewed by others nearby, taste is experienced privately; in this way, the divine is experienced most intimately. It may be for this reason that apocalyptic texts tend to include hierophagic events more frequently compared with texts outside of the genre; intimate access to divine realms is a precondition of acquiring the kind of hidden knowledge so many apocalypses include. In Rev 10 John internalizes the open scroll; its contents are thereby rendered inaccessible to every other being. Only John, then, is in possession of both the contents of God's message and of the ability necessary to "prophesy again." In consuming the scroll, John is uniquely situated as the mouthpiece of the divine realm, since its ingestion has given him access to God in a way that no other human in Revelation has.

Given that taste plays such a role in John's experience with the divine, the specific flavor of the scroll is significant. John experiences the scroll as bitter when it leaves his mouth and enters his stomach even though it was sweet, like Ezekiel's, at first. This sweet taste operates as a symbol by which the eater interprets his experience.[27] Many other texts in antiquity use sweetness to signal the divine origins of a food experience (Wis Sol 19:21; History of the Rechabites 7.2; 11.4; 12.5; Pss 19:10; 119:103; Prov 16:24; 24:13–14).[28]

Whereas Ezekiel's taste experience is unambiguously sweet, John is forced to reinterpret his taste experience with the scroll, whose sweetness

---

27. This same kind of sweetness is tasted by other participants in hierophagic events, as we have already seen in Persephone (Hom. Dem. 360–369; Ovid, *Metam.* 5.534–537) and as will be discussed later on in the example of Aseneth (Jos. Asen. 16.15–16), and Perpetua (Pass. Perp. 4.8–10).

28. See also Muir and Tappenden, "Edible Media."

turns bitter once ingested. When scholars of Revelation interpret the tastes metaphorically, as noted above, sweetness corresponds to the salvation to be expected by the Christian community while the bitterness indicates the necessary suffering to be experienced in order for salvation to be accomplished.[29] However, I propose that the bitter taste, in light of contemporary medical knowledge, represents the efficacy of God's message in John's mouth. Medical texts from antiquity are clear that bad-tasting remedies are more effective in delivering cures.[30] This passage from Pseudo-Julian indeed suggests that bitterness is inherent in medicinal substances:

> Indeed Hippocrates says that honey, though it is sweet to the taste, is quite bitter to the digestion, and I can believe this statement; for all agree that it produces bile and turns the juices to the very opposite of its original flavour, which face even more surely convicts it of being in its origin naturally bitter. For it would not change to this bitterness if in the beginning this quality had not belonged to it, from which it changed the reverse. (Pseudo-Julian, *Letter to Sarapion* 391.A–B [Wright])

Honey, according to this text, tastes sweet, but it must be inherently bitter.[31] This is confirmed by Dioscorides, who believes that honey's "properties are purgative, opening, stimulating of the humours, and for that reason it is helpful to rinse for dirty wounds and ulcers" (*Mat. med.* 2.82.1). Julian and Dioscorides know this because honey is very effective medicine and because the most effective medicine is bitter in flavor; therefore, honey must actually be bitter to digest. This logic lays bare the reasoning behind the sensory imagery in Revelation. In other words, the bitter taste that John experiences marks this hierophagic experience as the most effective, even over that of Ezekiel, who only experiences the sweetness of divine

---

29. Koester provides three alternative interpretations of the use of sweetness in Revelation (*Revelation*, 482). The one to which he subscribes proposes that the sweetness corresponds to the salvation to be expected by the Christian community while the bitterness indicates the necessary suffering to be experienced in order for salvation to be accomplished (483).

30. Laurence Totelin, "Tastes in Botany, Medicine and Science in Antiquity: Bitter Herbs and Sweet Honey," in Rudolph, *Taste and the Ancient Senses*, 60–71.

31. The average pH of honey is 3.9, making it about the same acidity as wine. See Stefan Bogdanov, "Honey Composition," in *The Honey Book* (Bee Product Science, 2016), ch. 5, p. 2, http://www.bee-hexagon.net/honey/.

interaction. John's charge to prophesy again therefore carries authority through this sensory description.

Conclusions

Hierophagy, I argue, is the rhetorical mechanism by which "the angel conveys to the seer the message he is to communicate."[32] This highlights one specific feature of hierophagy, which is the transmission of divine knowledge. John is further transformed in his ability to prophecy "again." While he does not undergo assumption into another realm as Ezra and Persephone do, he shares Ezra's internalization of the divine message through the ingestion of his scroll. As such, examining Rev 10:8–10 in the context of hierophagy illustrates how this text fits within the framework of this category of culturally understood narrative consumption; this study of Revelation, however, also showcases an important aspect of how hierophagy functions, which is through taste. The widespread use of this genre, not only in apocalyptic texts such as Revelation, but across multiple genres in antiquity also illustrates the importance of carrying out this kind of analysis on other texts that include this type of sensory experience. Examining the genre of hierophagy allows us to more fully understand how ancients thought about interactions between human beings and the divine realm, and specifically, how taste is used in narrative to mediate or breach the boundary between these two realms. Further, hierophagy highlights the importance of analyzing taste as a means of internalizing and absorbing knowledge. The prevalence of this mechanism of gaining divine knowledge in ancient texts indicates that hierophagy played a role in how ancients thought about their relationship to divine realms.

Revelation makes use of hierophagy to express how John gains access to the divine realm and shares an intimate relationship with the divine—in this way, the text legitimates the divine origins and contents of the revelations that John has written down in the book of Revelation. The ingestion of the scroll participates in a culturally understood way of interacting with the divine realm, one which grants the eater both direct transmission of divine knowledge and also the means of transmitting the knowledge to a community. The revelation that John puts into words, and indeed, puts into visions, is identifiable as the contents of the open scroll

---

32. Collins, *Combat Myth*, 21.

that he consumes. The message of God has changed form, from being edible to being visible and from being visible to being audible in the form of the text of Revelation. John first ingests the scroll and then visualizes its contents, the rest of Revelation. He likewise writes down what he sees and transmits this to his audience. This change of form—from edible to readable—is significant.

John shares his intimate access to the divine when he transforms his taste experience into the visions that make up Revelation. The fact that Revelation is written to "the seven assemblies" confirms that the contents of the book (i.e., John's revelatory experiences) are to be shared with an audience. But John alone experiences God's message directly. When he consumes the scroll it allows him to ingest, digest, and internalize the divine revelation; that he is asked to prophesy "again" indicates that the rest of the book, with its specific details about the timeline for the end times, emerges from the consumption of the little scroll.[33]

John's ingestion of the scroll signifies his special access to the divine realm in a way that his audience cannot participate in directly, although they understand its rhetorical force. They are put at arm's length from God and access God's revelation through John, their mediator, just as John has accessed God's revelation through the mediator of the angel who feeds him the little scroll. That the content of John's revelation is the result of hierophagy, that it has been imparted from the divine realm and internalized by John, lends authority to its message. Examining this scroll meal as hierophagy demonstrates how John's ability to understand and communicate the divine message is closely tied to his ingestion of heavenly food.

---

33. Koester, *Revelation*, 483.

4
Joseph and Aseneth

The next example of hierophagy I propose to include in this category of transformative eating occurs in the Greek romance Joseph and Aseneth. A text fraught with issues around dating, provenance, and the religious beliefs of its author(s), its complex and bizarre symbolism has long puzzled scholars. The hierophagic scene in question is the notorious section where the protagonist, Aseneth, is fed a piece of miraculous honeycomb by an angelic visitor. Aseneth is greatly affected by this small taste of heaven: she receives divine knowledge, her name is written in a book of those who live in heaven, and her features are transformed so that her household staff fail to recognize her. A superficial glance suggests that this incident fits well within the bounds of the category of hierophagy. To say what this conclusion might mean for the text and its interpretation, however, requires much deeper engagement with the narrative itself, its recensions, and the wealth of recent scholarship on the topic.

Because current consensus views the honeycomb scene as central to the plot of the text, it has been the focus of much of the discussion for all aspects of the text. Whether as conversion narrative, as code for the establishment of a new temple, as transformation to angelic being or to priestly status, as an indication of the text's Christian origins, or something else entirely, the honeycomb scene is central for an understanding of the text. The symbolism of the honeycomb scene must undergird any reading of the text as a whole; at the same time the narrative as a whole must be used to situate any reading of the honeycomb episode in particular. To date, no one has connected this scene of transformational eating to the other scenes of this type described in the other chapters of this book; it seems to me, then, that a crucial clue for understanding how the ingestion of the honeycomb works to transform Aseneth has been overlooked. Examining this clue will help us move beyond debates about provenance toward the larger worldview that lies behind the text.

Overview: The State of Joseph and Aseneth Studies

In an extremely useful turn of events, Angela Standhartinger has summarized the scholarship produced on Joseph and Aseneth between the years 1988 and 2013 in an article published in 2014.[1] Her overview is exhaustive at fifty-three pages long, and I could not hope to improve on her thorough discussion of the complex debates that took place in the field during that time. However, for those unfamiliar with the text and its scholarship, there are largely two camps: one group of scholars considers Marc Philonenko's shorter text family to be more original and favors a later date of no earlier than the third century CE;[2] the other group considers Christoph Burchard's longer text family to be the more original, with an earlier associated date of between the second century BCE and the second century CE.[3] The text was preserved by Christians, leading many to be suspicious of the earlier consensus that Joseph and Aseneth is the product of Jewish authorship. This is the view of several recent publications, most notably those of Ross Kraemer and Rivka Nir.[4]

Instead of revisiting the minutiae of date, recension, and provenance, I will focus on the interpretation of the honeycomb scene in particular,

---

1. Angela Standhartinger, "Recent Scholarship on *Joseph and Aseneth* (1988-2013)," *CurBR* 12 (2014): 353–406.

2. Marc Philonenko, *Joseph et Aséneth: Introduction, texte critique, traduction et notes*, SVTP 13 (Leiden: Brill, 1968). See also, recently, John C. Poirier's conference paper, "Apicultural Keys to *Joseph and Aseneth*: An Argument for the Priority of the Shorter Text" (paper presented at the Annual Meeting of the Society of Biblical Literature, 19 November 2017); in it Poirier argues that the *d* family of manuscripts, the shorter form of the text, represents "the earliest recoverable form." I am grateful to John for generously sharing this paper with me.

3. Christoph Burchard, *Untersuchungen zu Joseph und Aseneth: Überlieferung—Ortsbestimmung*, WUNT 8 (Tübingen: Mohr Siebeck, 1965); Burchard, "Joseph and Aseneth," *OTP* 2:177–247.

4. Kraemer, *When Aseneth Met Joseph*; Rivka Nir, *Joseph and Aseneth: A Christian Book*, HBM 42 (Sheffield: Sheffield Phoenix, 2012). James R. Davila suggests that assuming a late antique Christian provenance requires the least amount of "decoding" work but acknowledges that the evidence at present is inadequate to make any firm claims about the text (*The Provenance of the Old Testament Pseudepigrapha: Jewish, Christian, or Other?*, JSJSup 105 [Leiden: Brill, 2005], 195).

while outlining more recent contributions since Standhartinger's 2014 article. Following Standhartinger's practice, I will indicate which version is under discussion by marking Philonenko's text and its versification with "Ph" and Burchard's with "B."[5] The differences between the shorter and longer texts are especially important for certain elements of Aseneth's transformation after the honeycomb incident; in such cases side-by-side comparisons will clarify significant variations. By focusing on scholarly readings of the honeycomb scene, I will demonstrate the diversity of interpretations scholars have offered for this scene while highlighting the benefit of using hierophagy as a lens through which to view the event.

The Honeycomb Scene

The honeycomb scene takes place toward the middle of the book, in chapter 16. The chapter begins with Aseneth preparing a table for her other-worldly guest, the *anthropos*, who asks that she bring a honeycomb for the table rather than the bread that she is about to fetch. While Aseneth is sure that she has no honeycomb for her guest, the guest is convinced that she will find one in her storeroom. When there is indeed a comb there, Aseneth is amazed, not only at its presence but also at its appearance, which the author describes as "white as snow and full of honey, ... like dew from heaven and its exhalation like breath of life" (B 16.8–9).[6] Aseneth is convinced that the visitor spoke the comb into being. At this point, the angelic being takes her head in his hand and shakes it, with sparks coming from his fingers. He tells Aseneth that the mysteries of God have been revealed to her and that she will be blessed for attaching herself to God because she will eat the comb (B 16.12–14). The visitor explains that the honeycomb was made by bees of paradise and that the angels of God, God's chosen ones, and the sons of the Most High all eat this honeycomb, because "this is a comb of life, and everyone who eats of it will not die for ever (and) ever" (B 16.14). With that, the heavenly visitor

---

5. Standhartinger, "Recent Scholarship on *Joseph and Aseneth*," 355. Burchard's 2003 edition revised its textual tradition, using Syr, Arm, L2, and *f*, formerly referred to as family *b*. Christoph Burchard, *Joseph und Aseneth*, PVTG 5 (Leiden: Brill, 2003).

6. Translations of the longer text (B) are from Burchard, "Joseph and Aseneth," *OTP* 2:177–247. Translations of the shorter text (Ph) are from Ross S. Kraemer, *When Aseneth Met Joseph: A Late Antique Tale of the Biblical Patriarch and His Egyptian Wife, Reconsidered* (New York: Oxford University Press).

breaks off some of the honeycomb and eats some and then offers some to Aseneth.[7]

The longer text includes instruction from the visitor for Aseneth to eat the comb, whereas that command is not in the shorter version. This has led John C. Poirier, for one, to conclude that Aseneth does not eat the honey in the shorter text. In his view, Aseneth does not eat but rather the angelic visitor merely touches her mouth with it. He suggests that later Christian copyists "mistakenly suppose[d] the angel to be *feeding* Aseneth a morsel of honeycomb."[8] This reading supports his overall argument that the honey represents the establishment of a new city on Aseneth's mouth. Poirier makes a good case for linking this action with Aseneth's title of "City of Refuge," since, as he observes, beekeepers would use a smear of honey to relocate bees to a specific location, and in turn ancient authors associated bees with the founding of new cities.[9] Poirier's connection of the honey and the city imagery may well be correct, but I disagree that the shorter text only implies the placing of the comb on Aseneth's mouth. The Greek of the shorter version reads: καὶ ἐξέτεινε τὴν χεῖρα αὐτοῦ ὁ ἄνθρωπος τὴν δεξιὰν καὶ ἀπέκλασεν ἐκ τοῦ κηρίου, καὶ ἔφαγε καὶ ἔδωκε τῇ χειρὶ αὐτοῦ ἐκ τοῦ κηρίου εἰς τὸ στόμα Ἀσενέθ. Philonenko himself translates the phrase: "et de sa main il en porta un morceau à la bouche d'Aseneth." Kraemer's translation, on the other hand, renders it: "he put (a piece of) the comb into Aseneth's mouth with his hand."[10] The word in question appears to be εἰς. Kraemer translates it as "into" while Philonenko's French would be better understood as "toward" or "to." Poirier's understanding of the activity appears to rely on Philonenko's understanding of the preposition, but this is by no means clear in the Greek; the word can indeed imply motion into Aseneth's mouth and not simply the placing of the honeycomb on it.[11]

In addition, it is important to point out that even if Aseneth were not described as having *eaten* any honeycomb in the shorter text (and I believe

---

7. At this point, Aseneth is said to have eaten the same bread and cup combination that Joseph describes in chapter 8.
8. Poirier, "Apicultural Keys to *Joseph and Aseneth*," 2, 3.
9. Poirier, "Apicultural Keys to *Joseph and Aseneth*," 4, 6.
10. Kraemer, *When Aseneth Met Joseph*, 65.
11. LSJ, s.v. "εἰς"; F. C. Conybeare and St. George Stock, *Grammar of Septuagint Greek: With Selected Readings, Vocabularies, and Updated Indexes* (Peabody, MA: Hendrickson, 2007), 80–82; Herbert Weir Smyth, *Greek Grammar* (Cambridge: Harvard University Press, 1984), 376.

the Greek establishes that she has), that is not to say that she has not *tasted* any. The placing of the honeycomb on her mouth is reminiscent of Persephone's experience in Ovid's *Metamorphoses*, where we read that Hades presses the pomegranate seeds to Persephone's lips (5.537). Emily Gowers observes that lips were considered organs of taste in antiquity, especially when the tasting in question represents potential danger.[12] In addition, as with other texts from the ancient world, we should not be surprised that taste is implicit rather than explicit. Thus, when the heavenly visitor brings the morsel of honeycomb (in)to Aseneth's mouth, we should infer that its sweet taste was experienced by her. Indeed, the phrasing may reflect the perilous nature of her taste experience, which transforms her in physical and ontological ways. Thus, while the longer text is more explicit that Aseneth ingests the honeycomb, we should not infer that the shorter text implies no internalization of the honey, since (1) lips taste as well as tongues and (2) the preposition εἰς can imply that the honey enters her mouth.

After presenting her with promises of strength, youth, powers, and beauty, the visitor marks the honeycomb with two intersecting lines that resemble blood.[13] He then summons snow-white bees with purple wings and golden diadems on their heads out of the damaged part of the comb; the bees are described as "chosen." Alighting on Aseneth's mouth, they build another heavenly comb on it and proceed to eat from it. The visitor dismisses the bees; all of them return to heaven except those who wanted to harm Aseneth, who first die but are then resurrected and sent out to Aseneth's garden. When the angel asks Aseneth if she has seen these things, she says she has (B 17.1–2). Later, in chapter 18, Aseneth looks into a bowl of water[14] and realizes that she has changed. Her staff also notice this physical change (B 18.7–9).

Previous Readings

Many scholars, as I do, examine the scene from the perspective of the narrative, seeking to uncover what the ingestion of the honeycomb does to Aseneth at the level of text rather than at the level of symbolic meaning

---

12. Gowers, "Tasting the Roman World," 96.
13. Poirier offers a convincing explanation of this event, which will be discussed below.
14. While in the short recension of Joseph and Aseneth, Aseneth only asks for a bowl of water, Burchard's longer recension notes that this is for washing.

outside the text, an approach I will outline below. Of these, the majority view the scene as one of conversion, or at least confirming a conversion that occurs earlier during the scene of Aseneth's repentance and prayer. Indeed, conversion is the dominant mode of understanding the text, as shown in the multitude of publications with *conversion* in the title. In these readings, the ingestion of the honeycomb is symbolic of some ritual meal practiced in some existing Jewish or Christian community. Randall Chesnutt's 1995 book, *From Death to Life: Conversion in Joseph and Aseneth*, and in particular his careful discussion of characteristic features of conversion in antiquity and in Joseph and Aseneth, remains influential.[15] Chesnutt is correct in pointing out that the general symbolic meal imagery of bread and cup cannot reflect an existing Jewish ritual initiation meal, since Joseph is described as already eating those things. In other words, the bread and the cup represent ongoing meals that mark a person as Jewish rather than one-time ritual elements, according to Chesnutt. Since the honeycomb is described as representing these elements in B 16.16, "Behold, you have eaten bread of life, drunk a cup of immortality, and been anointed with ointment of incorruption," he suggests avoiding reading the honeycomb as an initiatory meal such as that offered to newly baptized Christians.[16] While I agree with Chesnutt that the honeycomb should not be read as pointing to an initiatory meal, I disagree that it merely symbolizes Aseneth's full participation in Jewish life. The honeycomb clearly affects some kind of transformation once eaten and is described as a food from heaven, marking it as exceptional.

Much previous scholarship on the honeycomb scene reads it allegorically, as a place-holder for another meaning that is not explained to the reader. For example, Gideon Bohak has suggested that the scene is symbolic of the establishment of Onias's temple in Heliopolis. In this argument, the bees in their elaborate clothing stand in for the temple priests and the honeycomb for the temple, destroyed and then rebuilt upon the mouth of a City of Refuge; the marks of blood that appear on the honeycomb, Bohak argues, represent the difficulties among priests between 170 and 160 BCE.[17] At face value, Bohak's argument maps well onto the imag-

---

15. Randall D. Chesnutt, *From Death to Life: Conversion in Joseph and Aseneth*, JSPSup 16 (Sheffield: Sheffield Academic, 1995), 118–50.
16. Chesnutt, *From Death to Life*, 130. This will be discussed further in chapter 6.
17. Gideon Bohak, *Joseph and Aseneth and the Jewish Temple in Heliopolis* (Atlanta: Scholars Press, 1996), 13.

ery in chapter 16. However, it does not explain the symbolic use of bread and cup imagery elsewhere in the text and suggests a very early date for the text, in the second century BCE.

Other symbolic readings have taken the scene to refer to early Christian variations of the Eucharist, such as Nir's recent contribution. Nir also understands Aseneth's experience in terms of conversion, although in Nir's case she views it as a conversion to Christianity rather than Judaism.[18] Nir interprets each symbol as reflecting a third- or fourth-century CE Syrian context. Of the honeycomb, she writes, "I believe that the Christian character of our scene is so obvious that it needs no demonstration at all; it corresponds perfectly to our general interpretation of the work."[19] Nir views the fragrant honeycomb as an "obvious" symbol for Jesus's fragrant body and the blood-red lines as pointing to his blood.[20] Nir's understanding of Joseph and Aseneth makes several assumptions about Second Temple Judaism and early Christianity that weaken her reading of the honeycomb scene. Namely, she assumes that "all scholars who maintain that *Joseph and Aseneth* is a Jewish work assume that Aseneth's conversion has to be seen as a Jewish *giyyur*."[21] On this understanding, Nir seeks to point out significant differences between talmudic representations of conversion, which all require immersion, and the event depicted in Jos. Asen. 16.[22] This is problematic on several levels. First, by assuming the event is conversion, Nir is limited to understanding the event in terms of other examples of transformational eating and risks reading back into the narrative elements from later practices. Second, and perhaps more importantly, using rabbinic texts as accurately reporting what diverse Jewish communities centuries earlier practiced is extremely problematic. Rabbinic memory of earlier ritual practices from the second temple period "is fundamentally bound up with the place the rabbis assert for themselves

---

18. Nir, *Joseph and Aseneth*, 91.
19. Nir, *Joseph and Aseneth*, 88.
20. Nir, *Joseph and Aseneth*, 89.
21. Nir, *Joseph and Aseneth*, 24.
22. E.g., b. Yevam. 47a–b; Sifre Num. 108; b. Ker 9a; m. Gerim 2:4. Although she focuses on a lack of immersion in Joseph and Aseneth, Nir sidesteps the issue of the postmeal water basin, which she connects with Christian baptism (Nir, *Joseph and Aseneth*, 176). It is unclear to me how the water basin in Joseph and Aseneth can be associated with baptism, on the one hand, and not with Jewish immersion, on the other, but that is beside the point for my argument.

in post-destruction society."²³ In other words, it is very dangerous to take at face value any claim rabbinic texts make about preserving or documenting practices from much earlier. As such, we cannot assume that the Talmud's or the Mishnah's or other rabbinic texts' description of conversion practices reflects anything other than the practices upheld at the time of their composition. Nir's use of these texts to establish a lack of continuity between early Jewish conversion rituals and Joseph and Aseneth, then, really only establishes that the text does not seem to reflect fourth-century CE rabbinic ritual ideals. It does not seem cautious to me to disregard a Jewish provenance for this text on this basis alone.

An example of a symbolic reading that does not connect the honeycomb ingestion to the Eucharist, and one which, as this study does, focuses on alternative interpretations to conversion, is Tyson Putthoff's 2014 article. Although I disagree with Putthoff's conclusion, which is that the text "establishes a model for an elite Jewish unit, set apart from the general populace, who mediate between God and humanity,"²⁴ I agree that they key to understanding the significance of the honeycomb event rests in sharing divine food. Putthoff calls this theophagy and links it to mystical practices in which God's presence is ingested symbolically.²⁵ The distinction between what Putthoff identifies as *theophagy* and what I articulate as *hierophagy* is: (1) that Putthoff links this practice to a ritual emulated in real life whereas I view hierophagy (and Aseneth's experience as a whole) as a literary occurrence; and (2) that in privileging sociological examples of this time of commensality Putthoff neglects literary parallels that would have illustrated the significance of the ingestion more clearly.

In general, the issue I take with readings of Joseph and Aseneth that privilege conversion as a lens for reading the text's symbols is that conversion in antiquity is often read as an earlier version of what conversion means

---

23. Naftali S. Cohn, *The Memory of the Temple and the Making of the Rabbis* (Pennsylvania: University of Pennsylvania Press, 2012), 39. Additionally, if Joseph and Aseneth is the product of the diaspora, there can be no guarantee that Jews outside of the land followed the same regulations or to the same degree as they are set out in rabbinic texts (Davila, *Provenance of the Old Testament Pseudepigrapha*, 33, 36; Tessa Rajak, "Jews and Christians as Groups in a Pagan World," in *The Jewish Dialogue with Greece and Rome: Studies in Cultural and Social Interaction*, AGJU 48 [Leiden: Brill, 2001], 355–72, esp. 358–62).

24. Tyson L. Putthoff, "Aseneth's Gastronomical Vision: Mystical Theophagy and New Creation in *Joseph and Aseneth*," *JSP* 24 (2014): 96.

25. Putthoff, "Aseneth's Gastronomical Vision," 98.

today—that is, a complete shift of life, behavior, and identity from before and after an event.[26] Frequently, the concept operates, even in antiquity, within the idea that the conversion is from one religion to another; given how problematic it is to assume a category of religion for the ancient world,[27] this alone should give us pause. Regardless, Joseph and Aseneth resists this mode of understanding of her devotion and identity. She certainly repents and offers her devotion to the God of Joseph. She removes herself from the public sphere (or in her case, the household sphere), changes clothing, offers prayers, and removes symbols of her previous devotion. However, these actions share parallels with initiation rituals, including for associations that did not attempt to enforce exclusive devotion from their members. Further, Aseneth's name change (B 15.7; Ph 15.6), included by Chesnutt and others as supporting a reading of the scene as conversion,[28] is temporary, as the text resumes calling her by her birth name as soon as the angel departs. She and Joseph are even married by Pharaoh himself (B 21.3-8; Ph 21.3-7), indicating that complete abandonment of non-Jewish (or non-Christian) rituals has not taken place. Wariness about conversion as a lens through which to view Joseph and Aseneth is rare but not unheard of; Shaye J. D. Cohen, for example, prefers to view the text as "venerating the god of the Jews and denying or ignoring the pagan gods" rather than conversion, which entails actually "becoming a Jew."[29] This may well support Kraemer's

---

26. For further discussion of conversion and its issues for antiquity, see chapter 5.

27. Annette Yoshiko Reed, "Partitioning 'Religion' and Its Prehistories: Reflections on Categories, Narratives, and the Practice of Religious Studies" (paper presented at the annual meeting of the North American Association for the Study of Religion; available at https://tinyurl.com/SBL4211b); Vaia Touna, *Fabrications of the Greek Past: Religion, Tradition, and the Making of Modern Identities* (Leiden: Brill, 2017); Carlin A. Barton and Daniel Boyarin, *Imagine No Religion: How Modern Abstractions Hide Ancient Realities* (New York: Fordham University Press, 2016); Maia Kotrosits, *Rethinking Early Christian Identity: Affect, Violence, and Belonging* (Minneapolis: Fortress, 2015); Brent Nongbri, *Before Religion: A History of a Modern Concept* (New Haven: Yale University Press, 2013); Nongbri, "Dislodging 'Embedded' Religion: A Brief Note on a Scholarly Trope," *Numen* 55 (2008): 440–60; Jonathan Z. Smith, *Drudgery Divine: On the Comparison of Early Christianities and the Religions of Late Antiquity* (Chicago: University of Chicago Press, 1990).

28. Chesnutt, *From Death to Life*, 127–28.

29. Shaye J. D. Cohen, "Crossing the Boundary and Becoming a Jew," in *The Beginnings of Jewishness: Boundaries, Varieties, Uncertainties*, HCS 31 (Berkeley: University of California Press, 1999), 150–55. Cohen points out that Joseph and Aseneth is in no way interested in the legal aspects of being Jewish, something one might expect of

and Nir's suggestion that the text is Christian; however, I would urge caution in pigeon-holing too early a text that seems to resist classification in this way. The boundaries between Christianity and Judaism were in flux in many areas at least up until the fourth century, as texts attempting to clarify those border lines show.[30] It is not at all clear, then, that the text needs to be identified as one or the other or that we would recognize its identity based on our knowledge of communities and texts from other places and other times.

While Cohen's approach problematizes describing Aseneth's experience as a conversion, it does so by pointing to other methods of worshiping the Jewish God (e.g., godfearers) rather than by suggesting that modes of becoming Jewish vary or by unpacking the appropriateness of conversion as a category for antiquity. In other words, while Aseneth's experience does not appear to match what we know of rabbinic conversion procedures or conform to the adherence to law we might expect in early Jews, we need not limit the text to rabbinic Jewish expectations nor to conforming with earlier Jewish practices when we know how much practices and beliefs varied by location, chronology, and author. However, in centering godfearers as a category, Cohen does allow for a nonbinary approach to the question of conversion; conversion as a concept appears to rest on the idea of a radical transformation from one category to another, categories that are opposed: Jew or non-Jew? The existence of godfearers illustrates that questions of allegiance to a god are not as simple as conversion suggests and as later texts appear to promote.

In essence, the issue of conversion when applied to Joseph and Aseneth is actually a distraction, since even late dates for the text still allow for a great diversity in modes of belonging to either (or both) Judaism or Christianity.[31] The central mechanism of Aseneth's experience, whether or not

---

a recent convert—this latter observation, however, assumes that rabbinic texts accurately reflect wider trends among diverse groups of Jews, something we cannot at all assume with certainty.

30. E.g., Daniel Boyarin, *Border Lines: The Partition of Judaeo-Christianity*, Divinations (Philadelphia: University of Pennsylvania Press, 2004); Wayne A. Meeks, *The First Urban Christians: The Social World of the Apostle Paul* (New Haven: Yale University Press, 1983); Yoshiko Reed, "Partitioning 'Religion' and Its Prehistories."

31. Jill Hicks-Keeton also problematizes the overarching scholarly approach of evaluating a "Jewish *or* Christian" authorship of Joseph and Aseneth. She rightly points out that such a dichotomy assumes a clear boundary between what are, in reality, two slippery and overlapping categories and proposes instead to look for whether the text might show signs of authorship by a Jewish (including Jewish Christian) or

we view it as a conversion, still requires some explanation: how exactly does ingesting honeycomb bring about this kind of transformation? The answer, I propose, rests in hierophagy.

Honey, Bees, and Transformation

The obscurity of the meaning of the text means that we must unpack the meaning of the compound symbols used in the honeycomb scene in order to understand how the act of ingestion functions within the broader narrative—honey, honeycomb, bees, blood, fire, and the cardinal directions may all serve metaphorical meanings that support the way that ingestion works to transform Aseneth. As such, even though I suggest that overall the ingestion is the key moment of transformation, the ways in which Aseneth is transformed and the association with divine knowledge reside in the characteristics of her experience with the angelic visitor.

The comb is described as divine food, which makes sense given the numerous associations in the Bible and elsewhere in early Jewish and Christian literature, as well as in Hellenistic traditions, between sweet-tasting things, especially honey, and the divine realm.[32] The honeycomb is described as being "like dew," which is not unusual for a text emerging from the context of the Greco-Roman world.[33]

Muir and Tappenden's article, "Edible Media: The Confluence of Food and Learning in the Ancient Mediterranean," provides the connection that must have existed in the ancient worldview between ingestion and knowledge. Specifically, they outline a number of instances in biblical texts where metaphors of food and eating are used to express internalizing God's wisdom. Metaphor, they observe, "structures and characterizes the nature of how the human animal experiences, obtains, and makes sense of

---

gentile (Christian) author; she concludes that the former is more likely than the latter (Jill Hicks-Keeton, *Arguing With Aseneth: Gentile Access to Israel's "Living God" in Jewish Antiquity* [Oxford: Oxford University Press, 2018], 26).

32. Patricia D. Ahearne-Kroll, "Joseph and Aseneth and Jewish Identity in Greco-Roman Egypt" (PhD diss., University of Chicago, 2005), 250–62. Sweetness and honey are also associated with erotic pleasures. Anathea E. Portier-Young, "Sweet Mercy Metropolis: Interpreting Aseneth's Honeycomb," *JSP* 14 (2005): 133.

33. Portier-Young, "Sweet Mercy Metropolis," 143. See Aristotle, *Hist. an.* 5.22.29–30; Pliny, *Nat.* 11.7. Portier-Young cites H. Chouliara-Raïos, *L'abeille et le miel en Egypt d'après les payrus grecs* (Jannina, Greece: Université de Jannina, 1989), 47 n. 42.

the world and their presence therein."[34] In other words, metaphors allow human beings to understand the world and to express that experience meaningfully; they function precisely because metaphors are intelligible to other people in a given society. The use of food and ingestion imagery in Joseph and Aseneth then rests on existing cultural knowledge that makes use of metaphors of ingestion as a means to divine wisdom, among other things.

In light of their conclusions, then, the various aspects of the honeycomb are significant in interpreting its meaning. This analytical method is not new, as others have already investigated the symbolism associated with the comb; however, I suggest that the significance of the comb's descriptive association with the heavenly realm operates in the context of a hierophagic meal, signaling to the reader that this is indeed heavenly food being ingested by a mortal person. An ancient reader would then be prepared to understand what happens to Aseneth next, not in the context of conversion, but in the context of other incidents of transformational eating.

That the honeycomb is heavenly is supported by several aspects of the text.[35] First, the being who appears in Aseneth's room is described as "from heaven"/ἐκ τοῦ οὐρανοῦ, a claim that is backed up by the being's appearance. He is shining like a flame or like lightning (B 14.1–2, 9), a pervasive symbol of divine origin or ontology.[36]

Sharing a meal with a divine being has important ramifications, which are particularly visible in the present text.[37] Meal practices are already identified in Joseph and Aseneth as an important boundary marker, since

---

34. Muir and Tappenden, "Edible Media," 125. See also George Lakoff and Mark Johnson, *Metaphors We Live By* (Chicago: University of Chicago Press, 1980); Lakoff and Mark Johnson, *Philosophy in the Flesh: The Embodied Mind and Its Challenge to Western Thought* (New York: Basic Books, 1999); and Mark Johnson, *The Body in the Mind: The Bodily Basis of Meaning, Imagination, and Reason* (Chicago: University of Chicago Press, 1987).

35. It is worth noting that, unlike other characters who ascend to heaven (e.g., Enoch [2 En. 1–22]), heaven comes to Aseneth directly (Putthoff, "Aseneth's Gastronomic Vision," 100).

36. Meredith J. C. Warren, *My Flesh Is Meat Indeed: A Nonsacramental Reading of John 6:51–58* (Minneapolis: Fortress, 2015), 86–87.

37. Andrea Beth Lieber, "I Set a Table before You: The Jewish Eschatological Character of Aseneth's Conversion Meal," *JSP* 14 (2004): 64; Putthoff, "Aseneth's Gastronomic Vision," 102.

Joseph will not eat with Egyptians who do not worship the same God, and since bread and cup (and ointment) imagery is used to distinguish between right and wrong religious practices. It should be no surprise, then, that sharing a meal with this heavenly visitor is significant to Aseneth's identity. As I discussed in the introduction, other ancient texts express anxiety about angels and humans sharing the same table. In the Testament of Abraham, the archangel Michael has to ask God's advice when Abraham invites him to stay for dinner; God supplies the angel with a solution so that Michael does not have to ingest any corruptible, mortal food (T. Ab. 4). In Joseph and Aseneth, Aseneth's visitor provides his own food, in the form of the honeycomb. But it is Aseneth who is invited to transgress divine-mortal boundaries by eating the heavenly food, rather than the other way around.

We know that the honeycomb is heavenly food because it is described as such: "And the comb was big and white as snow and full of honey. And that honey was like the dew from heaven and its exhalation like breath of life" (Jos. Asen. B 16.2–3). The white color of the honeycomb associates it with heaven.[38] The honey is also described as being like dew from heaven, implying that it is similar to nectar or ambrosia, such as is found in the History of the Rechabites where sweet nectar bubbles up from the ground (7.2; 11.4; 12.5). That it has a scent like the breath of life confirms that this is no ordinary honeycomb. Further, the visitor declares that the honeycomb "is the spirit of life" (Jos. Asen. B 16.14).[39] While Burchard softens this connection between the comb and the divine realm by translating it as "this comb is (full of the) spirit of life," the text nevertheless seems explicit about the extraordinary nature of this honey.[40] Moreover, as will be discussed further below, bees and honey have strong associations in the ancient Mediterranean world to the heavenly realm.[41]

But what associations should we connect with the honey, other than those already made explicit in Joseph and Aseneth? Three major trends in

---

38. This association also occurs in the Passion of Perpetua and Felicitas (chapter 6) where the white clothing of the people in the garden in associates them with the heavenly realm.

39. Διότι τοῦτο τὸ κηρίον ἐστὶ πνεῦμα ζωῆς.

40. Putthoff goes so far as to identify the comb as the presence of God, which is not actually what the text says directly but is not out of the realm of possibility ("Aseneth's Gastronomical Vision," 103).

41. Ahearne-Kroll, "Joseph and Aseneth and Jewish Identity."

scholarship on Joseph and Aseneth connect the honey to either wisdom traditions or to manna traditions or both.[42] Philo connects manna to the color white and to the taste of honey (Philo, *Fug.* 138), parallels we can easily identify in the description of the honeycomb in Joseph and Aseneth; likewise, the manna comes directly from heaven, which is also true of the honeycomb. It is likened to the bread of life (Jos. Asen. B 15.5), a further point of contact. On the other hand, the sweetness of God's words in wisdom texts is also a trope likely to inform Joseph and Aseneth's symbolic description; Philo says that God's word and reason are sweeter than honey and whiter than snow (Philo, *Fug.* 138). Kraemer notes rabbinic sources that connect honey with mystical experiences, such as b. Hag. 14b.[43] Four sages enter Pardes, and one, Ben Zoma, is described in this way:

> Ben Zoma glimpsed at the Divine Presence and was harmed, i.e., he lost his mind. And with regard to him the verse states: "Have you found honey? Eat as much as is sufficient for you, lest you become full from it and vomit it" (Proverbs 25:16). (trans. Steinsaltz)

This excerpt reflects a tradition that has several implications for Aseneth's experience. First, a potentially later Jewish text connects the divine presence with honey. Second, that text connects the divine presence with transformation, albeit in a less than positive way. Third, that text grounds these connections in biblical citations, which in turn preserve metaphors of speaking, words, and wisdom. Thus, the connection between ingestion of honey-flavored foods clearly has a wide range of interpretive links aside from (1) conversion or (2) Eucharist; but further, the connection between receipt of divine knowledge and ingesting heavenly honey persists in Jewish traditions. Aseneth's use of this imagery should not therefore be too hastily associated with any one religious tradition.

Kraemer also connects the bees in this scene to a Greek philosophical-mythological tradition known as the "myth of *begonia*." She points out that Greek philosophical thought associates bees with the souls of the dead (e.g.,

---

42. Putthoff, "Aseneth's Gastronomical Vision," 104; V. Rabens, *The Holy Spirit and Ethics in Paul: Transformation and Empowering for Religious-Ethical Life*, WUNT 2/283 (Tübingen: Mohr Siebeck, 2010), 61–62; Ross S. Kraemer, "Aseneth as Wisdom," in *Wisdom and Psalms*, ed. Athalya Brenner and Carole R. Fontaine, FCB 2nd series (Sheffield: Sheffield Academic, 1998), 219–39; Philonenko, *Joseph et Aséneth*, 25–27.

43. Kraemer, *When Aseneth Met Joseph*, 169.

Ovid, *Fast.* 1; *Metam.* 15; Pliny, *Nat.* 11.23). Citing Vergil (*Georg.* 4), Kraemer recounts a tradition where bees would spontaneously generate from the flesh of a dead ox, the bees being the newly transformed life force of the now dead animal. Porphyry develops the concept, since honey as nectar, the food of the gods, allows for the preservation and therefore immortality of the soul. Their association with honey prompts Porphyry to identify bees as the souls of righteous individuals awaiting resurrection (*Antr. nymph.* 8). Kraemer draws a parallel to the imagery of the bees in Vergil and Porphyry and in Joseph and Aseneth. While she admits that much of the philosophical reflection around bees and souls predates her proffered date for Joseph and Aseneth, Kraemer uses Porphyry's innovation of the bee as *righteous* soul to shore up her dating of the text after the third century CE.[44] However, as Anathea E. Portier-Young points out, "there is nothing shared between Porphyry and *Joseph and Aseneth* which must have originated within a Neoplatonic context. Porphyry has simply followed a common rule for allegorical interpretation, articulated by Philo and others, whereby the properties of the thing being interpreted provide clues to its allegorical meaning."[45] In other words, these properties of honey that Porphyry makes use of are part of a common tradition shared also by earlier thinkers; the extrapolations he makes are the logical outcome of common allegorical practices.

Moyer Hubbard has suggested that there is also another text that uses honey to symbolize renewal of the soul, that is, the Epistle of Barnabas, tentatively dated toward the end of the first century CE.[46] While the Epistle of Barnabas is undoubtedly a product of what came to be known as Christianity, it is also possible that its ideas emerge from a Jewish milieu—or rather, what scholars tend to call a Jewish-Christian milieu.[47] The section

---

44. Kraemer, *When Aseneth Met Joseph*, 169.
45. Portier-Young, "Sweet Mercy Metropolis," 144.
46. Moyer Hubbard, "Honey for Aseneth: Interpreting a Religious Symbol," *JSP* 16 (1997): 97–110. Moyer points out that Joseph and Aseneth and the Epistle of Barnabas are generally assumed to have been composed in the same area, namely, Egypt (104). Ellen Aitken instead suggests a Syrian context. Ellen Aitken, "'The Basileia of Jesus Is on the Wood': The Epistle of Barnabas and the Ideology of Rule," in *Conflicted Boundaries in Wisdom and Apocalypticism*, ed. Benjamin G. Wright III and Lawrence M. Wills, SymS 35 (Atlanta: Society of Biblical Literature, 2005), 200, 202. See also Peter Richardson and Martin B. Shukster, "Barnabas, Nerva, and the Yavnean Rabbis," *JTS* 2/34 (1983): 33.
47. Moyer, "Honey for Aseneth," 104; William Horbury, "Jewish-Christian Relations in the Epistle of Barnabas and Justin Martyr," in *Jews and Christians: The Parting*

of the epistle that Hubbard invokes in his discussion of Joseph and Aseneth is 6.8–7.2, a section that discusses an interpretation of "a land flowing with milk and honey" (Exod 33:1–3; Lev 20:4; Deut 6:18; etc.). For Hubbard, "the parallels between *Barnabas* and *Joseph and Aseneth* point strongly in the direction of seeing Aseneth's consumption of honey as a symbol of her new birth."[48] Certainly, the Epistle of Barnabas connects being made new to the ingestion of honey; interspersed with this exegesis of the "milk and honey" phrase is a discussion of creation (6.12) and renewal through forgiveness of sins (6.11). The inheritance of the land is connected, in this text, with renewal and salvation through Christ. The most telling line, in my view, is 6.17: "Why then does he speak of milk and honey? Because the child is first nourished by honey and then milk. So also when we are nourished by faith in the promise and then by the word, we will live as masters over the earth" (trans. Ehrman). Hubbard is correct to bring this text into discussion with Joseph and Aseneth, since it adds to our discussion of the significance of honey as a food of renewal; however, this line, 6.17, indicates that honey functions differently in the Epistle of Barnabas than it does in Joseph and Aseneth. Where the Epistle of Barnabas connects this renewal to conquest and dominion, Aseneth is described as a City of Refuge (B 15.7; 16.16; Ph 15.6; 16.9); rebirth is not a prominent descriptor in Aseneth's experience. This represents two diverging understandings of the ramifications of eating honey, whether metaphorical in the case of the Epistle of Barnabas or narratively real in the case of Joseph and Aseneth. Aseneth's transformation is not discussed in terms of mastery or ownership over a land, nor in terms of birth or rebirth, but rather in terms of knowledge and divine appearance.

Kraemer comes close to the idea of Aseneth's receipt of heavenly knowledge but in my view takes the association too far.[49] She is correct to draw parallels between Joseph and Aseneth's description of the honeycomb and

---

of the Ways A.D. 70 to 135, ed. James D. G. Dunn, WUNT 66 (Tübingen: Mohr, 1992), 315–45; L. W Barnard, "The Epistle of Barnabas in Its Contemporary Setting," *ANRW* 27.1:159–207; cf. James Carleton Paget, *The Epistle of Barnabas: Outlook and Background*, WUNT 2/64 (Tübingen: Mohr, 1994), 7–9, who ultimately decides against a Jewish-Christian origin.

48. Hubbard, "Honey for Aseneth," 106.

49. Kraemer, *When Aseneth Met Joseph*, 26. See also John J. Collins, *Between Athens to Jerusalem: Jewish Identity in the Hellenistic Diaspora* (Grand Rapids: Eerdmans, 2000), 236.

the description of personified Wisdom in Sir 24:19 and in Prov 2:6, since in all cases it emerges from the mouth of God. While I think these connections are invaluable for understanding the process Aseneth undergoes during her transformation, especially as it has implications for the event's participation in hierophagy as a genre, I do not follow Kraemer's conclusion that Aseneth herself becomes Wisdom, since, as Portier-Young observes, this goes beyond what the text itself says about Aseneth's identity.[50]

Finally, Jill Hicks-Keeton proposes a convincing connection between the description of the honeycomb and creation language found in the LXX Genesis. She argues that the description of the honey links its origins not just with heaven but more specifically with the garden of Eden (rendered παράδεισος in Gen 2:8, 15 with the additional modifier of τῆς τρυφῆς in Gen 3:23–24)—literally, the "orchard of delight" (NETS).[51] In Joseph and Aseneth, this same phrase is used to describe the comb: B 16.14 reads, "for this comb is (full of the) spirit of life. And the bees of the paradise of delight have made this from the dew of the roses of life that are in the paradise of God," while Philonenko renders it, "car ce miel, ce sont les abeilles du Paradis de délices qui le font."[52] For Hicks-Keeton, it is not surprising that eating the honeycomb renders Aseneth transformed in splendor, since the honeycomb recalls God's creating breath and a world spoken into being.[53] I am convinced generally by Hicks-Keeton's conclusion that the bees in Jos. Asen. 16 come from Eden and that the paradise referred to in the narrative is none other than the original orchard of creation; Hicks-Keeton further suggests that this event in the narrative represents the provision of life to non-Israelites.[54] For my own analysis, however, what is perhaps more significant about her analysis is the possibility that Aseneth's ingestion of heavenly food harvested from Eden marks an inversion of the ingestion of the fruit, the result of which was Adam and Eve's expulsion from paradise.[55]

---

50. Kraemer, *When Aseneth Met Joseph*, 26; Portier-Young, "Sweet Mercy Metropolis," 145.

51. Hicks-Keeton, *Arguing with Aseneth*, 51.

52. B 16.14: διότι τοῦτο τὸ κηρίον ἐστὶ πνεῦμα ζωῆς. καὶ τοῦτο πεποιήκασιν αἱ μέλισσαι τοῦ **παραδείσου τῆς τρυφῆς** ἐκ τῆς δρόσου τῶν ῥόδων τῆς ζωῆς τῶν ὄντων ἐν τῷ παραδείσῳ τοῦ θεοῦ. Ph 16.8: διότι τὸ μέλι τοῦτο πεποιήκασιν αἱ μέλισσαι τοῦ **παραδείσου τῆς τρυφῆς**. Kraemer translates the short version as follows: "This honey the bees of the paradise of delight have made" (*When Aseneth Met Joseph*, 38).

53. Hicks-Keeton, Arguing with Aseneth, 54.

54. Hicks-Keeton, Arguing with Aseneth, 55.

55. I briefly discuss the potential hierophagic event in Genesis in chapter 1.

Her argument, then, strengthens my suggestion that hierophagy functions to relocate the eater. Where Adam and Eve are relocated to the world outside Eden, here Aseneth is brought into paradise through her ingestion.

After Aseneth consumes the comb, and the heavenly visitor announces that Aseneth has been changed in some way by it, the visitor restores the honeycomb's broken edge and then draws two intersecting lines across the comb, apparently in blood (B 16.17):

> And again the man stretched out his right hand and put his (fore)finger on the edge of the comb looking east and drew it over the edge looking west, and the way of his finger became like blood. And he stretched out his hand the second time and put his finger on the edge of the comb looking north and drew it over the edge looking south, and the way of his finger became like blood.

To compare, Philonenko's edition (Ph 16.10–11):

> Et l'homme étendit sa main et posa son doigt à l'extrémité du rayon qui regardait vers l'est, et la trace de son doigt devint sanglante. Et il étendit sa main une seconde fois et posa son doigt sur l'extrémité du rayon qui regardait au nord, et la trace de son doigt devint comme du sang.[56]

It has been pointed out many times that if you draw two intersecting lines according to the cardinal directions, what you draw is in fact a cross. Nir, for example, understands the honeycomb to be bread and the mark drawn on it to be a cross of wine; the cross represents the eschatological character of what she views as the eucharistic scene of Joseph and Aseneth. Again, Nir believes "that the Christian character of our scene is so obvious that it needs no demonstration at all."[57] However, it is crucial to remember with ancient texts, and therefore worth repeating with regard to Joseph and Aseneth and this scene, that symbols that have later significance for

---

56. Kraemer translates the passage in the following way: "And again the figure stretched forth his right hand and put his finger on the edge of the comb facing east, and drew it over the edge looking west and the path of his finger became like blood. And he stretched forth his hand a second time and put his finger on the edge of the comb facing north, and drew it over the edge facing south and the path of his finger became like blood" (*When Joseph Met Aseneth*, 66–67).

57. Nir, *Joseph and Aseneth*, 88.

Christianity or Judaism should not be read into texts whose provenance is contested.[58]

In my view, Poirier's proposal that the intersecting lines on the comb are reminiscent of the marks left by honey-presses on actual honeycombs in antiquity holds just as much weight as any other proposal offered so far.[59] According to his findings, and using material evidence for support, a board or plunger was used to crush the honeycomb, releasing its contents. The plunger pressed the comb against a stand grooved with intersecting lines, which would result in a cross shape being imprinted on the harvested comb. The marks may then represent the extraction of honey from the comb.[60] This rather ordinary explanation for the marks serves as a warning against assuming that every obscure reference in a text necessarily has deeper symbolic meaning.

Honeycomb and Hierophagy

Examining the honeycomb scene using the lens of hierophagy isolates a key ramification of ingesting the honeycomb that is often downplayed. If we put to the side for the moment anachronistic categorization issues about Jewish and Christian authorship, the narrative itself yields information about how ingesting honeycomb advances the plot and characterization of its protagonist. In doing so, this analytical perspective illustrates how the ingestion, rather than being a cipher for conversion or some kind of

---

58. The cross as a symbol associated primarily with Christianity is relatively late. See Robin M. Jensen, *The Cross: History, Art, and Controversy* (Cambridge: Harvard University Press, 2017), esp. 41–42; Ross S. Kraemer, "Jewish Tuna and Christian Fish: Identifying Religious Affiliation in Epigraphic Sources," *HTR* 84 (1991): 141–62; Oliver Larry Yarbrough, "The Shadow of an Ass: On Reading the Alexamenos Graffito," in *Text, Image, and Christians in the Graeco-Roman World*, ed. Aliou Cissé Niang and Carolyn Osiek (Eugene, OR: Pickwick, 2012), 239–54; Bruce W. Longenecker argues for the early use of the symbol. Bruce W. Longenecker, *The Cross before Constantine: The Early Life of a Christian Symbol* (Minneapolis: Fortress, 2015). But many of the pre-Constantinian examples offered are highly contested by other scholars. See John Granger Cook, review of *The Cross before Constantine*, by Bruce W. Longenecker, *Int* 72 (2018): 88–89.

59. Poirier, "Apicultural Keys to *Joseph and Aseneth*," 11–12. See also Haralampos V. Harissis and Anastasios V. Harissis, *Apiculture in the Prehistoric Aegean: Minoan and Mycenaean Symbols Revisited*, BARIS 1958 (Oxford: Hedges, 2009), 30–32.

60. Poirier, "Apicultural Keys to *Joseph and Aseneth*," 13.

eucharistic event, in fact represents a shared understanding across the ancient Mediterranean about the effects of eating otherworldly food.

Chapters 15–17 provide descriptions of three promises made to Aseneth by the angelic visitor that may or may not overlap in what they refer to. The first is the writing of Aseneth's name in the Book of Life (B 15.4; Ph 15.3); the second involves Aseneth and the bread/cup/ointment; the third is her identification as City of Refuge. At the end of his visit, the visitor asks Aseneth if she has understood his actions and their meaning, and Aseneth affirms that she has (B/Ph 17.1–2), although it takes the present scholarly audience considerably more effort to say the same. While the first promise, the Book of Life, emerges from Aseneth's repentant prayer, the second two promises appear to be connected to the honeycomb; when the visitor announces that Aseneth's name was written in the Book of Life, it is an event that has already taken place (ἐγράφη), while the second and third promises are to take place in the future, after the honeycomb. The futurity of these promises is apparent in the way the angel expresses them. The eating of the bread, the drinking of the cup, and the anointing are expressed in future verbs (φάγῃ; πίεσαι; χρισθήσῃ [B 15.5; Ph 15.4]), as is her future renaming (ἔσται [B 15.7; Ph 15.6]). It is only when Aseneth has ingested the honeycomb and understood these things that the angelic visitor speaks into reality these promises made prior to the honeycomb event: "So shall be the words I have spoken to you" (B/Ph 17.2), referring to his earlier promises.[61] As such, Aseneth's change in identity and in understanding both come about as a result of her ingestion of the honeycomb and are confirmed in the change to her physical appearance in chapter 18.

Prior to the visitor's appearance in the chamber, Aseneth has already uttered her prayer (B/Ph 11–13) and has already thrown away the statuettes of the gods she previously worshiped (B/Ph 10.13–14). In some sense, then, the ingestion of the honeycomb in the next section is distinct from any decisions Aseneth has made concerning whom she will worship; the text locates the appearance of the visitor and the beginning of the next scene *after* Aseneth's solitary activities: "And as Aseneth finished confessing to the Lord...."[62] As such, while it seems likely that Aseneth's actions

---

61. Kraemer, *When Joseph Met Aseneth*, 38. Ph: καὶ εἶπεν ὁ ἄνθρωπος· οὕτως ἔσται τὰ ῥήματα ἃ ἐλάλησα πρὸς σέ. B: καὶ εἶπεν ὁ ἄνθρωπος· οὕτως ἔσται πάντα τὰ ῥήματά μου ἃ λελάληκα πρὸς σέ σήμερον.

62. Kraemer, *When Joseph Met Aseneth*, 28. Burchard renders it similarly: "and when Aseneth had ceased making confession to the Lord."

lead to the arrival of the visitor and the honeycomb meal, the ingestion occurs in a distinct section of the text rather than in the midst of the prayerful behavior.

The angelic visitor introduces himself, and the text depicts his appearance in such a way that associates him with both Joseph and images of God or angels: the light imagery describing his face, hands, and feet is closely connected with ancient ways of articulating divine presence.[63] Aseneth recognizes this, falling down in worship, and follows the visitor's instructions to change her clothing and clean the ashes off her head and face (B/Ph 14.7–15; in the longer version, Aseneth also washes her hands). The visitor tells Aseneth that her seven-day mourning period has resulted in her name being written in the Book of Life (ἐν βίβλῳ ζωῆς). A second promise is then made to Aseneth, which is that she will eat the (B: blessed) bread of life and drink the (B: blessed) cup of immortality and be anointed with the (B: blessed) ointment of incorruptibility.

Aseneth invites the visitor to share a meal with her, offering bread and fragrant wine (B/Ph 15.14). At this offer, the visitor also asks for a honeycomb, which Aseneth assumes she will need to send out for; the visitor reassures her that, on the contrary, one is already in her storeroom. The comb in question has a remarkable appearance. Like the visitor, it is described as white (λευκὸν; B 16.8; Ph 16.4), and because of this and its fragrance, Aseneth wonders at its origins. In the longer text, Aseneth's internal dialogue asks whether the comb has come out of the mouth of her angelic visitor in addition to her explicit question to the visitor about the comb's origin in the shorter version (B 16.9, 11; Ph 16.6). Regardless, Aseneth suspects that the honeycomb has heavenly origins, just like her visitor. Her insight into the heavenly honeycomb prompts the visitor (with or without molten hands, B 16.13) to take hold of Aseneth's head and bless Aseneth. The visitor states that it is a result of repentance (μετάνοια; B 16.14; Ph 16.7) that she has the opportunity to eat the honeycomb, reinforcing the idea that the two events—repentance and ingestion—are distinct and that one does not represent the other. The angelic guest confirms that the honeycomb comes from paradise and is made by heavenly

---

63. Meredith Warren, "A Robe Like Lightning: Clothing Changes and Identification in *Joseph and Aseneth*," in *Dressing Judeans and Christians in Antiquity*, ed. Kristi Upson-Saia, Carly Daniel-Hughs, and Alicia J. Batten (Farnham: Ashgate, 2014), 140.

bees and is the food for God's heavenly angels;[64] ingesting the honeycomb results in immortality.

We have now arrived at the core scene of the episode, wherein the angelic being takes and eats some of the honeycomb and then feeds Aseneth some as well. As noted above, Burchard's longer version is explicit about Aseneth's ingestion of the piece of honeycomb, using a direct command from the angel ("eat"; B 16.15), but the shorter version also includes Aseneth in this little taste of heaven. The longer text also doubles up on the significance of the ingestion. Where the shorter text leaves it somewhat up to the reader what this mouthful means, the longer text associates it with the bread of life and the cup of immortality and the ointment of incorruptibility (B 16.16). It uses a lot of pastoral imagery to describe Aseneth's favor with God, much of which bears similarity to language found in Song of Songs.[65] The longer text also restores the broken honeycomb and makes it whole again. The shorter text, by not stating any connection to the bread/cup/ointment previously mentioned in Ph 15.4 leaves open what this meal means within the narrative; the longer text makes it clear that the honeycomb confirms the promise made by the angelic visitor when he first arrived.

At this point, the angelic visitor performs certain actions on the comb (the two intersecting lines, discussed in detail above [B 16.17; Ph 16.10–12]), and the bees associated with the comb emerge from it. There is no indication in the text that the bees' activities in any way alter Aseneth herself, although it is clear that their behavior is meaningful; Aseneth is asked if she has understood and Aseneth says that she has (B/Ph 17.1). It is possible that the object of Aseneth's understanding in this line (τὸ ῥῆμα τοῦτο) is the entire event, from ingesting the honeycomb to the marking of the comb to the behavior of the bees, but it is unclear from the text. Kraemer translates the phrase as referring to something spoken: "Have you perceived what was said?"[66] This translation highlights the possibility of the understanding referring to the most recent words spoken by the angel, which is the command to go away to their place in B 16.20–22; Ph 16.15–17. Given that at this stage the angelic being sets the honeycomb on fire (its sweet fragrance confirming its divine origins) and the

---

64. Burchard's version includes "all the chosen of God and all the sons of the Most High" with the angels who eat heavenly honeycomb (16.14).

65. See Kraemer, *When Aseneth Met Joseph*, passim.

66. Kraemer, *When Joseph Met Aseneth*, 67.

narrative changes focus from Aseneth to her "seven virgins" in the next section, I am inclined to believe that the understanding encompasses the three distinct events of eating the comb, marking the comb, and the bees emerging from the comb. The question remains whether the three events, the eating, the marking, and the bees, each have a distinct meaning or whether they point to the same "thing" or ῥῆμα, but I leave that question to the side for the moment in order to showcase the effects of eating the heavenly honeycomb.

After her heavenly visitor departs in his fiery chariot (B 17.7–10; Ph 17.6), Aseneth changes her clothing in preparation for dinner with Joseph. As I have written elsewhere, her change in clothing here (B 18.5–7; Ph 18.3–6) is indicative of her new association with the divine realm as a result of her honeycomb experience.[67] The shining radiance of her attire, which is described as being "like lightning" (B 18.5; Ph 18.3), connects Aseneth with other divinely associated figures through its use of the ancient literary trope of shining brilliance as a way to identify divine or semi-divine beings. This element of her transformation is not merely sartorial, nor does the descriptor "like lightning" (ὡς ἀστραπὴ) merely refer to the fine quality of her clothing. Rather, the text's use of light in this context echoes markers of epiphany that are common literature across religious communities.

Her shining robe is matched by her shining face, confirming that Aseneth's change is not merely in her dress but in her being. In both the short and long recensions, Aseneth notices that her face has been changed by her experience. In the short text, Aseneth puts on her radiant attire and then asks for a basin of water. As she bends over it, Aseneth notices her brilliant visage: her face "was like the sun," and her eyes "like the rising morning star" (Ph 18.7).[68] There is no mention in the short text of why Aseneth wants the water. In Burchard's version, Aseneth has the water brought in order to wash her face, which she needs to do because her servant has pointed out to her before her change of clothing that her face has been affected by her period of mourning (B 18.3–4). In this longer text, she bends over the water in order to wash but stops abruptly when she notices her shining face and eyes.[69] As I have discussed elsewhere,

---

67. Warren, "Robe Like Lightning," 137–53.

68. Trans. Kraemer, *When Joseph Met Aseneth*, 39. Philonenko's translation: "Son visage était comme le soleil, et ses yeux comme l'étoile du matin à son lever." Greek: καὶ ἦν τὸ πρόσωπον αὐτῆς ὡς ὁ ἥλιος καὶ οἱ ὀφθαλμοὶ αὐτῆς ὡς ἑωσφόρος ἀνατέλλων.

69. Reading the two texts' version of this scene together for this project has con-

Aseneth's transformation is highlighted by the fact that her clothing in chapter 18 is almost identical to the finery she dons in order to prepare for Joseph in 3.6: robe, golden girdle, bracelets, buskins, necklaces with costly stones, and a head-dress (either tiara or crown).[70] The difference is not in the items of clothing but in their description as radiant with light, like Aseneth's face and like the face of the heavenly visitor: they are both ὡς ἀστραπὴ, like lightning. Where the lack of Egyptian religious iconography on her gemstones confirms her rejection of her family's gods, these brilliant elements confirm Aseneth's association with the divine realm. Her appearance, therefore, confirms that the hierophagic transformation she experienced as a result of ingesting or tasting the honeycomb has taken place.

Conclusion

The texts discussed previously, as well as the ones in the next chapters, not only depict the eating of special foods which transform a person; they also shed light on the knowledge shared by the various communities to which these texts belong. None of these texts, including Joseph and Aseneth, take pains to explain to their readership precisely what takes place when a character eats, nor do they give reasons as to why this type of eating does what it does. It is assumed that the audience understands the norms that govern eating in such a framework—that naturally, if one eats food given to one by a heavenly being one will be transformed in some way. If the relationship between food and transformation is a common theme in the literature of antiquity, there still remains the question of how Joseph and Aseneth uses that known relationship in its own narrative. It is clear that in Joseph and Aseneth eating and food ritual are important markers for defining categories.[71] We can see that Joseph defines himself in relation to Aseneth using culinary terminology: while he eats "blessed bread of life and drink[s] a blessed cup of immortality" (B 8.5), she eats "from

---

vinced me of the priority of the shorter text. It makes more sense that an editor has added justification for the basin of water than that an editor has removed all mention of washing; it also does not make sense that Aseneth's radiant face only occurs after her change of clothing.

70. Warren, "Robe Like Lightning," 149–51; see especially the chart comparing the passages on p. 150.

71. Lieber, "I Set a Table before You," 65.

their [i.e., the idols'] table bread of strangulation and drink from their libation a cup of insidiousness" (B8.5). Since the novel structures itself in terms of food and eating, our analysis of its meaning should engage this important aspect.

The mystery of the honeycomb becomes clear when examined in this light; readers of Joseph and Aseneth would have understood the comb's transformative properties when administered by an otherworldly visitor and would have expected Aseneth's transformation, when she becomes chosen like her visitor, the bees, and Joseph, her betrothed. Her physical transformation and newfound abilities would also have been anticipated, as Ovid's *Metamorphoses*, 4 Ezra, and Revelation suggest. Joseph and Aseneth—in particular chapter 16—can therefore be understood through its affinities with other texts from the ancient Mediterranean, since these texts appear to preserve a shared understanding of hierophagy. Aseneth's categorization as heavenly is determined in the narrative by the same ritual that governs the transformations of other Greco-Roman characters. Joseph and Aseneth shares the understanding with the texts examined above that hierophagy is transformative; it is not only physically transformative but also shifts a person's belonging. Persephone, for example, is made a citizen of the underworld, while Aseneth becomes a devotee of the Most High God, not just a worshiper but also associated with heaven through her shining appearance. It would not only have been clear but also anticipated by the ancient readers, then, that Aseneth's transformation from ordinary Egyptian to exceptional heavenly creature is tied to the food she has been fed and that her transformation occurs only because of this meal.

If we take it seriously that Joseph and Aseneth is participating in a shared genre of transformational eating, known as hierophagy, shared by many texts—Jewish, Christian, and others—it seems less necessary to view Aseneth's experience as a conversion, a category which requires an attempt to divine what her religious affiliations were before as well as what they become after her experience. The question of this text's religious affiliation has been a bee in the bonnet, so to speak, of scholarship up until this point;[72] however, if we step away from imagining the text as creating commentary on religious affiliation *through this ritual in particular*, we may come in some way closer to understanding what Joseph

---

72. See, for example, Barbara Diane Lipsett, *Desiring Conversion: Hermas, Thecla, Aseneth* (Oxford: Oxford University Press, 2011); and Chesnutt, *From Death to Life*.

and Aseneth can tell us about how religious transformation takes place in the context of the Hellenistic world. In a milieu where actual conversions were, if not rare, at least anomalous in terms of the general culture, it seems appropriate to approach this text in a way that cautiously respects the difficulties in talking about religion at a time when such a designation did not exist. That is, in examining Joseph and Aseneth's participation in this genre of transformational eating, it is possible to move beyond questions of the religious authorship of Joseph and Aseneth and toward the issue of how this text reflects a particular social worldview. For Joseph and Aseneth, this does indeed look different when compared with the current Jewish/Christian dichotomy through which the text is most often analyzed. Instead of continuing to view Aseneth's transformation in terms of historical ritual practices—conversion rituals that require the opposition of religious identities—examining Joseph and Aseneth in terms of its literary predecessors allows for an interpretation of this scene as a participant in the genre of hierophagy that was clearly prevalent in ancient literature and cultural understanding. When the honeycomb scene, which is the fulcrum of Joseph and Aseneth, is examined using hierophagy as an analytical category, it is no longer necessary to label the text as either the product of Jewish or Christian concerns. In this light, conversion is not a natural category for reading Joseph and Aseneth—her transformation is of a different kind. This approach allows for a reading that not only reflects the complex interactions of religious genres in literature but also respects Aseneth's transformation as one which endows her with the new abilities common to others who have undergone hierophagic transformation: new knowledge, new appearance, and new location.

5
Apuleius's *Metamorphoses*

Apuleius's hapless character Lucius is well known among scholars of ancient literature for his adventures and mishaps in the *Metamorphoses*. Among the most remarkable in a series of unfortunate and then fortunate events is Lucius accidental metamorphosis into a donkey, the result of his curiosity about magic, and his eventual restoration to human form, thanks to his invocation of the goddess Isis. For the purpose of this study, what is important is that Lucius's return to human form takes place because Isis provides him with divinely-sent roses to ingest.

This scene has been the topic of much discussion; in this chapter I will suggest that the most appropriate lens to examine Lucius's transformation is hierophagy, since this approach explains why eating roses makes sense as a mechanism of change. Like Aseneth's, Lucius's experience in the *Metamorphoses* has frequently been read in terms of conversion. Again, however, limiting our understanding of what food-induced transformations mean to conversion events prevents us from seeing the important connections this literary genre has across religious borders. Lucius's transformation certainly ends up with his initiation into the cult of Isis and his eventual appointment as priest, but the physical transformation he experiences is set apart from those later experiences. As a hierophagic event, the ingestion of the roses in *Metam.* 11 points to a common understanding of the transformative effects of ingestion and also highlights one element of hierophagy, namely, that the food is given from one of higher ontological status to a recipient of lesser ontological status, in this case a donkey.

Preliminary Matters

Apuleius appears to have written several texts in the second century CE, although many of these have been lost, and some extant works attributed to him are likely spurious.[1] He was an orator born in the North African town of Madauros; his education in Greek and Latin took him to Carthage and then to Athens, among other locations around the ancient Mediterranean. After he married a wealthy widow, he was put on trial for witchcraft, accused by the widow's avaricious relatives of using magic to seduce his wife.[2] He spoke in his own defense and was very likely acquitted.[3]

Apuleius's writings range from philosophical treatises, poetry, novels (including *Metamorphoses* but also the now-lost *Hermagoras*), histories, biological and medical texts, and other cultural and scientific texts.[4] It is not clear where exactly the *Metamorphoses* fits in his literary career. While Erwin Rohde believes it to be part of his earlier *oeuvre*, it is more likely that the novel was written after his trial for witchcraft, since it does not appear that *Metamorphoses* was used against Apuleius at his trial, and since some events that take place in the novel appear to echo events in Apuleius's own life.[5] Indeed, in book 11, the so-called Isis Book under discussion here, the protagonist-narrator Lucius seems to conflate his own identity with that of the author, Apuleius: with the protagonist being called "a man from Madauros" (*Metam.* 11.27) the readers might lose any distinction between character and composer.[6] This slip (or perhaps hint?) strengthens potential arguments about autobiographical elements in *Metamorphoses*, but at the same time we should not be so quick to take at face value any claims from an author with such skill in allusion and turns of phrase. Keeping this in mind is important, since it helps us as critical readers see through the author's attempts at conflating author and narrator and therefore at conflating history and narrative.

---

1. S. J. Harrison, "Apuleius' *Metamorphoses*," in *The Novel in the Ancient World*, ed. Gareth Schmeling (Leiden: Brill, 2003), 491–93.

2. Harrison, "Apuleius' *Metamorphoses*," 491–92.

3. S. J. Harrison, *Apuleius: A Latin Sophist* (Oxford: Oxford University Press, 2000), 7.

4. Harrison, "Apuleius' *Metamorphoses*," 491–92.

5. Erwin Rohde, "Zu Apuleius," *Reinisches Museum* 40 (1885): 66–95. For the alternative position, see Harrison, "Apuleius' *Metamorphoses*," 493; Apuleius, *Cupid and Psyche*, translated by E. J. Kenney (Cambridge: Cambridge University Press, 1990), 203; P. Walsh, *The Roman Novel: The "Satyricon" of Petronius and the "Metamorphoses" of Apuleius* (Cambridge: Cambridge University Press, 1970), 250.

6. Keith Bradley, "Contending with Conversion: Reflections on the Reformation of Lucius the Ass," *Phoenix* 52 (1998): 316.

The unity of the text has been hotly debated, since the Latin novel is at face value an expansion of a slightly earlier (second-century) Greek story, The Ass, which centers on Lucius as a first-person narrator but lacks the inserted stories that punctuate the Latin text.[7] As S. J. Harrison indicates, the matter is further complicated by the fact that a ninth-century Christian writer, Photius of Constantinople, alludes to a Greek novel by one Lucius of Patras titled *Metamorphoses*, which does contain "astonishing stories." It is possible that The Ass, then, is itself an epitome that was later expanded by Apuleius, but Harrison suggests that it is more likely that Apuleius used the longer Greek *Metamorphoses* directly and that The Ass independently epitomized the same longer Greek text.[8] Apuleius's version inserts numerous stories that "help bring out Lucius' foolishness in his pursuit of magic."[9] It is also Apuleius who innovates by adding Isis as bestower of true form; in the Greek, Lucius as ass manages to secure the roses on his own.[10]

In terms of genre, the novel presents a curious predicament: the first ten books seem comic in tone, while the end of the book turns sharply towards religion, suggesting a more serious tone. I will discuss a specific implication of this apparent tension between comic and religious elements towards the end of the chapter, but for the present it is important to recognize that this interplay of serious and comic is not unique to *Metamorphoses*; Stefan Tilg has argued convincingly that a philosophical component in some ancient novels provides a model for reading both silly and serious aspects of Apuleius's text.[11] These elements, in reality, are not segregated into a set of comic books from 1–10 and a set of serious books in the second portion of the novel; rather elements of each can be found throughout the seriocomic tale.[12] Taking this into consideration will be of use when analyzing how

---

7. Harrison, "Apuleius' *Metamorphoses*," 500.

8. Harrison, "Apuleius' *Metamorphoses*," 501; Stavros Frangoulidis, *Witches, Isis, and Narrative: Approaches to Magic in Apuleius' Metamorphoses* (Berlin: de Gruyter, 2008), 13.

9. Frangoulidis, *Witches, Isis, and Narrative*, 13.

10. Joel C. Relihan, ed. and trans., *The Golden Ass: Or, A Book of Changes* (Indianapolis: Hackett, 2007), xxvii.

11. Stefan Tilg, *Apuleius'* Metamorphoses*: A Study in Roman Fiction* (Oxford: Oxford University Press, 2014), esp. 85–105. For a discussion of potentially philosophic novels, see 57–68. An example he lists is Euhemerus's fragmentary work, *Sacred History*, but Tilg also identifies elements in the other extant Greek novels.

12. Tilg, *Apuleius'* Metamorphoses, 99; Luca Graverini, *Literature and Identity in the Golden Ass*, trans. Benjamin Todd Lee (Columbus: Ohio State University Press,

this text uniquely communicates its version of hierophagy, since some elements are inverted rather than expressed positively.

Isis Initiation?

A primary focus of study for *Metamorphoses* has been book 11, commonly called the Isis Book. This book details the restoration of Lucius back to his human form and describes his subsequent initiation as a devotee of Isis, whose patronage facilitates his transformation. Unfortunately for scholarship, most of what we understand about how individuals were initiated into the mysteries of Isis comes from this text; we have nothing substantial with which to compare Apuleius's account.[13] As Richard G. Summers observes,

> The question of verisimilitude in the *Metamorphoses* of Apuleius always has presented difficulties. The work clearly is indebted to sources other than the author's own creative instincts, as the epitome *Lucius sive asinus* found in the corpus of Lucian demonstrates and Apuleius himself admits, and this fact has complicated further the attempt to establish the existence in the novel of any foundation of historical or autobiographical truth relative to its writer or the Roman Empire in which he lived.[14]

In other words, it is difficult to establish what elements of the narrative reflect the historical reality of Apuleius's world, and yet scholars (for lack of other sources) tend to use book 11 as a template for actual initiation practices for the Isis cult.[15] This results in rather a circular discussion of whether the text represents or diverges from historical initiation processes. The cult of Isis was extremely popular in the second century CE,[16] and so

---

2012), 133; Carl C. Schlam, *The* Metamorphoses *of Apuleius: On Making an Ass of Oneself* (Chapel Hill: University of North Carolina, 1992), 7.

13. Luther H. Martin, *Hellenistic Religions: An Introduction* (New York: Oxford University Press, 1987), 80; Walter Burkert, *Ancient Mystery Cults* (Cambridge, MA: Harvard University Press, 1987), 97.

14. Richard G. Summers, "Apuleius' *Juridicus*," *Historia* 21 (1972): 120.

15. Martin, *Hellenistic Religions*, 80; Burkert, *Ancient Mystery Cults*, 6, 17; E. R. Dodds, *Pagan and Christian in an Age of Anxiety* (Cambridge: Cambridge University Press, 1965), 2–3.

16. James Gollnick, *The Religious Dreamworld of Apuleius'* Metamorphoses (London, ON: Wilfrid Laurier Press, 1999), 138; Sharon K. Heyob, *The Cult of Isis among Women in the Graeco-Roman World* (Leiden: Brill, 1975), 36.

5. Apuleius's Metamorphoses 105

it is not out of the realm of possibility that Apuleius was familiar with the rites. Nevertheless, we should remain cautious about assuming too much about the relationship between the text and historical reality. What the text does describe, however, is a narratively real process that the author assumes will hold cultural water for his readers. In other words, while we may not have a record of actual Isis cult initiation rites, we have something that communicates the expectations of what such a ritual might entail. In some sense, and at least for the purpose of this study, the narrative aspects of the initiation are more important than whether or not they are historical; hierophagy, too, is a narrative-level experience whose existence at the historical level I do not presume to explore. Thus, the narrative function and narrative effects of the rituals are what is important to analyze regardless of their relation to reality.

In light of a narrative-level approach, then, Lucius's initiation into the Isis cult has a complex relationship with his experience with the roses, which he ingests at the instruction of Isis. His initiation is one result of his vision of the goddess, but it is not the only result, and it is not identical with his participation in the procession where he ingests the roses and regains his human form. The fact that the text goes into great detail about the process of his later initiation, presenting the rituals as representative of real historical initiation procedures, indicates that the hierophagic event is actually distinct from the initiation event. The general consensus about these initiation rites, even if they emerge largely from Apuleius's own text, is that they do not commence with ingesting roses. Generally, the absence of this initial ingestion of roses, present in Lucius's transformation but omitted from scholarly descriptions of Isis cult initiation, is important to recognize: this suggests that we need to firmly establish that the two events, the initiation and the transformation, are separate and need to be considered separately in terms of their narrative significance.

At the level of narrative, the events transpire in stages, with the vision leading to the ingestion event and the ingestion event allowing the initiation to take place; each step, however, is distinct. Indeed, the priest who carried the roses offers Lucius the chance to serve the goddess only after Lucius is returned to human form (11.15). The goddess herself, communicating with Lucius in dreams, has to urge Lucius to become initiated: "Not a night passed, not even a nap, devoid of a vision of admonition [*monitus*] from the goddess. With repeated commands she urged [*censeo*] me now at last to be initiated, since I had long been destined for her rites"

(11.19).[17] In other words, the passage from hierophagy to initiation is not automatic; the two events are narratively separate and perform different functions in the text.[18]

The fact that these two events are distinct has not gone entirely unnoticed; as Stavros Frangoulidis notes, the initiations—which are not one, but three in number—seem almost unnecessary additions to the story, "most especially because the goddess has fulfilled her role as saving deity after restoring Lucius to his human form."[19] In a certain sense, what occurs after Lucius's return to his human form—namely, his devotion to Isis and his success as a lawyer—reflects the physical changes he underwent in transforming from ass to human. Book 11 represents positive metamorphoses to counterbalance all the negative changes Lucius experienced in the first ten books,[20] all of which hinge on his hierophagic transformation in 11.13. However, to understand the ramifications of this transformation, it is necessary to unpack what the process actually entails, which comparisons to other texts illuminate its meaning, and which comparisons obscure it with anachronism.

Conversion

As with Aseneth's hierophagic experience, scholars tend to regard Lucius's transformation event as pointing towards a conversion, in no small part because his transformation leads directly (though not automatically) to his initiation into the Isis cult.[21] James Gollnick identifies "new beliefs and inner peace" as key hallmarks of a religious conversion.[22] However, it is not clear that either Aseneth's or Lucius's transformation brings

---

17. Text and translation from Apuleius, *Books 7–11*, vol. 2 of *Metamorphoses (The Golden Ass)*, ed. and trans. J. Arthur Hanson, LCL (Cambridge, MA: Harvard University Press, 1989).

18. This argument is one I have also made regarding Aseneth's experience; for her, the decision to worship Joseph's god precedes the hierophagic event, but they are nevertheless distinct in the same way that Lucius's two experiences are.

19. Frangoulidis, *Witches, Isis, and Narrative*, 200–201. Frangoulidis notes that the second and third initiations could function to highlight Lucius's continued naïveté but alternatively to juxtapose Lucius's frivolous and superficial flirtations with magic with his sophisticated and committed Isis devotion.

20. Frangoulidis, *Witches, Isis, and Narrative*, 175.

21. E.g., Gollnick, *Religious Dreamworld of Apuleius' Metamorphoses*, 136–38.

22. Gollnick, *Religious Dreamworld of Apuleius' Metamorphoses*, 136.

about this kind of feeling; in both cases, the characters already pray to the divinities in question and already believe in their power to rescue them. Putting aside for the moment the Christian-centric and anachronistic prioritization of belief as a marker of conversion or religious experience, and even if, as some propose, Lucius gains new knowledge about Isis from her visitation by the sea,[23] the transformation effected by the roses remains distinct; physical transformation of that sort is not typically part of a conversion event. Lucius's interaction with the priest of Isis certainly kicks off the beginning of his deeper devotion to Isis in the form of his initiation but that transformational event takes place because of the ingestion of the roses. I have not found any indication that rose-eating is a mark of conversion or of initiation to that specific cult, and so the moment of transformative eating accomplishes something different and overlooked: hierophagy.

Arthur Darby Nock's influential contribution to the study of religious conversion includes a detailed discussion of *Metamorphoses* by way of example. This text remains an important benchmark study on the topic despite its Christian categorizations and worldviews. Nock situates the idea of a spiritual and emotional religious experience of transformation over and against the "adhesions" he identifies as part of "paganism":

> Our survey of paganism has given us little reason to expect that the adhesion of any individual to a cult would involve any marked spiritual reorientation, any recoil from his moral and religious past, any idea of starting a new life. For adhesion to acquire the emotional values of conversion special personal circumstances were necessary, and we find such in the story told in the eleventh book of the *Metamorphoses* of Apuleius.[24]

For Nock, Lucius is the exception that proves the rule, namely, that so-called pagan devotional practices were devoid of emotional or spiritual depth. His views on conversion were influenced by the psychology of religion approach exemplified by William James, whose understanding of religion prioritizes interiority, the individual self, and emotion.[25] James's influence on Nock's definition of conversion is clear, as James writes:

---

23. Gollnick, *Religious Dreamworld of Apuleius'* Metamorphoses, 137.
24. Arthur Darby Nock, *Conversion* (Oxford: Oxford University Press, 1969), 138.
25. William James, *The Varieties of Religious Experience* (New York: Penguin, 1984).

To be converted, to be regenerated, to receive grace, to experience religion, to gain an assurance, are so many phrases which denote the process, gradual or sudden, by which a self hitherto divided, and consciously wrong inferior and unhappy, becomes unified and consciously right superior and happy, in consequence of its firmer hold upon religious realities.[26]

James and Nock use the same language, influenced by a Christian vernacular (e.g., grace), to define religious conversion: the emphases in both cases are on renewal, grace, the interior emotions of the individual (the self), and on a moment or a process that transforms a singular person in ways that are psychologically, morally, emotionally, or spiritually knowable by that one person.[27] The first person narrative of *Metamorphoses* certainly lends itself well to this kind of argument, since it allows the reader access to the internal experiences of the protagonist, Lucius. However, as Zeba Crook observes, these categories of analysis are in no way organic to the ancient world and rather emerge from James's understanding of the self as a modern Western category.[28] The same is true of Nock's study, which distinguishes between religions to which a person belonged "body and soul" and philosophies like Mithraism, which were only used for personal gain.[29] In addition, the idea of personal gain (protection and good fortune

---

26. James, *Varieties of Religious Experience*, 189.
27. As Keith Bradley points out, James's "converts were fully familiar before conversion with the dominant religious framework of the society in which they lived, Christian and monotheistic as it was … this already familiar framework came to occupy a principal place in the converts' lives" (Bradley, "Contending with Conversion," 321. The preexisting cultural framework guides and shapes the interpretation of religious experience, which means that this framework, whether nineteenth-century Christian Protestant or second-century Roman, is fundamental to understanding what any kind of transformation signifies (322).
28. Zeba Crook, *Reconceptualising Conversion: Patronage, Loyalty, and Conversion in the Religions of the Ancient Mediterranean*, BZAW 130 (Berlin: de Gruyter, 2004), 23–24. Paula Fredriksen also notes that the typical translation of the Greek term ἐπιστρεφῶ does not reflect ancient understandings of religious devotion, and that the idea of conversion is "anomalous" in the first century CE (*Paul: The Pagan's Apostle* [New Haven: Yale University Press, 2017], 75–77).
29. Nock, *Conversion*, 14; Crook, *Reconceptualising Conversion*, 25. The false division between what Nock views as religions, namely, Judaism and Christianity, and what he views as philosophies, pagan associations devoted to a particular deity, breaks down with the recognition that both James and Nock anachronistically envision that

in this life) points to inauthentic religious experience, distinguished by the level of emotional crisis that brings about the conversion.[30] It is this emotional crisis that is, for Nock, what distinguishes so-called real religious experience from the superficiality of other types of religious affiliation. Nock writes that while Lucius would not have shunned other worship practices expected of him in public (i.e., in contrast to the exclusivism prescribed by Christianity), "any other worship must appear to him tame and inferior"[31] because of what Nock views as this deep, emotional experience. In this way, Lucius's experience maps well onto Nock's established (if anachronistic) categories, since Lucius is in anguish throughout the novel leading up to book 11, but it only maps well if one ignores the personal, immediate gain achieved through the experience. Lucius's aretalogy, the one that invokes the goddess to appear out of the ocean, reminds the goddess of her good works specifically in delivering people from concerns of this world—pain in childbirth, agriculture, moonlight—in order to bring about his transformation. Lucius asks not for personal, emotional, or moral transformation when he begs her, "rid me of this dreadful four-footed form, restore me to the sight of my own people, restore me to the Lucius I was" (11.2). He requests a return to his former self, not the beginning of a new life.[32]

Given the methodological difficulties inherent in both Nock's and in James's work on conversion, it is problematic that many current analyses of Lucius's experience still rely foundationally on their work. Nancy Shumate's 1996 work on the *Metamorphoses, Crisis and Conversion* contains a chapter titled "Book 11: Conversion as Integration," which clearly relies on James's idea of the reunified self as a hallmark of conversion. She writes, "Conversion is a change in one's center of energy, a shift in or rearrangement of one's mental system.... In other worlds, it is a process involving the dismantling of one cognitive structure and its replacement by another."[33]

---

nineteenth- and twentieth-century Jewish and Christian experiences are identical with first- and second-century ones.

30. Crook, *Reconceptualising Conversion*, 25–26.

31. Nock, *Conversion*, 155.

32. Walter Burkert writes, "The emphasis is, once again, on a "safe anchor" in this life. A redirection of religion toward other-worldly concerns, contrary to what is often assumed, is not to be found with the "Oriental" gods and their mysteries. At best they continue what was already there" (*Ancient Mystery Cults*, 28).

33. Nancy Shumate, *Crisis and Conversion in Apuleius' Metamorphoses* (Ann Arbor: The University of Michigan Press, 1996), 289.

Like her predecessors, Shumate frames her discussion of Lucius's experiences in terms of an individualistic and internal cognitive and emotional framework, a framework whose priorities are bound by Protestant values of faith and belief rather than ancient modes of religious identity. As Keith Bradley concludes about Apuleius's account, and I agree,

> There is no rejection of one and an embracing of a radically different system of religious knowledge, no heightened awareness of a single, dominant god already familiar to the worshipper, nothing to suggest that Lucius' previous religious knowledge was "wrong" (to use Nock's term) or that he turns away from his past religious life, or that he undergoes a radical and total change of religious allegiance.[34]

Even if Apuleius narratively describes a ritual for initiation, as discussed above, there is no guarantee that this imagined ritual corresponds to any actual historical ritual.[35]

Instead, and as Bradley suggests, Apuleius makes use of existing cultural assumptions and literary genres about how reconfiguring identity is accomplished. This means his process of experiencing Isis and his transformation are understandable through commonly shared assumptions about how transformation takes place. I argue that for Lucius, one culturally assumed mechanism for this process—indeed, the primary mode of transformation in this text and the others under discussion in this volume—is through ingestion: hierophagy. In a certain sense, then, conversion is more a metaphor for transformation as opposed to the other way around. This is clear when Apuleius's text is read alongside the stories of Persephone, Ezra, and John of Patmos, none of whose experiences is ever assumed to be a conversion experience despite the mechanisms of transformation mapping onto the same hierophagic pattern.

More recent scholarship on conversion has moved away from psychological approaches of shifting religious allegiances, but nonetheless I maintain that Lucius's transformation should be looked at without the anachronistic lens of conversion. Both Beverly R. Gaventa and Alan F. Segal exemplify the movement away from defining conversion as an inter-

---

34. Bradley, "Contending with Conversion," 326.

35. This is worth keeping in mind for other texts discussed in this book, in particular Aseneth's honey and Perpetua's cheese, both of which have tended to be examined through the lens of historical ritual.

nal or emotional experience.[36] Segal's more sociological approach toward Paul's religious experience—as described in Acts[37] as well as in Paul's own writings—does make moves towards prioritizing community immersion over and above the internal emotional experience. Segal writes, "By using the term *conversion* I wish to stress the wrenching and decisive change of Paul's entrance to Christianity, thereby linking Paul with many modern accounts of conversion."[38] Later on that same page, he tempers his definition slightly by allowing that this kind of "decisive change" can occur within the same religious tradition, as long as "the change is radical."[39] For Segal, even though Paul remained a Jew, he converted to "a new apocalyptic, Jewish sect" and then changed his social position by living with non-Jewish adherents of that same sect.[40] In applying this model to Apuleius's text we come across a few stumbling blocks, not least in what is defined as radical, but also in whether initiation into becoming a religious official for a "sect" can be counted as entering into a social community of the type Segal identifies. But further, the fact remains that even though Segal is cautious to locate his reading of Paul in the texts of antiquity, he acknowledges that modern conversion narratives are in the back of his mind, forming the lens through which he views religious experiences.

Gaventa's study is also extremely cautious, but still in my reading does not help us to better understand Lucius's transformation; she explicitly rejects the notion that there is a type of religious transforma-

---

36. Beverly R. Gaventa, *From Darkness to Light: Aspects of Conversion in the New Testament* (Philadelphia: Fortress, 1986); Alan F. Segal, *Paul the Convert: The Apostolate and Apostasy of Saul the Pharisee* (New Haven: Yale University Press, 1990. It is important to note that both Gaventa and Segal write about Paul/Saul, whose importance as a figure in later Christianity has impacted the very notion of conversion.

37. Numerous scholars have pointed out the dangers in approaching Luke-Acts as representing history, as does Segal himself (*Paul the Convert*, 3–5). See also P. Vielhaur, "Paulinisms of Acts," in *Studies in Luke-Acts*, ed. Leander E. Keck and J. Louis Martyn (Nashville: Abingdon, 1966), 35–50.

38. Segal, *Paul the Convert*, 6.

39. Daniel Boyarin's book, *A Radical Jew: Paul and the Politics of Identity*, Contraversions 1 (Berkeley: University of California Press, 1994) alludes to a similar notion. Other work on Paul has highlighted just how aligned Paul's views are with the Judaism of his time. See, for example, Gabriele Boccaccini and Carlos A. Segovia, eds., *Paul the Jew: Rereading the Apostle as a Figure of Second Temple Judaism* (Minneapolis: Ausberg Fortress, 2016).

40. Segal, *Paul the Convert*, 6–7.

tion that is more genuine than another, which is an important step away from the previous generation of scholarship such as James and Nock.[41] She also articulates a type of conversion that centers on a transformation by which a person reinterprets their past life in light of their present affiliation: "Transformation applies to conversions in which a new way of perception forces the radical reinterpretation of the past. Here the past is not rejected but reconstrued as part of a new understanding of God and world."[42] Despite the capitalization of the word God, which indicates a monotheistic theological perspective on religious experience, it is possible to apply this approach to Lucius's experience; however, the question remains whether Lucius (1) develops a new understanding of the role of the divine or (2) uses this understanding retrospectively. Photis reveals the cure to Lucius's erroneous transformation early on (3.25), so in this respect the goddess only provides the remedy that Lucius has been searching for all along. And, like most if not all novels from the first and second centuries, the gods are involved in one way or another from the beginning; Fate and Providence, in particular, are invoked throughout the tale as responsible for Lucius's fate, most notably in 11.1, when Lucius is readying to pray to Isis for release; Isis, for her part, confirms that she is in control of all that moves in the universe (11.5). So, for Lucius, his acceptance of Isis's role in his fortunes is not so much new, but rather he has decided to work with the will of the goddess rather than against it. Gaventa's category, then, does not fully explain the transformation outlined in *Metamorophoses*.

Bradley's work on *Metamorphoses* also calls into question the relevance of conversion as an analytical category useful for understanding Lucius's experience.[43] Bradley provides an excellent critique of the Protestant Christian background that informs both James's and Nock's approach to religious change, pointing out that

> neither the world of Apuleius' novel nor the real world in which he himself lived were worlds generally characterized by rival systems of religion. Rather, both worlds knew a multiplicity of co-existent gods who comprised a pantheon that always had the potential to expand, and in which the incorporation of new gods never required the expulsion of

---

41. Gaventa, *From Darkness to Light*, 148.
42. Gaventa, *From Darkness to Light*, 148.
43. Bradley, "Contending with Conversion," 315–34.

the old or demanded from worshippers a choice between one form of divinity and another.[44]

Bradley observes that there is a potential example of one character who, closer to what Nock would envision, has rejected other gods in favor of a deity of her own; this character is maligned in the text rather than held up as an example and therefore strengthens the critique of conversion as a descriptor of Lucius's devotion to Isis. In other words, even if there were such a thing as conversion per se in antiquity, the text sets up rejection of other gods as something deviant and wrong (9.14).[45]

Zeba Crook's critique of the scholarship around conversion is important for understanding the significance of how the poetics of this transformation function in the context of the novel and in the wider ancient world that produced it and the other texts under discussion. In the context of the ancient Mediterranean, even Nock admits that multiple religious affiliations are simultaneously possible and even likely. The aspect of psychological or inward, self-facing transformation that is so important to those who would label Lucius's transformation as such emerges from the first-person narrative. This perspective allows insight into the thoughts Lucius has as he transforms. In this respect, the work of Segal and Gaventa shows its limitations, as Crook points out. In his reading, both Segal and Gaventa imply that, had Paul been more like *Metamorphoses* in revealing Paul's inner thinking, a psychological approach would have illuminated the psychological effects of his conversion.[46] However, this perspective has allowed three distinct events to be conflated into one under the umbrella of conversion: the invocation of the goddess, the shift from donkey to human, and the initiation into the Isis cult. Using Crook's critique of the psychological approach to religious transformation and affiliation is significant in that it allows us to tease apart what undergirds *Metamorphoses*'s

---

44. Bradley, "Contending with Conversion," 318. I disagree with Bradley's claim on p. 319 that conversion in what he describes as monotheistic Christianity would be possible in the second century. Because of what we know of the difficulties defining the boundaries of Christianity (if we can even call it that at this time) and Judaism, this amounts to special pleading based on anachronistic exclusivity claims apologetically demanded by later church fathers and other rhetorically charged attempts to control grass-roots Christian praxis.

45. Bradley, "Contending with Conversion," 320–21.

46. Crook, *Reconceptualising Conversion*, 30; Segal, *Paul the Convert*, 5; Gaventa, *From Darkness to Light*, 20.

cultural assumptions. Crook points out that the ancient world, the one in which Apuleius writes, is really a foreign culture and further that cross-cultural psychology brings with it numerous problematic assumptions about universal patterns of thought and experience.[47] Because psychology as a discipline is the result of research done on individual, Western selves, there are problems for its application within cultures where individualism and selfhood are not prominent ontological or social categories of meaning, which lead to additional difficulties when emotion is brought into the equation, since emotional categories and experiences are also culturally defined and bounded.[48] Instead, Crook offers what he calls an "emic category and an alternative to the dominant psychological paradigm with which the West typically approaches conversion."[49] Again using Paul as the grounding character for analysis, Crook offers a social analysis of how patronage and reciprocity offer a better set of categories for analyzing religious adherence and new devotional events than previous modes of emotional and psychological change. Crook points out that ancient writing about gods and their assistance has to do with the same elements of protection and generosity with which human benefactors might also assist: "Humans addressed the gods for general and daily needs—food, protection, comfort, strength, assistance—in addition to those things which only the gods could deliver—great crops, health, and most frequently, salvation."[50] As such, the role of the gods is not categorically different from the role of patrons; it is a question of scale. Crook even notes that Isis specifically is an example of this kind of divine benefaction, operating within a patron-client system. Citing an inscription from the second century BCE, he demonstrates that Isis's responsibilities include things also expected of human patrons and benefactors, such as justice and social and familial norms.[51] If we take this model to Apuleius's account of Lucius's experiences in book 11, the model fits, since Isis is the benefactor and patron of Lucius from the time that he requests, and Lucius is the client of the goddess, fulfilling his responsibilities as such.[52] The agreement made between the goddess and Lucius is transactional. As Friedrich Solmsen

---

47. Crook, *Reconceptualising Conversion*, 31–33.
48. Crook, *Reconceptualising Conversion*, 34–47.
49. Crook, *Reconceptualising Conversion*, 52.
50. Crook, *Reconceptualising Conversion*, 76.
51. Crook, *Reconceptualising Conversion*, 76; SEG 2.821; *NewDocs* 1:10–21.
52. See Crook, *Reconceptualising Conversion*, 53–89.

observes, "Lucius without hesitation accepts Isis' claims and trusts her promise," which is to provide the roses that will restore him to human form in exchange for his service.[53] Separating the question of emotional or spiritual transformation from the process of conversion is important for understanding Lucius's experience since his spectacular change from donkey to human is frequently taken for a symbol of an inward transformation as well. What this leaves us with is the question of the role of the ingestion and transformation, since using Crook's social model of what conversion looks like allows us, at last, to separate out Lucius's devotion to Isis from his ontological shift from donkey to human.

Ontological Hierarchy

If Lucius's experience is not of conversion but of some other kind of transformation, it is necessary to closely examine the various aspects of that transformation. Teasing out the process by which the ass becomes human allows for an analysis that puts this transformation in conversation with other examples of the time period, which better situates Apuleius's literary choices within the cultural milieu and its accepted genres of experience. One of the components of hierophagy that I propose in this book is that the ingested item be given by a character belonging to a higher ontological category to a character belonging to a lower ontological category. As I discussed in my introduction, there are examples in the literature of the first and second centuries of higher-category beings expressing anxiety about potentially ingesting lower-category food items, which I understand as contributing to the cosmological framework in which hierophagy operates. However, since it is not directly related to the mechanisms I am attempting to underscore in this example and in the other examples in this book, I put to the side for the moment any discussion of the ramifications of higher-category beings ingesting lower-category food. Instead, I will focus on the ontological hierarchies implicit in Lucius's ingestion of the roses. In the other texts analyzed in this volume, and in particular the ones composed by Jews and/or Christians, the ontological hierarchy between the giver of the ingested item and the eater is relatively clear. In 4 Ezra, Revelation, the Passion of Perpetua and Felicitas, and Joseph and Aseneth,

---

53. Friedrich Solmsen, *Isis among the Greeks and Romans* (London: Harvard University Press, 1979), 88.

the ones who ingest are all mortal human beings, ordinarily residing on earth, the mortal plane. The feeders all belong to the divine realm: they are angels, or agents of the divine, or perhaps the divine hand itself, especially, as we shall see, in the case of Perpetua.[54]

In these other cases the hierarchy is clear, but it is more complicated in the case of Apuleius's *Metamorphoses*. The complications arise first because of the multiple ontological identities of the eater: Is Lucius truly human or truly donkey? Or is he both simultaneously? Second, we have three individuals involved in the process of ingestion rather than just two: Lucius, the priest, and Isis. In the case of a hierophagic event with three characters, who is considered to be the one providing the hierophagic food? Answering this latter question actually resolves the former at the same time. In many other texts discussed in the present volume, intermediaries between gods and mortals are frequently responsible for handing over the ingested item; like the *angelus interpres* in 4 Ezra, then, the priest can be understood as an agent of Isis, since he is instructed by her in a dream to allow Lucius access to the roses. He is merely an intermediary, then; in reality, the goddess is the character who provides the ingested item, and it is clear that she is a higher-category being than the priest and therefore of Lucius. As such, for the purpose of the hierophagic pattern being met, Lucius's "true" identity at the moment of ingestion is not important, since whether he is ass or human, he still belongs to a lower category of beings than does the goddess.

Analysis

As with Joseph and Aseneth, there is a distinction between the transformation due to hierophagy and the renewed religious devotion. Aseneth, if we remember, prays to God, which brings about the visit from the heavenly man. Only then is she transformed by his honeycomb. For Lucius, these two steps are represented by three: first by his prayer, then by his Isis-granted transformation, and then thirdly by his initiation into the actual rites of Isis at Cenchreae. While his prayer to the goddess in 11.2 certainly facilitates his transformation by way of one of her

---

54. The Persephone myths are outliers in this sense, as Hades/Pluto and Persephone/Proserpina both exist in the same ontological category, as they are gods; rather, the shift in that example comes in the Chthonic versus Olympian distinction between the divine beings.

priests, that aspect of his transformation is discrete from his later choice to become initiated. As with Joseph and Aseneth, then, it is important not to conflate the hierophagy with any surrounding religious devotion; while in both texts the allegiance to a new god is important, focusing on that allegiance misses the separate significance of what transformational eating accomplishes.

Prayer

Lucius's prayer begins book 11 and marks the beginning of a new section of the novel as a whole. It is widely agreed that this book represents the climax of the narrative, all of which has led Lucius to this point on the beach. He purifies himself in the ocean under the full moon; Lucius is prompted to action by the realization that some yet-to-be-named "supreme goddess" (*deam praecipua*; 11.1) holds the power over life, the universe, and everything. This realization takes place prior to his transformation; as with Aseneth, his acceptance of the power of the goddess anticipates any ritual action including prayer. The prayer praises the goddess for numerous qualities embodied by multiple goddesses, including Ceres, Venus, Proserpina, and others; like Lucius, we do not learn that the object of his prayer is Isis until she responds by appearing to him. When she appears, she is distinguishable from other goddesses, whose attributes are also visible in the goddess' appearance,[55] by two features: the distinctive knotted robe and the bronze rattle she holds in her right hand (11.3–4). John J. Winkler offers three reasons behind Apuleius's choice of the goddess Isis for his novel.[56] First is the association between the ass and the Egyptian goddess.[57] Next is the popularity and visibility of Isaic worship in the Roman Empire, with distinctive Egyptian paraphernalia.[58]

---

55. The description of the moon on her crown indicates Luna; the coils of snakes and ears of wheat on her crown suggest Demeter.

56. While there has been some scholarly conjecture that Apuleius was a devotee of the goddess himself, there is no external evidence for this. See John J. Winkler, *Auctor and Actor: A Narratological Reading of Apuleius' Golden Ass* (Berkeley: University of California Press, 1985), 276–79.

57. Winkler notes that "the mere presence of the ass in the Greek *Metamorphoses* ought to have been sufficient to suggest … the specific retwisting of the tale toward the ass-god of Eypt" (*Auctor and Actor*, 277).

58. This emphasizes the momentous change Lucius experiences, argues Winkler (*Auctor and Actor*, 278).

Finally, Winkler notes that Isis is often found in "tales of saving."[59] These narrative (rather than historically grounded) reasons for using Isis as the patron deity of Lucius's transformation highlight the importance of recognizing the narrative-level function of the rose event, separate from issues of initiation or conversion.

Dreams

At the end of his prayer, Lucius falls asleep. As in the hierophagic incident we shall examine in the Passion of Perpetua and Felicitas, dreams play an important role in Lucius's transformation.[60] Dreams were important ways for gods to communicate with human beings in literature, as is demonstrated by their presence in a range of texts but especially novels, a genre to which *Metamorphoses* belongs. The text is clear that when Lucius initially experiences a vision of the goddess Isis as the Moon, prior to his prayer, this is not in a state of dreaming. Rather, Lucius has just awoken on the shore of the ocean: "About the first watch of the night *I awoke* in sudden fright and saw" (11.1).[61] But here what he sees is the image of Isis, the moon. It is after his prayer and his ritual bathing (11.2) that Lucius goes back to sleep, and in sleep he at last sees the anthropomorphic image of the goddess herself emerge from the sea, just as the moon had emerged from the waves of the sea in his initial vision.[62] It is in this form and in this medium—the dream—that the goddess provides the instructions that bring about Lucius's transformation. Gollnick observes that the presence of Isis as savior and her presence in a dream both fit well with the ancient expectations of that goddess and of salvific dreams as preserved in Artemidorus, who specifically identifies Isis as one of the gods known to appear in dreams in order to rescue people from dire situations—people "who have tried every resort and who find themselves in utmost peril" (*Onir.* 2.123).[63] In this dream context, Isis's instructions to Lucius make perfect sense: "go right up to the priest and gently, as if you were going to kiss his hand,

---

59. Winkler, *Auctor and Actor*, 278. See M. Barrigón Fuentes, "Les dieux egyptiens dans l'*Onirocriticon* d'Artémidore," *Kernos* 7 (1994): 29–45, esp. 33. See also Artemidorus, *Onir.* 2.39.
60. Gollnick, *Religious Dreamworld of Apuleius'* Metamorphoses, esp. 53–79.
61. *Circa primam ferme noctis vigiliam experrectus pavore subito, video.*
62. Compare 11.1 (*emergentem fluctibus*) with 11.3 (*emergit divina facies*).
63. Gollnick, *Religious Dreamworld of Apuleius'* Metamorphoses, 136.

pluck the roses and cast off at once the hide of that wretched beast which I have long detested" (*Metam.* 11.6).[64] The instructions provide the means by which Lucius will be rescued from his perilous situation. The matter is not simply one of restoring human form, but also of removing Lucius from the harmful situations from which, throughout the novel, he has barely escaped. But as the goddess's rescue is not simply about a return to the human form (but rather promises rescue from future and past dangers) so too is it not limited to the moment of transformation. As in Joseph and Aseneth, the deity promises ongoing blessedness and protection:

> You will clearly remember and keep forever sealed deep in your heart the fact that the rest of your life's course is pledged to me until the very limit of your last breath.... You will live in happiness, you will live in glory, under my guardianship. And when you have completed your life's span and travel down to the dead, there too, even in the hemisphere under the earth, you will find me ... and I will favour you and you will constantly worship me. (11. 6)

When the roses become a reality, we see the importance of tokens given or received in dreams sent by divine forces; the reality of the roses indicates the physical fulfillment of a promise made in the dream.[65] That is, the additional promises that Isis makes to Lucius are shown to be real by the presence of the initial component of the dream, which is the roses proffered by Isis's priest.

As soon as the vision has ended, Lucius awakes (11.7). Things happen suddenly: Lucius is released from sleep "at once" (*nec mora*); the sun rises abruptly and crowds of people appear (*nec mora*). Time then slows down. The procession, filled with a variety of gods other than Isis all of whom are described in detail,[66] gradually brings Lucius his opportunity of transformation. Patiently, he approaches the priest with caution (11.12). Upon eating the roses from the wreath, time speeds up again: at once (*protinus*) Lucius is transformed back into his human form.

---

64. *Et de proximo clementer velut manum sacerdotis osculabundus rosis decerptis, pessimae mihique iam dudum detestabilis beluae istius corio te protinus exue.*

65. For examples elsewhere in ancient literature of tokens playing a role in the reality of dreams, see this volume, chapter 6 ("The Passion of Perpetua and Felicitas") note 34.

66. Bradley, "Contending with Conversion," 325.

Roses

The mechanism of Lucius's transformation is the garland (*corona*) of roses promised by Isis (11.6) and presented to him by the priest (11.13). Like Lucius, the priest has also received an "oracle" in a dream from Isis instructing him to offer the roses. Byzantine oneirocritica overwhelmingly associate dreams of roses (while in season) with good fortune.[67] The second- to third-century oneirocriticon of Artemidorus also indicates that dreams of rose-wreaths while in season indicate good fortune (*Onir.* 1.77). The text suggests that the fragrant scent of in-season roses[68] is significant in interpreting such dreams as fortuitous. Aside from their positive meaning in dream oracles, flower garlands were standard fare at religious rites such as processions.[69] They were braided together and worn as crowns by participants in the procession or used to decorate houses, altars, and other spaces.[70] It is not surprising, therefore, that they would be part of the Isiaic procession to which Lucius awakes after his dream vision.

Roses were not merely ornamental flowers whose appearance and scent could be enjoyed; they are also present in ingredient lists and menus in antiquity.[71] This makes Lucius's ingestion of the roses less like the ingestion of the scroll in Revelation and perhaps more akin to Ezra's fiery cup—certainly liquid served in cups must have been a regular part of daily life, and in that sense drinking a cup of liquid is ordinary, but the context and description in which the ingestion is embedded marks the event as particular. Likewise, garlanded roses are not normal food, so while they

---

67. Steven M. Oberhelman, *Dreambooks in Byzantium: Six Oneirocritica in Translation, with Commentary and Introduction* (Farnham: Ashgate, 2008), 27, 110, 162, 187, 188.

68. Roses are considered spring flowers. George F. Osmun, "Roses of Antiquity," *The Classical Outlook* 52.10 (1975): 115. Apuleius indicates that the procession takes place in the spring, since "there were women gleaming with white vestments, rejoicing in their varied insignia, garlanded with flowers of spring [*vernus*]" (11.9).

69. Nicole Belayche, "Religious Actors in Daily Life: Practices and Related Beliefs," in *A Companion to Roman Religion*, ed. Jörg Rüpke, Blackwell Companions to the Ancient Worlds (London: Blackwell, 2007), 275–91, esp. 211, 280.

70. See Charlotte R. Potts, "The Art of Piety and Profit at Pompeii: A New Interpretation of the Painted Shop Façade at IX.7.1–2," *Greece and Rome* 56 (2009): 55–70. They are used in this context elsewhere in *Metamorphoses*, e.g., 3.27, where they are decorating the shrine of Epona.

71. Osmun, "Roses of Antiquity," 115.

are technically edible (especially for a donkey) their ordinary function within the context of a procession is not that they be eaten. Since roses were an ordinary part of processions and were sometimes used in cooking, the roses that Lucius eats are therefore not distinct to Isis; their significance is not in what they symbolize, but rather in how they are used.[72]

Several scholars have indicated that the goddess' role in Lucius's transformation is not entirely the result of her own powers, but rather relies on the same magic with which Lucius was transformed in the first place.[73] As Brigitte B. Libby observes, Lucius was already aware of the fact that roses would cure him from his predicament, since he is told so by Photis immediately after his transformation (3.25), and further "Isis must wait to offer roses until the next day, when she knows that flower garlands will be part of her parade."[74] However, rather than view this as an indication of Isis's impotence or of Apuleius's irreverence, I would suggest an approach to the event that focuses on the reason why eating roses brings about the effects that it does; in other words, even if the treatment is magical in some way, ingesting something (anything!) in order to bring about some transformation needs unpacking. It is certainly the case that Lucius attempts several times to eat roses as he goes through books 3–10 as a donkey. Directly after his transformation into the ass in 3.27, he spies the shrine of Epona adorned with roses but is comically thwarted from eating them and changing back to his human form by his own enslaved servant. Shortly after in 3.29, Lucius spots roses growing in a garden but decides it would be unwise to transform back into a human just at that moment because the robbers who have captured him might kill him; he counts on finding roses again but Fortune frustrates his luck. In book 4, he spies what look like

---

72. Interestingly, Artemidorus (*Onir.* 4.81) states: "it is not good to see or eat things served during festivals of the dead and funeral banquets or to prepare a funeral banquet. For it prophesies doom for the sick and, for those who are well, it foretells the death of someone in one's household" (trans. Harris-McCoy). The mention of eating (φαγεῖν) funerary food in a dream suggests a point of contact with the hierophagic ramifications of eating food from another world, since funerary food, when eaten in a dream, indicates the association of the dreamer/eater or one of their household with the realm of the dead.

73. Brigitte B. Libby, "Moons, Smoke, and Mirrors in Apuleius' Portrayal of Isis," *The American Journal of Philology* 132 (2011): 304; John A. North, "Novelty and Choice in Roman Religion," *JRS* 70 (1980): 191; Winkler, *Auctor and Actor*, 214; Solmsen, *Isis among the Greeks and Romans*, 88.

74. Libby, "Moons, Smoke, and Mirrors," 304.

roses off in the distance, but as he approaches, offering a prayer to Fulfillment, Fortune reveals that they are nothing but "laurel-roses" produced by some kind of shrub and not true roses that would bring about his return to human form.[75] So, while Lucius could eat normal roses and regain his true shape, he is prevented from doing so at every step of the way, most frequently with Fortune to blame. While his quest to find roses functions as a comedic plot device that keeps Lucius as a donkey long enough for the story to play out, the consistent invocation of other goddesses such as Fulfillment and Fortune, who are either unable to provide him with the cure or are actively working against him, serve to highlight the power of Isis, who is the only deity able to bestow Lucius with the remedy to his predicament. This is made especially clear in comparison to Lucius's earlier attempt at ingesting roses at the shrine of Epona;[76] there, he attempted to take the rose garland from the goddess without her permission. The situation is reversed in book 11, when Lucius earnestly prays for the goddess Isis's help. It is clear, then, that it would not have been possible for Lucius to use roses to transform himself without the assistance of (and therefore supplication to) a divine patron.[77]

Excursus: Another Instance of Transformational Eating?
Cupid and Psyche

The text of *Metamorphoses* is riddled with stories told not by the narrator but rather by the characters in that overarching narrative. One such story is that of Cupid and Psyche (4.28–6.24). The recounting in Apuleius's text represents an older Greek tale preserved here in the mouth of an old woman as "an old wife's tale" (*anilis fabula*; 4.27). Whether or not the tale was well known prior to Apuleius's text, the narrative presents it as such.[78]

---

75. Roses are also invoked in 10.29 as a metaphor for hope.
76. Michael von Albrecht, *Masters of Roman Prose: From Cato to Apuleius—Interpretive Studies*, trans. Neil Adkin (Leeds: Francis Cairns Publications, 1989), 173.
77. If the goddess is a necessary component of this transformation, the hierophagic criteria of high-low ontology feeding is strengthened by this example.
78. See Luca Graverini, "An Old Wife's Tale," in *Lectiones Scrupulosae: Essays on the Text and Interpretation of Apuleius' Metamorphoses in Honour of Maaike Zimmerman*, ed. M. Zimmerman et al., Ancient Narrative Supplementum 6 (Groningen: Barkhuis, 2006), 86–110.

There are two instances of potentially transformative ingestion in the tale. First, when in Proserpina's hall, Pysche is instructed by Venus to decline any offer of sumptuous dinner and instead request plain bread to eat (6.19); Theseus is trapped by such a meal in the *Aeneid* 6.617–618, which suggests that if Psyche had eaten the banquet, she too would have been trapped in Hades. The text indicates that Psyche obeys these instructions (6.20), and the matter is passed over without too much comment by the narrator of the story. While Proserpina is a goddess who is well aware of the effects of eating food from another realm, as discussed in an earlier chapter at length, this small amount of bread or cake (*panem*) does not seem in this story to relocate Psyche in the way the pomegranate did Proserpina. Psyche is able to return from the underworld after her visit because she has resisted the lure of an underworld banquet. The second example from this text perhaps suggests the reason why: Psyche is offered a celestial banquet by Jupiter after she drinks a cup of ambrosia (6.23–24). The cup of ambrosia transforms her into an immortal being, and the banquet is a wedding banquet for Psyche and Cupid. While this portion of the text does not articulate a theory of transformational eating as clearly as other texts in this monograph, the fact that these small examples of divine ingestion by a human (Psyche) are included adds support to the idea that the genre was known not just by ancient literary culture in general but by Apuleius specifically.

Transformation through Eating

At last, Lucius achieves his transformation back into human form. Unlike in some hierophagic incidents discussed in this volume, Lucius does not give any hint as to the taste of the roses. When sensory imagery does play a role, it is fragrance, sound, and touch rather than taste that impact how Lucius understands his transformation. Scent is important among the descriptors used in book 11, in particular to describe Isis. She is described as smelling like the "fragrances of Arabia" and as having "ambrosial feet" in 11.4, indicating divine providence and luck. Likewise, sweet sounds indicate Lucius's fortune in the goddess' patronage. Her sistrum jingles in time, and when Lucius awakes, he notices the sounds of people, birds, and even trees producing joyous noises (11.7). The scents and noises of the procession likewise play a role in constructing the narrative context in which the transformation takes place. Participants strew flowers on the path, sprinkle scented ointments, play musical instruments, and sing

(11.9–10). The sensory cacophony of the procession comes to a still point when Lucius makes his move toward the priest; the roses are described as "lovely" (*amoenis*) rather than with explicitly marked sensory adjectives. However, as soon as Lucius "most eagerly devour[s]" (*devoravi*) the wreath, haptic imagery becomes prominent. The descriptions emphasize the textured experience of his existence as the ass: his coarse hair and thick hide, his rock-like teeth and his tail all disappear (11.13). The physicality of this description inverts the intensely physical experiences Lucius has had while in his transformed state.

It is not entirely surprising that taste appears to play no role here. As I have observed elsewhere, taste descriptions are not abundant in ancient sources, since higher values were placed on quantity rather than quality of food available. It is remarkable that in several of the texts examined in this volume taste plays such a prominent role; but its absence here does not prevent the hierophagic genre from playing a role in Lucius's transformation. Taste is not the only functioning aspect of ingestion that brings about transformation; rather, the act of ingestion in and of itself alters the person who ingests it. As Maggie Kilgour has demonstrated, ingestion even aside from taste is transformative in that it collapses the distinction between the body and what is outside of it; the opposition dissolves as the external object is dissolved into the ingesting body.[79] In putting the roses into his "greedy mouth" (*avido ore*) and devouring them, Lucius devours the patronage of the goddess. He has broken down the division between himself and her divine patronage. Lucius is transformed by the roses as a result of internalizing Isis's promise, a promise which his body physically repays by his later service in the form of an initiand.

After Effects

But the absence of sensory description at this pivotal moment of transformative eating is surprising, given how it is surrounded with scent, vision, touch, and sound. Winkler observes another point of "silence" in the *Metamorphoses* that might shed light on what has occurred, since Lucius's transformation is not just physical, but also has an effect on his demeanor. As Winkler points out, after Lucius is transformed back into

---

79. Maggie Kilgour, *From Communion to Cannibalism: An Anatomy of Metaphors of Incorporation* (Princeton: Princeton University Press, 1990), esp. 239.

a human from the unspeaking ass, he continues to be silent, saying nothing.[80] Indeed, the narrator makes a point of reminding us that Lucius keeps his tongue:

> But I, fixed on the spot with a profound numbness, kept silence, my mind not comprehending so sudden and so great a joy. I hesitated, thinking what word would be best to begin with, what opening lines should I employ my new voice on, what would be the most happy and auspicious speech for my born-again tongue, what words—and just how many—should I use to give thanks to so great a goddess. (11.14)

This is a rather long passage describing Lucius's decision not to speak, suggesting that there is some significance in Lucius's continued silence even after he is returned to his human form. This allows the priest, Mithras, to speak with the prophetic force of the goddess herself, summarizing Lucius's misfortunes and reiterating the goddess' promise (11.15–16). For Winkler, the fact that the priest speaks and that the crowd directly following misinterprets Lucius's divine favor for virtuous living (11.16) highlights that, while other parties understand (or think they understand) the implications of books 1–10 and everything leading up to his transformation, Lucius as character and as narrator does not; he continues to play the dupe throughout his subsequent initiations.[81] This is an inversion of the bestowal of divine truth we have seen in other examples of hierophagy. In most of the other cases, the eater is granted privileged knowledge that is only accessible because of the ingestion. Here, we are surprised by Lucius's seeming lack of awareness. The ambivalence of the text speaks to its comic tone and, following from Winkler, further subverts the seriousness of the religious devotion by pointing to the ignorance of the initiand. While Winkler points to the ambivalent signifier of the bald head as support for this double reading,[82] I would suggest that subverting the hierophagic genre in regard to specialized knowledge also contributes to the author's subversive tale.

But further, it is possible that the absence of taste language in the hierophagic moment might also have surprised readers. After all, the text actually does describe flavors in other descriptions of food. For example,

---

80. Winkler, *Auctor and Actor*, 209.
81. Winkler, *Auctor and Actor*, 214–15, 218.
82. Winkler, *Auctor and Actor*, 225–27.

after Lucius's transformation occurs and he begins the process of initiation into the Isis cult, a priest instructs him to observe a set time of fasting (11.23); secret rituals are pointedly not described. Lucius celebrates with a feast and then a sacred breakfast three days later (11.24) marking the conclusion of the initiation. None of the food is described here, although the banquet is described as "delicious" (*suavis*; pleasing to the senses). In instructing Lucius to fast, the priest tells him "to restrain [his] pleasure [*voluptas*] in food for the next ten days, not to partake of animal food [*neque ullum animal essem*], and to go without wine" (11.23). These descriptive elements can be read two complementary ways. First, they serve to highlight the distinction I attempt to make here between ordinary ritual eating and hierophagy. The food marks different stages in the process of initiation but does not effect, in itself, any changes in status; those rituals are not described. Second, because the food is variously described as delicious and pleasurable, the lack of a description of the taste of the roses in 11.13 is marked as all the more surprising, bearing in mind, as I highlight above, just how vivid other sensory elements surrounding the event are. It is possible, then, that Apuleius intentionally avoids taste descriptors as a way of inverting expectations around the implications of taste in special categories of eating, both ritual and hierophagic. This playfulness through silence is supported by (and supports) Winkler's observations about the verbal silence of the ego-narrator at exactly this point.

Conclusion

The use of roses in Apuleius's *Metamorphoses* to effect transformation participates in the genre of hierophagy in several apparent ways. While the text also subverts the genre, similarly to how it subverts other elements of its narrative and plot, it does so in ways that are recognizable because defining and identifying hierophagic elements makes the subversion recognizable. As part of this subversion, the sensory language that is frequently a core element of other instances of this kind of transformational eating is markedly absent in *Metamorphoses*; this absence allows us to see how ingestion, and not just taste, functions to bring about these physical and ontological changes. Making divinely-given items internal to the eater is a powerful way of bringing about transformation just as taste is another way of dissolving the foreign into the familiar. Lucius's transformation changes him physically from animal to human because he internalizes the promises of Isis in the form of the roses; the unavailability of roses throughout the early portion of the text confirms that the protection and patronage of Isis was always necessary for Lucius to be fully restored. The second and third components of hierophagy, aside from physical transformation, are less straightforward in this text. Lucius is eventually associated firmly with the realm of the goddess, although in a very different way than we have seen in, for example, Joseph and Aseneth or 4 Ezra. While in those cases characters who were transformed became subsumed into the heavenly realm, in the case of Lucius his life is promised to Isis. This is presented as a choice in the text, but his transformation would not have taken place without Lucius agreeing to it. The third component, that of gaining privileged knowledge, is likewise slightly slippery in this text. As discussed above, this aspect of hierophagy is inverted so that the ambiguity of religious truth is highlighted. However, together these core elements of hierophagy indicate Apuleius's awareness of the implications of eating divinely-given food, well enough to play with them.

Examining the text using the lens of hierophagy has also confirmed the instability of conversion as a way of understanding Lucius's experience. In doing so, this chapter also suggests that conversion does not work well as a lens to read other texts using the genre of hierophagy from the same time period. In particular, I would suggest that if it is inappropriate to use conversion to understand Lucius's experiences here, it is likewise inappropriate to use it regarding Joseph and Aseneth, especially given the marked parallels drawn out in this chapter between the two texts' use of prayer and invocation prior to transformation.

6
The Passion of Perpetua and Felicitas

This final chapter will examine whether Perpetua's cheese ingestion in the Passion of Perpetua and Felicitas gains clarity when viewed in light of the hierophagic pattern I have set out above. As the previous chapters have illustrated, hierophagy is a mechanism by which characters in narrative cross boundaries from one realm to another. The basic event of hierophagy involves the eating of something otherworldly, which associates the eater with another world in one or more of three ways. First, hierophagy might bind the eater to the realm in which the food originated, for instance, heaven or, in the case of Persephone, Hades. Second, the eater might be physically or psychologically transformed by the food—they might gain new abilities like John of Patmos or Ezra or have a new appearance like Aseneth. Third, hierophagic ingestion can grant divine knowledge, for example, Ezra or John of Patmos. Perpetua's ingestion of the cheese given to her by a heavenly figure facilitates her transformation in two of these ways, namely, she becomes associated with the heavenly realm and loses her connection to the earthly realm, and she receives divine knowledge that she is then able to share with her companions.

Introduction to the Text

It is generally accepted that the diary portion of the Passion of Perpetua and Felicitas dates to 203 CE, potentially making it the latest of the texts under examination here. Likewise, although the text itself is not clear about a precise geographical location for its events, the description of the large amphitheater attached to a soldiers' barracks has convinced most scholars that Carthage in North Africa is the most likely provenance.[1] The

---

1. See Jan N. Bremmer and Marco Formisano, introduction to *Perpetua's Passions:*

original language of composition of both the diary and the editorial portions is almost certainly Latin, although some scholars support a Greek original.[2] The authorship of the text has been contested. The text purports to be the diary of Perpetua herself, with an editor's introduction and conclusion depicting the actual martyrdom, about which it would have been impossible for the martyr herself to write. Augustine is suspicious of the authorship of the account (*An. orig.* 1.10.12), as are more recent scholars, citing rhetorical, generic, and philological problems with the composition of the text.[3] Although it has been suggested that Tertullian is the editor, responsible for writing the introduction, conclusion, and certain other sections (Pass. Perp. 14, 15, 16–21), this is very unlikely given his distaste for women and their bodies; however, the editor appears to share many of Tertullian's views, and it is therefore possible that he or she was closely connected to Tertullian.[4] It is now generally accepted that the diary portions of the text were indeed authored by Perpetua.[5] As Jan N. Bremmer and Marco Formisano point out, prison letters from Christians are known from antiquity, including those of Paul and Ignatius; this in itself, then, is not enough to discount Perpetua's authorship, but it is crucial to keep in mind that whatever words Perpetua herself wrote, they were heavily edited after her death.[6]

Multidisciplinary Approaches to the Passio Perpetuae et Felicitatis, ed. Jan N. Bremmer and Marco Formisano (Oxford: Oxford University Press, 2012), 2–7.

2. For arguments that the original language was Latin, see Bremmer and Formisano, introduction, 3; Jacqueline Amat, *Passion de Perpétue et de Félicité suivi des Actes*, SC 417 (Paris: Editions du Cerf, 1996), 51–66; Reinhart Herzog and Peter L. Schmidt, eds., *Handbuch der Lateinischen Literatur der Antike*, vol. 4 (Munich: Beck, 1997), 425. For scholars arguing a Greek original, see, e.g., L. Robert, "Une Vision de Perpétue Martyre à Carthage en 203," *CRAI* (1982): 256; Robin Lane Fox, *Pagans and Christians* (London: Harmondsworth, 1986), 401; Glen Warren Bowersock, *Martyrdom and Rome* (Cambridge: Cambridge University Press, 1995), 34.

3. Augustine: "Concerning Dinocrates, however, the brother of St. Perpetua, there is no record in the canonical Scripture; nor does the saint herself, or whoever it was that wrote the account, say that the boy, who had died at the age of seven years, died without baptism." See, more recently, Thomas J. Heffernan, "Philology and Authorship in *The Passio Sanctarum Perpetuae et Felicitatis*," *Traditio* 50 (1995): 315–25.

4. Bremmer and Formisano, introduction, 5. See also René Braun, *Approches de Tertullien* (Paris: Institute des Études Augustiniennes, 1992), 287–99.

5. Bremmer and Formisano, introduction, 5.

6. Bremmer and Formisano, introduction, 5–6; Bremmer, "The Vision of Saturus in the *Passio Perpetuae*," in *Jerusalem, Alexandria, Rome: Studies in Ancient Cultural*

Although some hierophagic texts under discussion in this book, such as Revelation, Ezekiel, and 4 Ezra, can properly be called apocalypses, the Passion of Perpetua and Felicitas is not categorized as belonging to that genre. The text is distinct from an apocalypse, given that it is primarily a record of Perpetua's imprisonment and eventual martyrdom. However, certain aspects of the Passion of Perpetua and Felicitas do overlap with similar features in apocalyptic texts. The divine visions and the otherworldly journey are both hallmarks of the genre of apocalypse.[7] In comparing the Passion of Perpetua and Felicitas with the definition offered by John J. Collins, which is generally accepted,[8] the present text lacks an otherworldly mediator and the salvation envisaged is not eschatological but imminent, the result of an impending martyrdom that is not universal, but individual.

Scene within the Narrative

The Passion of Perpetua and Felicitas is a martyrdom text that describes the experiences not only of Perpetua but also her "brothers" and "sisters." The text records the martyrdom of several Christians on about 7 March 203 CE in the amphitheater of Carthage. The date, 7 March, is connected in the text with Emperor Septimus Severus's son's birthday, Geta Caeasar (9.7)—this date is confirmed as Geta's birthday, making the dating of the text remarkably certain.[9] The composite text includes a first-hand account from the perspective of the formerly respectable Roman matron Perpetua. Perpetua's prison diary records the hardships faced by her fellow male and female Christians, including the pregnant slave Felicitas,[10] and also several visions experienced by Perpetua while in prison.

Interaction in Honour of A. Hilhorst, ed. Florentino García Martínez and Gerard P. Luttikhuizen, JSJSup 82 (Leiden: Brill, 2003), 55–73; Fox, *Pagans and Christians*, 468–70; Bremmer, "Perpetua and Her Diary: Authenticity, Family and Visions," in *Märtyrer und Märtyrerakten*, ed. Walter Ameling, Altertumswissenschaftliches Kolloquium 6 (Wiesbaden: Franz Steiner Verlag, 2002), 84.

    7. J. J. Collins, *The Apocalyptic Imagination: An Introduction to Jewish Apocalyptic Literature* (Grand Rapids: Eerdmans, 1998), 5.

    8. See chapter 2, n. 3.

    9. Bremmer and Formisano, introduction, 2; Timothy David Barnes, *Early Christian Hagiography and Roman History* (Tübingen: Mohr Siebeck, 2010), 68.

    10. Notably, Felicitas is only mentioned in the sections written by the editor and not in the diary portions written by Perpetua, although she mentions other brothers and sisters imprisoned with her. This could indicate that Felicitas is more a liter-

Unlike the revelations experienced by Ezra in 4 Ezra, Perpetua's visions do not progress in intensity or in intimacy with the divine; the visions do not bring Perpetua ever closer to God except in that they bring her further along the path to "victory" (i.e., death).[11] However, what seems to unite the visions is their common theme: Perpetua experiences physical changes or sensations in her visions that have ramifications in her waking life; her physical transformation in the vision of the Egyptian signals her victory just as the ingestion of the cheese somehow signals her martyrdom.[12] Thus, Perpetua's vision of eating cheese, the vision under discussion here, should be understood as primarily indicating some change, both cosmic and earthly.

The vision begins with a request: Perpetua is encouraged to ask for a vision to know whether she will be martyred. With confidence, Perpetua requests the vision and is given one. In it, Perpetua climbs a ladder up to heaven, where she is greeted by the inhabitants and fed cheese:

> Then I saw an immense garden, and in it a grey-haired man sat in shepherd's garb; tall he was, and milking sheep. And standing around him were many thousands of people clad in white garments. He raised his head, looked at me, and said: "I am glad you have come, my child." He called me over to him and gave me, as it were, a mouthful of the milk [*caseo*] he was drawing; and I took it into my cupped hands and consumed it. And all those who stood around said: "Amen!" At the sound of this word I came to, with the taste of something sweet still in my mouth. I at once told this to my brother, and we realized that we would have to

---

ary creation than historical person. Judith Perkins also infers this possibility in "The Rhetoric of the Maternal Body in the *Passion of Perpetua*," in *Mapping Gender in Ancient Religious Discourses*, ed. Todd Penner and Caroline Vander Stichele, BibInt 84 (Leiden: Brill, 2007), 330.

11. Instead, the visions progress Perpetua toward a shedding of her womanhood; Elizabeth Castelli, "'I Will Make Mary Male': Pieties of the Body and Gender Transformation of Christian Women in Late Antiquity," in *Body Guards: The Cultural Politics of Gender Ambiguity*, ed. Julia Epstein and Kristina Straub (Routledge: London, 1991), 35.

12. For instance, in chapter 10 Perpetua has a waking vision in which she is summoned to the arena to face a fearsome Egyptian opponent (10.6–8). When Perpetua is stripped of her clothes, she becomes a man, and her assistants rub her with oil, as for athletic competition (10.7). Castelli observes that both the vision of the cheese and the vision of the Egyptian result in Perpetua shedding some aspects of her womanhood (Castelli, "I Will Make Mary Male," 34).

suffer, and that from now on we would no longer have any hope in this life. (Pass. Perp. 4.8–4.10)[13]

Dreams and Visions in Antiquity

Perpetua's hierophagic event takes place in a vision. According to the text, Perpetua's brother suggests that she ask God for a vision that will clarify whether she will be killed or released (4.1–2). Perpetua is confident that her request for divine knowledge will be granted. Visions sent by the divine were accepted as common (literary) occurrences. That divine knowledge is transmitted through dreams and visions was part of the cultural understanding of the relationship between the divine and human worlds.[14] Tertullian notes that this is common: "just about the majority of people get their knowledge of God from dreams" (*An.* 47.2 [trans. Cox Miller]).[15] Perpetua's visions are therefore meant to be taken as true predictions of what is to come.[16] But likewise, prophecy and visions are associated with religious authority.[17] Perpetua is not unique in having visions or dreams about her impending martyrdom. Polycarp and Cyprian both received information about their deaths in dreams.[18] Ancient dream analysis often assumes a body-soul division in which the soul can separate itself from the body while asleep and encounter both the souls of those

---

13. Translations by Joseph Farrell and Craig Williams, "The Passion of Saints Perpetua and Felicity," in *Perpetua's Passions: Multidisciplinary Approaches to the Passio Perpetuae et Felicitatis*, ed. Jan N. Bremmer and Marco Formisano (Oxford: Oxford University Press, 2012), 14–23.

14. Patricia Cox Miller, "A Dubious Twilight: Reflections on Dreams in Patristic Literature," *Church History* 55 (1986): 157.

15. Quoted in J. H. Waszink, ed., *Quinti Septimi Florentis Tertuliani: De Anima* (Amsterdam: Meulenhoff, 1947), 65.

16. Katharina Waldner, "Visions, Prophecy, and Authority in the *Passio Perpetuae*," in Bremmer and Formisano, *Perpetua's Passions*, 210.

17. Laura Nasrallah, *An Ecstasy of Folly: Prophecy and Authority in Early Christianity* (Cambridge: Harvard University Press, 2003); Waldner, "Visions, Prophecy, and Authority in the *Passio Perpetuae*," 201–19.

18. Patricia Cox Miller, *Dreams in Late Antiquity: Studies in the Imagination of a Culture* (Princeton: Princeton University Press, 1994), 150; Martine Dulaey, *Le Rêve dans la vie et la pensée de Saint Augustin* (Paris: Études Augustiniennes, 1973), 22–44; Jacqueline Amat, *Songes et Visions: L'au-delà dans la littérature latine tardive* (Paris: Études Augustiniennes, 1985), 62–66.

already deceased as well as divine beings.[19] This is potentially important for the significance of Perpetua's experience in her vision, namely, the ramifications of hierophagy on Perpetua's place in the world. Perpetua's visions gain authority in this respect by her having a witness, her brother, to whom she explains the ramifications of the vision. However, Perpetua's vision gives her knowledge through a very special mechanism, which is the cheese she is given by the heavenly shepherd.

The symbols found in Perpetua's dreams have communicable meanings that made sense both to Perpetua (who correctly interpreted them) and to her readers, given the popularity of the text particularly in North Africa.[20] Several manuals for interpreting dreams, including the second-century CE oneirocriticon of Artemidorus, also suggest that there were commonly held understandings of what different elements of dreams meant for the waking life.

Perpetua's vision begins with Perpetua seeing a tall bronze ladder (4.3).[21] The ladder is so narrow that only one person at a time would have been able to climb it and so tall that it reaches the sky. It is embedded with various sharp weapons on the rails. The implements attached to the rails appear to be the kinds of weapons that might have been used in the arena to torture potential martyrs: swords, javelins, hooks, daggers, and lances (4.3). At the foot of the ladder is an enormous serpent to deter those who would ascend the ladder. In Perpetua's vision, she is with Saturus, who climbs up the ladder ahead of Perpetua and encourages her once he gets to the top (4.6). Perpetua defiantly uses the head of the serpent as the first rung and climbs the ladder (4.7). The image of the ladder situates the heavenly realm as physically above the mortal realm. Fritz Graf notes that this spatial representation of heaven as "above" is prevalent in antiquity—the idea that one might use a bridge, that the other realm is somehow on the same plane as this realm—does not occur until much later despite the very real structural popularity of actual bridges in the ancient world.[22] The spa-

---

19. Dulaey, *Le Rêve dans la vie et la pensée*, 23.

20. Jan N. Bremmer, *The Rise and Fall of the Afterlife: The 1995 Read-Tuckwell Lectures at the University of Bristol* (London: Routledge, 2002) 58.

21. Most readers and translators interpret *scala* as ladder rather than staircase since the *scala* is described as very narrow and very tall, although it technically includes both in its semantic range.

22. Fritz Graf, "The Bridge and the Ladder: Narrow Passages in Late Antique Visions," in *Heavenly Realms and Earthly Realities in Late Antique Religions*, ed.

tial structure of ancient cosmological realms is arranged on a vertical axis; ladders are therefore occasionally necessary, either for gods or angels to descend, as in Jacob's dream (Gen 28:10–22), or for those, like Perpetua and Saturus, who would ascend.[23] Graf also points out the agency involved in Perpetua's unique take on the ladder image; whereas Jacob is the passive recipient of the divine message in Genesis, Perpetua's vision requires her own effort.[24]

We know the destination is heaven for several reasons.[25] The image of the garden is frequently associated with the idea of heaven. The Greek παράδισος, itself a Persian loanword,[26] can mean both pleasure-garden and the abode of the blessed. Luke 23:43 appears to use the term in this way, for example, as does 2 Cor 12:4 and Rev 2:7.[27] The Latin *hortus* does not appear to have this same connotation that the Greek term has, but nonetheless garden imagery is pervasive in late antique visions of heaven, beginning with the New Testament. Although the provenance of 2 Enoch is far from certain,[28] the text does offer a detailed account of the third heaven and/or paradise, an association also made by 2 Cor 12:4. Second Enoch describes a pleasant garden with flowering trees and ripe fruits and describes the sweet smells of flowers and food. It is a plentiful pleasure-garden where work is unnecessary—angels are the guardians or caretakers (2 En. 8.1–12). Likewise, when Revelation clarifies in 22:1–5

Ra'anan Boustan and Annette Yoshiko Reed (Cambridge: Cambridge University Press, 2004), 19–20.

23. Graf notes that it is extremely rare for human beings to ascend to the heavenly realm and that no other martyr texts use the image; the ladder image, beginning with the interpretation in the Passion of Perpetua and Felicitas, became a symbol for the effort required for ascetic living in later antiquity, with rungs becoming identified with each progressive step in lifestyle ("Bridge and the Ladder," 20, 30, 32).

24. Graf, "Bridge and the Ladder," 32.

25. Bremmer, *Rise and Fall of the Afterlife*, 57–58.

26. LS, sv. "παράδισος."

27. See Grant McGaskil, "Paradise in the New Testament," in *Paradise in Antiquity: Jewish and Christian Views*, ed. Markus Bockmuehl and Guy G. Stroumsa (Cambridge: Cambridge University Press, 2010), 64–81; and Martin Goodman, "Paradise, Gardens, and the Afterlife in the First Century CE," in Bockmuehl and Stroumsa, *Paradise in Antiquity*, 57–63.

28. F. I. Anderson writes, "There must be something very peculiar about a work when one scholar, Charles, concludes that it was written by a hellenized Jew in Alexandria in the first century B.C., while another, J. T. Milik, argues that it was written by a Christian monk in Byzantium in the ninth century A.D." ("2 Enoch," *OTP* 1:95).

what it apparently means by the paradise referenced in 2:7, we are shown a city with flowing rivers and the tree of life, providing twelve kinds of fruit throughout the year. Gardens as an image for heaven tend to evoke the restoration or return of Eden, with the tree of life and flowing rivers being prominent images. Thus, although the Passion of Perpetua and Felicitas does not describe the garden she sees in detail (there are no further descriptive elements other than that it is a "wide open space" [4.8]), the fact that (1) it is spatially elevated and requires access by ladder and (2) it is viewed as a garden are enough to suggest that *hortus* here also implies heavenly paradise.[29]

Confirming this suspicion are those present in the garden when Perpetua arrives. The crowd of people whom Perpetua sees in the heavenly garden are dressed in white, just like the angels Saturus sees in his later vision in chapter 11. White clothing can symbolize purity, but it also signifies holiness. In Dan 7:9, Matt 17:2, John 20:12, Acts 1:10, and 1 En. 14.20, for example, heavenly beings wear white, and the blessed in Rev 7:9 are also wearing white.[30] First Enoch 62.15–16 also depicts those who have been raised as wearing bright clothing.[31] The central figure that Perpetua sees is a tall man with grey hair who is dressed like a shepherd; this is presumably God.[32] He welcomes her to paradise and feeds her some of

---

29. Later, in 11.5–7a, Saturus's vision also depicts a garden with angels: "And while we were being carried by the same four angels, a great space opened up before us that was just like a park [*viridiarium*] with rose trees and all kinds of flowers. The trees were as tall as cypresses, and their leaves kept falling and falling. And there in the park were four more angels brighter than all the others."

30. In the Greco-Roman world, white was considered the color most appropriate to the gods, and so people taking part in religious rites often wore white, e.g., Plato, *Leg.* 956a; Aelius Aristides, *Or* 48.30; Plutarch, *Amat. narr.* 1 (771d); and P.Oxy 471.101.

31. On white garments as signifiers of blessedness, see Gabriel Sanders, *Licht en duisternis in de Christelijke grafschriften*, 2 vols (Brussels: Paleis der Academiën, 1965), 2.674–78.

32. Rev 1:14 describes "one like a human being," that is, God, as having white hair; likewise see also Dan 7:9; 1 En. 46.1, 71.10. Angels have white hair in 1 En. 106.2–6 and in Apoc. Ab. 11:2. Tertullian also uses the image of a shepherd to describe God (*Pud.* 10.12). The image of the good shepherd is pervasive in antiquity, including early Christianity. See Jennifer Awes Freeman, "The Good Shepherd and the Enthroned Ruler: A Reconsideration of Imperial Iconography in the Early Church," in *The Art of Empire: Christian Art in Its Imperial Context*, ed. Lee M. Jefferson and Robin M. Jensen (Minneapolis: Fortress, 2015), 166–84. Miller observes that iconographic representa-

the cheese that he has produced from the sheep he is milking (Pass. Perp. 4.9). This is the central hierophagic event, the significance of which will be discussed shortly. In brief, she is fed by the hand of a heavenly being in a heavenly environment. These heavenly people watch her eat, but they do not themselves participate in her meal; they are not offered cheese from the shepherd figure. These people, or perhaps angels, are in a separate category from Perpetua; they already belong to the heavenly realm. This is clear not only because they are present and waiting for Perpetua when she arrives in the garden, but also because their white clothing directly associates them with the angels—and therefore with the heavenly realm.

Awaking from her vision, Perpetua retains a sweet taste in her mouth that reminds her of what she has uncovered. Tokens, items received in dreams, were expected in ancient prophetic dreams; Flannery-Dailey writes that these tokens "illustrat[e] the *shifting borderline between dream-world and waking-world.*"[33] In Greek dreams, it is fairly common for physical tokens to continue to "remain in the waking world."[34] There are two aspects to Perpetua's receipt of the token: the cheese on its own represents a token in that it is something given to her in the dream world; the taste is the persistent part of the token that remains with Perpetua upon waking. This taste, as token, confirms the reality of the dream world, the heavenly realm to which Perpetua now finds herself belonging

---

tions of Jesus as Good Shepherd in Perpetua's era usually depict him as a young man rather than the old shepherd described in the text, which would make it unlikely that the shepherd in the vision is Jesus (*Dreams in Late Antiquity*, 156–57). Nevertheless, Bremmer identifies the shepherd as Christ—the Son rather than the Father (*Rise and Fall of the Afterlife*, 62), as does Thomas J. Heffernen (*The Passion of Perpetua and Felicity* [New York: Oxford University Press, 2012], 169, 180–81).

33. Flannery, *Dreamers, Scribes, and Priests*, 63, emphasis original.

34. R. G. A. Van Lieshout, *Greeks on Dreams* (Utrecht: HES, 1980), 21–23; Flannery, *Dreamers, Scribes, and Priests*, 21; A. Leo Oppenheim, *The Interpretation of Dreams in the Ancient Near East* (Piscataway: Gorgias, 2008). E.g., Pindar, *Ol.* 13.61–80, where the golden bridle Athena gives Bellerophon is still there when he wakes up; Herodotus, *Hist.* 6.69 where Demaratus's mother's dream is confirmed with "real" garlands of flowers upon waking; Suetonius, *Aug.* 91 (Atia, future mother of Augustus, awakes with a mark on her body left from intercourse with a snake), *Galb.* 4 (Fortune leaves behind a bronze statue as proof of her visit); Vergel's *Aeneid* (8.27–68) also depicts the physical fulfillment of a promise made in a dream, here in the guise of a sow with piglets. Healing dreams in particular are likely to include tokens, e.g., inscription A13 from Lynn R. LiDonnici, *Epidaurian Miracle Inscriptions*, SBLTT 36 (Atlanta: Scholars Press, 1995).

spiritually, if not yet bodily.³⁵ Divine interaction in dreams, as established by the presence of this token, yields "extraordinary knowledge, healing, divine sanction, or their opposites."³⁶ In Perpetua's case, her ingestion of the token grants her special divine knowledge, but also allows her to relocate symbolically to the heavenly realm. This token, the cheese, is at the heart of Perpetua's vision. Its symbolism, associations, and significance thus require unpacking.

Heavenly Cheese?

As far as I am aware, there is no direct parallel in extant literature to heavenly cheese. Thus, in order to understand what this peculiar scene signifies, scholars have sought answers in texts that are not exactly parallel; this, indeed, is what I also attempt—the difference being that previous scholarship has largely turned to historical ritual examples as possible parallels whereas the present chapter attempts to situate Perpetua's experience with the shepherd within its narrative context.

To date, much of the discussion around the cheese Perpetua ingests is contextualized in the milk imagery prevalent in the Passion of Perpetua and Felicitas. As Judith Perkins has outlined, the maternal body, including its lactating breasts, is a pervasive theme in the martyrdom account.³⁷ Perpetua is breastfeeding when she enters the prison, while Felicitas gives birth just before she is martyred and is described as having dripping breasts when she is entering the arena (20.2). Perkins interprets the first vision to be an inversion of the maternal role Perpetua has performed thus far; whereas before she provided milk to her child, she is called a child and given cheese.³⁸ However, while there may indeed be a connection between the milking of the sheep and the recently postpartum woman's leaky breasts, several factors point to additional if not alternative understandings of Perpetua's cheese meal.

When Herbert Anthony Musurillo translated the Passion of Perpetua and Felicitas, he mistranslated *caseus* as "milk" rather than cheese, as it

---

35. Flannery notes the phenomenon of the "auditory message dream," which is a kind of auditory (rather than visual) token given to the dreamer in the dream world (*Dreamers, Scribes, and Priests*, 21).
36. Flannery, *Dreamers, Scribes, and Priests*, 106.
37. Perkins, "Rhetoric of the Maternal Body," 313–32.
38. Perkins, "Rhetoric of the Maternal Body," 327.

should have been.[39] His translation was likely influenced by his belief that the *caseus* was related to baptismal imagery, taking his cue from Tertullian's description of postbaptismal milk-drinking (*Cor.* 3.3). However, this is not what the text says, and as I will suggest below, baptismal imagery may not be the best lens through which to view this type of eating. This connection, however, persists in much of the scholarly discussion of this scene. Curdled milk offers a sort of midpoint, where the food is a mixture of liquid milk with solid curds in the same mouthful; this allows Jacqueline Amat, for example, to draw connections to milk's role in prebaptismal rituals and other, biblical, imagery.[40] The straightforward reading of this word, however, is cheese. Roman North African descriptions of cheese and dairy agriculture are scarce, but according to Cato there are two main types of cheese consumed by Romans: *caseus aridus* and *caseus molli* (*Agr.* 150). As we will see below, these two categories also feature in the *oneirocritica* of antiquity, making them applicable to a wide cultural range rather than specific to Cato's (sometimes eccentric) understanding of agriculture.[41] *Caseus aridus* is dry, aged cheese that is hard and travels well; this was prized in Rome and could make good money for a dairy farmer. Fresh cheese, *caseus molli*, was softer, but according to Columella, still pressed—more like feta, although ricotta-style cheeses were also enjoyed by aristocrats in the Roman period (*Agr.* 7.8).[42] This cheese was often made directly as the shepherd was milking the sheep, with a coagulating agent added to the milking bucket in advance: "Some people, before they put the shackles on the she-goats [to keep them still during milking], drop green pine-nuts into the pail and then milk the she-goats over them and

---

39. Herbert Anthony Musurillo, *Acts of the Christian Martyrs* (Oxford: Clarendon, 1979), 113 and n. 8; Miller, *Dreams in Late Antiquity*, 157. The Greek edition published by Harris reads: καὶ ἐκ τοῦ τυροῦ οὗ ἤλμευγεν ἔδωκέν μοι ὡσεὶ ψωμίον. J. Rendel Harris and Seth K. Gifford, *The Acts of the Martyrdom of Perpetua and Felicitas* (London: Clay & Sons, 1890).

40. Amat, *Songes et Visions*, 75–76; Miller, *Dreams in Late Antiquity*, 157.

41. Cato's *placenta* (a type of cheesecake) recipe calls for an unrealistic 6.4kg of cheese and 2kg of honey to produce a pastry 0.3m by 0.6m by 5cm (*Agr.* 76). Paul Kindstedt, *Cheese and Culture: A History of Cheese and Its Place in Western Civilization* (White River Junction, VT: Chelsea Green, 2012), 97; Joan M Frayn, *Sheep-Rearing and the Wool Trade in Italy during the Roman Period* (Liverpool: Cairns, 1984).

42. Kindstedt, *Cheese and Culture*, 99; John H. D'Arms, "The Culinary Reality of Roman Upper-Class Convivia: Integrating Texts and Images," *Comparative Studies in Society and History* 46 (2004): 436.

only remove them when they have transferred the curdled milk into the moulds" (*Agr.* 7.8.6 [Ash, Forster, and Heffner]). While we should not read too much into the accuracy of dreams regarding cheese production, the fact that this practice was common enough for Columella to describe it suggests that the "insta-cheese" eaten by Perpetua is more plausible than previously assumed.[43]

The *Oneirocritica* of Artemidorus associates cheese with treachery.[44] In Byzantine oneiromanca, however, receiving soft cheese in a dream signifies profit. For example, in the *Oneirocriticon* of Germanus, eating fresh cheese is auspicious, whereas eating dry cheese is inauspicious (T.228–229; see also Oneirocriticon of Daniel T.449).[45] Although it is possible that Perpetua's dream cheese reflects symbolism found in these later, Byzantine dream manuals, this would be impossible to establish, and indeed, there are other, more relevant contexts to consider.[46]

The pastoral setting of the milking and cheese-making in Perpetua's vision can also shed light on its meaning. Milk and cheese frequently seem to represent an idyllic, antedeluvian world in which animal sacrifice has not yet become a practice.[47] By juxtaposing the idyllic cheese of the garden with the violent weapons on the ladder, the Passion of Perpetua and Felicitas represents divine peace with lactation, motherhood, and

---

43. Heffernan argues that the chronology of the dream has collapsed the time between milking and cheese-making (*Passion of Perpetua and Felicity*, 182–83), but this is not necessary given the cheese production techniques I have outlined.

44. Oberhelman, *Dreambooks in Byzantium*, 111. The Oneirocriticon of Manuel II Palaeologu 33 (Oberhelman, *Dreambooks in Byzantium*, 212) says the opposite: cheese denotes anxiety except in the case of dry cheese, and the *Oneirocritica* of Artemidorus states that cakes "seasoned with cheese signify trickery and ambushes" (1.72) since the verb of making cheese, ὁ τυρὸς προαγορεύει, can also mean to trick someone. See Artemidorius Daldianus, Oneirocritica: *Text, Translation, and Commentary*, ed. and trans. Daniel E. Harris-McCoy (Oxford: Oxford University Press, 2012), 456; LSJ, s.v. "τυρεύω."

45. Oberhelman, *Dreambooks in Byzantium*, 164; The Anonymous Oneirocriticon 10.418 agrees with this.

46. I should note that neither Louis Ginzberg, *Legends of the Jews* (Philadelphia: Jewish Publication Society, 2003) nor Dov Neuman (Noy), *Motif-Index of Talmudic-Midrashic Literature* (PhD diss., Indiana University, 1954) offers relevant parallels in Jewish literature or tradition about cheese.

47. McGowan, *Ascetic Eucharists: Food and Drink in Early Christian Ritual Meals* (Oxford: Oxford University Press, 1999), 94–97.

milk and the empire with weapons, pain, and bloodshed.[48] This juxtaposition is most apparent in the arena, where, as Perkins points out, the graphic depiction of Perpetua and Felicitas as maternal bodies dripping with the signs of recent motherhood comes head to head with the brutal violence of the sword.

These symbolic meanings likely all feed into the construction of the imagery of the cheese and the garden: a pastoral setting is the opposite of the arena the martyrs are about to enter and thus offers a dualistic understanding of this world and the next, with violence at its fulcrum. The maternal imagery of milking likewise serves to connect Perpetua's maternal body with the nurturing care offered by the shepherd, juxtaposed as it is with her own milk supply drying up. However, the image would be more directly related to both of these contexts if Perpetua drank the milk rather than ate the cheese, and therefore I suggest that this meal does more than simply evoke nurturing, pastoral images of the heaven Perpetua is about to enter. However, before offering up my own understanding, it is also important to examine the sociohistorical contexts used by other scholars to interpret the cheese meal.

Alternative Contexts: Early Christian Meals

Eucharistic Meals with Cheese

There are attested groups in antiquity that used cheese as part of eucharistic practice. Andrew McGowan, in his *Ascetic Eucharists*, outlines several groups. One group, called the Artotyritai (the "bread-and-cheesers"), who appear much later than 203 CE when Perpetua was experiencing her vision, is mentioned by Epiphanius of Salamis (*Pan.* 49.1.1).[49] Filastrius of Brescia locates these Artotyritai in Galatia and notes that they "offer bread and cheese" (*panem et caseum offerunt, Div. haer.* 74).[50] McGowan posits

---

48. McGowan, *Ascetic Eucharists*, 102; Judith Perkins, "Rhetoric of the Maternal Body," 313–32.
49. McGowan, *Ascetic Eucharists*, 95.
50. In the past, a connection between the Passion of Perpetua and Felicitas and Montanism has been posited, not unconnected to the apparent association between the Montanists and Artotyritai in certain sources. But McGowan rightly warns that there is some significant geographical and chronological distance between the practices of the Artotyritai and whatever the cheese meal in Perpetua reflects (*Ascetic*

that the cheese in question, at least in the context of the Artotyritai, would likely have been a very soft, even spreadable cheese, closer to milk than, say, *pecorino Romano*.[51] This would make the divergence from a bread-and-cup eucharistic practice less radical, as cheese in this form might have been understood as "an appropriate form of ritual drink, rather than an additional solid food."[52]

Ephrem the Syrian preserves a Marcionite practice that confirms the use of milk as a eucharistic beverage.

> Instead of that bread, the presence-bread of the new covenant,
> they offered honey or milk.
> Since all these things are natural, however
> They could not found their error this way either.
> Honey is not brought as an offering
> nor is milk used for sprinkling and libation.
> The presence-bread was offered symbolically,
> and blood and wine purified as types.
> The crucifiers and the teachers of error
> Have been contradicted by the symbol of which Moses wrote. (*Contra haer.* 47.6)[53]

It is unclear what precisely Ephrem is critiquing—whether the ritual refers to the Artotyritai using milk in place of ordinary eucharistic foods, or whether it refers to the postbaptismal meal discussed below.[54] Regardless, this hymn supports the other evidence that suggests that eucharistic meals with cheese did occur in antiquity in Asia Minor. However, no extant source documents cheese eucharists taking place in North Africa, and so it is not clear the extent to which this context should inform our reading of the Passion of Perpetua and Felicitas.[55]

Eucharists, 102); several other writers confirm this information, including Augustine, *Haer.* 28; Praedestinatus, *Haer.* 1.28; Pseudo-Jerome, *Indiculus de Daeresibus* 20.

51. McGowan, *Ascetic Eucharists*, 98.
52. McGowan, *Ascetic Eucharists*, 98.
53. As translated in McGowan, *Ascetic Eucharists*, 98.
54. McGowan, *Ascetic Eucharists*, 99.
55. McGowan is rightly cautious about using the Passion of Perpetua and Felicitas as evidence for actual meal practices: "Thus the *Martyrdom of Perpetua and Felicitas* may not really a witness to the actual use of milk or cheese in ritual meals, nor is it likely to be directly connected with the case of the Artotyritai, but the oppositions presented in the account, between bloodshed, meat-eating, and sacrifice on the one hand,

Baptismal Meals

More likely than a eucharistic parallel, which seems to be largely confined to Asia Minor, is a baptismal meal, which is attested in North Africa.[56] Several scholars identify the cheese meal with baptism, which for Perpetua takes place before her vision in 3.4. This connection is despite the fact that Perpetua does not directly connect her meal with her baptism.[57] Baptismal meals of milk and honey are known from the third century, and Tertullian is an excellent witness to the kinds of meals Perpetua and her fellow martyrs might have been familiar with, since he writes from the perspective of a Carthaginian of the third century, just like Perpetua. Tertullian mentions a meal of milk and honey after baptism in his *Cor.* 3.3:

> When we are going to enter the water, but a little before, in the presence of the congregation and under the hand of the president, we solemnly profess that we disown the devil, and his pomp, and his angels. Hereupon we are thrice immersed, making a somewhat ampler pledge than the Lord has appointed in the Gospel. Then when we are taken up (as newborn children), we taste first of all a mixture of milk and honey [*lactis et mellis*], and from that day we refrain from the daily bath for a whole week. We take also, in congregations before daybreak, and from the hand of none but the presidents, the sacrament of the Eucharist, which the Lord both commanded to be eaten at meal-times, and enjoined to be taken by all alike. (trans. Schaff, *ANF* 3:95)

In this ritual, the catechumens renounce Satan, are immersed in the waters, and then receive a drink of milk and honey as their first food as Christians. The newly baptized Christians take this meal all together as a cohort. Note that this meal is distinct from the Eucharist, which Tertullian mentions separately. Tertullian also notes that the Marcionites observe this kind of practice in *Marc.* 1.14.3, observing that Marcion is not opposed to using a honey and

---

and idyllic peace and avoidance of meat on the other, are a valuable and enlightening source for comparison" (McGowan, *Ascetic Eucharists*, 103).

56. Heffernan, *Passion of Perpetua and Felicity*, 169.

57. E.g., Andrew McGowan, *Ancient Christian Worship: Early Church Practices in Social, Historical, and Theological Perspective* (Grand Rapids: Baker, 2014), 160–63; Katharina Waldner, for instance, gives the cheese meal as an example to strengthen her claim of the importance of baptism in the text ("Visions, Prophecy, and Authority in the *Passio Perpetuae*," 215 n. 69).

milk (again, *lactis et mellis*) mixture as "nourishment for children," which is presumed to be a reference to postbaptismal ritual meals. In both texts, Tertullian does not use the word *caseus* as Perpetua does; rather he refers to milk (*lactis*). In addition, Perpetua's actual baptism occurs earlier in 3.4 with little fanfare: "It was during this period of a few days that we were baptized [*baptizati*], and the Spirit told me to ask for only one thing from the water: bodily endurance." It is possible that the usual postritual milk-ingestion was curtailed in the prison context, but her request for a vision in 4.1–2 does not seems to come out of this baptismal context.

There is one other milk-vision that should be brought up in order to shed light on the Passion of Perpetua and Felicitas. This is found in the Martyrdom of Montanus and Lucius, a text that shares many similarities with the Passion of Perpetua and Felicitas, including a Carthaginian provenance.[58] In the vision reported in this text, a woman sees her son, followed by a young man carrying two cups of milk. Everyone drinks from the cups, which never empty (8.3–5). This text, which is later than the Passion of Perpetua and Felicitas, seems more likely to reflect its own contemporary liturgical practice, given the number of cups and drinkers; whereas Perpetua is the sole participant in her meal, in this example, multiple people share the milk drink.[59] Further, the vision of the milk cups in Martyrdom of Montanus and Lucius does not occur in the context of baptism whatsoever.

What remains to be seen is whether the cheese-eating in the Passion of Perpetua and Felicitas should be understood as referring to either of these actual ritual meals, baptismal or eucharistic. McGowan includes the scene in his discussion of eucharistic meals using cheese but admits that "it is hard to say how seriously we might take this as an indication of what an actual eucharistic meal might have involved in Perpetua's community."[60] Nevertheless, he insists that the event must have some connection with historical reality given the physical placement of Perpetua's cupped hands and the chorus of "Amen" after. He thus locates the meal as participating in a baptismal, transformative event, related to Perpetua's earlier baptism

---

58. No relation to the mid-second-century founder of Montanism. The very close similarities between this text and the Passion of Perpetua and Felicitas have led to suspicions that the text might be a forgery (McGowan, *Ascetic Eucharists*, 103 n. 45; Musurillo, *Acts of the Christian Martyrs*, xxxiv–xxxvi).

59. McGowan, *Ascetic Eucharists*, 104.

60. McGowan, *Ascetic Eucharists*, 100–101.

in the narrative, although he calls it "exceptional" rather than normative.[61] McGowan is correct that the event as described in the narrative should be viewed as transformative. The mechanism of that transformation, however, is hierophagy. The cheese is not simply an allusion to baptismal meals or eucharists; it is a literary genre common to other texts of the ancient Mediterranean whereby individuals who ingest otherworldly food are affected in fundamental ways.

Of the two ritual contexts, postbaptismal meals seem a more likely parallel to Perpetua's cheese vision than eucharistic cheese meals found in other provenances. However, there are two problems with understanding Perpetua's meal as a postbaptismal one of the sort that Tertullian describes. First, the connection between baptism and the vision's meal is not explicit in the text; second, Tertullian consistently refers to milk (*lactis*) rather than cheese (*caseus*) as the appropriate first food, and honey is nowhere to be found in Perpetua's vision. Thus, it is not at all clear that these historical Christian ritual meals are the path to understanding the significance of the cheese meal in Perpetua's vision.

The most important aspect, in my opinion, to take into account is that Perpetua herself does not seem to interpret her meal in light of either of these known Christian rituals. The meaning she takes from the vision in which she eats the cheese does not emerge from her baptismal experience, nor does she explicitly or implicitly connect the meal to any eucharistic practice, which does not appear in the text elsewhere, either. Perpetua's other visions correspond to—rather than stand in for—real-world events; for example, her vision of the Egyptian foreshadows her experience in the arena. Her cheese meal, therefore, should not be understood as merely standing in for what might have been ordinary postbaptismal meal practice in her community. Instead, its significance should be understood as coming from the vision's role in the text: this cheese meal is interpreted correctly by Perpetua, as she interprets her other revelatory experiences. In other words, even if the ingestion of cheese in chapter 4 emerges from a real-world situation in which newly baptized catechumens were fed milk and honey, and I am not convinced that it does, the fact remains that in the Passion of Perpetua and Felicitas the vision of the meal effects a different result than simply her induction into the Christian community, heavenly

---

61. McGowan, *Ascetic Eucharists*, 101.

or otherwise; it is because Perpetua awakes from her vision still tasting "something sweet" (4.10) that she recognizes her fate.[62]

Rather than an initiatory meal, Perpetua's meal is transformational and belongs to this distinct category of eating found in ancient literature that I call hierophagy. Rather than reading historical practices back into Perpetua's hierophagic experience, I suggest that viewing her meal event as hierophagy might explain a lot about the nature of Christian ideas about event boundaries and belonging. That Perpetua is relocated to heaven by eating this cheese has important ramifications for how we reconstruct the *actual* ritual eating performed by early Christians living in a society that understood the implications of hierophagic eating.

The Narrative Context of Perpetua's Cheese

Analysis of the scene at the level of the narrative in which it is situated perhaps sheds more light on the significance of the meal than attempts to compare it with potential ritual meals from historical reality. As we saw most explicitly in Revelation, Perpetua's hierophagic experience also involves sweet-tasting food. Perpetua returns from her vision with that sweet taste in her mouth. This sweet taste, as I suggested above, is evocative of the heavenly realm all by itself, even apart from the heavenly location of the eating. That Perpetua tastes the sweetness of the cheese she ate in her vision even when she wakes up confirms that the vision was true and that the food she ingested has special ramifications for her relationship with the heavenly realm.

There are two important aspects of ancient dream analysis that have an impact on how we understand Perpetua's meal. The first is the fact that she emerges from her vision with something still in her mouth—something sweet (4.10). The presence of the sweet taste in her mouth even while conscious establishes the dream as a true dream, divinely granted, as discussed above. Second, ancient analysts of dreams worked on the understanding that the soul and body were distinct entities, capable of separating from one another in certain circumstances, particularly in death and in dreams.

---

62. As discussed elsewhere in this book, this sweet taste likely refers to heavenly food tasting sweet. Bremmer suggests a parallel in Celsus, *Med.* 4.16.1.8: "*dulcia omnia inimical sunt, item lac et caseus*" / "All sweet things are hurtful, also milk and cheese" ("Perpetua and Her Diary," 104). But this interpretation is incongruous with how Perpetua understands her fate.

Perpetua's soul is affected by this vision in that it is relocated to the heavenly realm by ingesting the cheese—an aspect of hierophagy in certain contexts. When the soul returns to Perpetua's body, Perpetua is aware of the change and responds to her earthly contexts accordingly.

Perpetua's relationship to the earthly realm has been altered in two ways. First, Perpetua is given heavenly knowledge. Given the position of this event in the text, it seems clear that it is through this taste that Perpetua realizes that she will be martyred: as soon as she relays her vision to her brother, they "realize that … from now on [they] would no longer have any hope in this life." This was the knowledge that she sought to receive in asking for the vision—whether to expect martyrdom or freedom (4.1). The knowledge that she will be presently martyred comes from the cultural knowledge that eating food belonging to a world of a different category somehow associates the eater to that other world, a ramification we also saw in the event of Persephone's pomegranate. The ladder might be enough to demonstrate to Perpetua that she will undergo violent trials; the cheese alerts her that heaven has already welcomed her.

As such, the second implication that emerges from the cheese vision is that Perpetua has become irrevocably associated with the heavenly realm. It seems clear that both Perpetua and her brother in verse 10 are familiar with the implications of eating otherworldly food and understand the consequences. The food presented to and eaten by Perpetua (and Perpetua alone out of all those watching her eat—note that Saturus is not described as eating) symbolically relocates her from the earthly realm to the heavenly realm. As in our other examples, this type of eating shares a cultural understanding of the significance of consuming otherworldly food. Perpetua's symbolic translocation is observable through several shifts in the text. It is clear through these shifts that because of her mouthful of cheese, given to her by a heavenly being, she is no longer concerned with her earthly family,[63] nor with this world at all. When Perpetua meets her earthly father again in the next section, it is he who has tears in his eyes, not Perpetua, who has no emotional response:

> A few days later a rumour went around that our hearing was imminent. At this point Father came from the city. He was worn out with grief and

---

63. Maureen A. Tilley, "The Passion of Perpetua and Felicity," in *A Feminist Commentary*, vol. 2 of *Searching the Scriptures*, ed. Elisabeth Schussler Fiorenza (New York: Crossroad, 1994), 839.

came up to see me in order to lead me astray.... Then he kissed my hands and threw himself at my feet and wept. (5.1, 5)

Perpetua coolly notes that her father's words, while not persuasive, are designed to try and convince her against martyrdom and are spoken "like a dutiful father" (5.5). She feels empathy for her father, not because of her own impending experience in the arena, but because his words signify that he has no confidence in God's role in the transpiring events.[64] Nevertheless, her father goes away "heartbroken" (5.6) while Perpetua apparently only feels badly for her father's lack of faith and understanding. Later, after he unsuccessfully attempts to use her baby to arouse her motherly affections in order to persuade her to prevent her martyrdom, Perpetua describes him as "a pitiful old man" (6.5); she again feels sorrow that her father is beaten for disrupting the hearing, but Perpetua's concern is no longer for any earthly thing. This becomes physically apparent when Perpetua later attempts to breastfeed her child. After the hearing, she requests that her Father bring the baby to the prison so that Perpetua can feed it:

> After that, since the baby was used to being breast-fed and to living with me in the prison, I sent the deacon Pomponius to Father as soon as I could, asking for the baby. But Father refused. It was God's will, though: not only did the baby stop wanting my breasts but they did not become inflamed. And so I was not subjected to the torment of anxiety for my baby and sore breasts as well. (6.6–8)

This lack of anxiety for her earthly family is in stark contrast to her worries about her child in chapter 3, prior to her vision, which are alleviated only when the baby is allowed to stay with Perpetua in her jail cell. In her own words, Perpetua describes that earlier interaction as follows: "As for me, I nursed the baby, who by that point was starving to death. Anxious for him, I spoke to Mother and tried to comfort Brother, and I asked them to take care of my son. I was devastated to see how devastated they were on my account" (3.8). After her vision, her father takes the baby and immediately her milk dries up and she has no anxiety for her child. Her physical response to the knowledge her vision gave her further separates

---

64. Castelli notes that the father's gender becomes feminized during his interaction with a post-cheese-vision Perpetua ("I Will Make Mary Male," 38–39).

Perpetua from the earthly realm, as represented by her body and paternal relationships.⁶⁵ Her allegiance has shifted because of her vision; her concerns belong to the heavenly realm, not the earthly one. Thus, there are two significant implications of Perpetua's meal, implications that are comprehensible when viewed through the lens of hierophagy. Perpetua is relocated—symbolically at first, but eventually materially—into the heavenly realm through her eating. She knows this because of her vision from God, which she correctly interprets as foretelling this relocation. Immediate physical changes also come about: she stops lactating and no longer cares for her child. This change in knowledge—that she is to be martyred—in location—that she will therefore leave her earthly existence—and in behavior—her lack of anxiety for her earthly family—is because Perpetua understands the implications of her hierophagic meal: that she now belongs to the heaven she experienced in her vision.

Perpetua's case illustrates some fundamental ramifications of hierophagy. Other scholars have observed that Perpetua is changed by her vision but have not identified the precise mechanism by which that change takes place. Maureen Tilley, for instance, notes that Perpetua "was immediately and radically transformed by this first vision."⁶⁶ Tilley, however, does not say how this transformation occurs. As I have shown here, though, it is hierophagy that serves as the mechanism for this change. It is only through the experience of tasting the cheese in the garden that Perpetua gains the foreknowledge of her martyrdom, a knowledge that takes for granted that eating food from another world binds the eater to that world, as we also saw with Persephone. The text and its characters accept this aspect of hierophagy as understood, implying that the mechanisms of this transformation needed no explanation for readers. Viewing Perpetua's vision of heaven in light of hierophagy therefore illuminates several aspects of the narrative: it is now clear that, aside from the pastoral associations governed by cheese, the taste of the cheese as sweet signals its association with the heavenly realm, and that, by eating it, Perpetua has accepted her place in that realm: in other words, hierophagy facilitates the relocation of the eater. Further, Perpetua is aware of her fate in that she recognizes that her path forward is to martyrdom: hierophagy transmits heavenly knowledge. These two aspects of hierophagy are present in the Passion of Perpetua and

---

65. Castelli, "I Will Make Mary Male," 39.
66. Tilley, "Passion of Perpetua and Felicity," 838.

Felicitas and become visible only when analyzed in the context of other such events of transformational eating.

Conclusion

When Alice takes her tumble down the rabbit hole on her way to Wonderland, she lands in a liminal hallway with doors she cannot open or fit through. She is trapped in a transitional zone between the real world and the world of Wonderland, represented by a lush garden. "'Oh,' said Alice, 'how I wish I could shut up like a telescope! I think I could, if I only knew how to begin.'"[1] When she turns around, she sees a small bottle labeled "DRINK ME" and then later a small cake with the words "EAT ME" spelled out in currants.[2] Alice eats and drinks as instructed and finds she now knows how to "shut up like a telescope." Alice's entry into Wonderland is facilitated, in the end, by her ingestion of the food and drink that appear in the liminal room, and quite possibly by their curious tastes.[3] I use this example when I try to explain to nonspecialists what it is this book discusses; for people without familiarity with the ancient texts analyzed here, Alice is but one example that easily points toward the ramifications of consuming otherworldly food. Alice gains the know-how of changing her physical appearance in some way by shrinking or growing; and she gains access to Wonderland in a way that she could not before she ingested the items provided by the liminal room.[4] It is an example,

---

1. Lewis Carroll, *Alice's Adventures in Wonderland* (New York: Gabriel Sons, 1916), 6.

2. Carroll, *Alice's Adventures in Wonderland*, 7–8.

3. The DRINK ME bottle "had a sort of mixed flavor of cherry-tart, custard, pineapple, roast turkey, toffee, and hot buttered toast" (Carroll, *Alice's Adventures in Wonderland*, 7). The original book combines a number of different shape-changing mechanisms that help Alice enter the other world, but Disney's 1951 film *Alice in Wonderland* eliminates competing mechanisms such as the White Rabbit's fan (Carroll, *Alice's Adventures in Wonderland*, 10–11) and retains only the hierophagic elements of Alice's access to Wonderland.

4. Other contemporary examples include, as noted in the introduction, *The Matrix* (1999) and *Spirited Away* (2001), but hierophagy might also be at play when

therefore, that also helps to refocus on the core elements of hierophagy that this book has defined.

Hierophagy Defined

In each of the texts examined in the chapters of this book, the characters are affected by their ingestion of certain edible products provided by a divine hand or emerging from an otherworldly location. Revisiting the definition I set out in the introduction, and invoked throughout the previous chapters, hierophagy is a mechanism by which characters in narrative cross boundaries from one realm to another through ingesting some item from that other realm. Hierophagy results in three specific types of transformations: (1) the binding of the eater to the place of origin of the food; (2) the transformation of the eater either in terms of behavior or physical appearance; and (3) the transmission of new knowledge. The chart below outlines clearly which texts display which characteristics.

Character	1	2	3
Aseneth (Joseph and Aseneth)	B 18.5–7/Ph 18.3–6	B 18.5–7/Ph 18.3–6	B/Ph 17.1
Ezra (4 Ezra)	14.50	14.40–42	14.40–42
John of Patmos (Revelation)		10:11	10:10–11
Lucius (Apuleius, *Metamorphoses*)	11.15	11.13	X[5]
Perpetua (Passion of Perpetua and Felicitas)	4.10	6.7–8	4.10
Persephone/Proserpina (*Homeric Hymn to Demeter* // Ovid, *Metamorphoses*)	390–400 // 5.564–567	390–400 // 5.564–567	

Indeed, hierophagy is a genre embedded in fiction used to advance the story. In this way, it is a social action[6] within an imagined scenario that

---

Edmund Pevensie accepts the Turkish delight from the White Witch in C. S. Lewis's *The Lion, The Witch, and the Wardrobe*.

    5. The inversion of this genre is discussed in chapter 5.

    6. Miller, "Genre as Social Action," 151–67; Auken, "Genre as Fictional Action," 19–28.

participates in patterns of action. In the case of hierophagy, the patterns laid out in the chart above suggest that there are three elements of the genre that are commonly found. As a social action, the genre transforms the relationship the character has with the world around them, including with the divine realm. As with any genre, variation is to be expected.[7] As the chart demonstrates, this is likewise the case with hierophagy.

Shared Worldview

As I stated in the introduction, I made a conscious decision to put texts from a variety of religious contexts in conversation with each other. I did so in order to demonstrate that artificial and anachronistic boundaries erected by centuries of scholarship can and do hinder our understanding of ancient texts. Hierophagy appears in Ovid and in Apuleius, but also in apocalyptic Jewish texts like 4 Ezra. It equally appears in the Christian martyrdom account of the Passion of Perpetua and Felicitas. In each of the texts I explored, I pointed out how scholars have often struggled to make sense of these peculiar scenes of eating because they tended to look for parallel examples only within the same religious category. I hope I have shown that as a genre, hierophagy transcends religious boundaries.

Genre and worldview are inseparable, since genre relies on the shared expectations between author and audience. Meaning-making in literature takes place because of the (many times effortless) assumptions that those on either side of the text make about how their common world works.[8] This does not mean that all actions take place according to these norms—rather, literature relies on bending, challenging, inverting, and parodying these norms in order to make meaning out of genre. Hierophagy relies on several cultural assumptions about the relationship between this world and other worlds, the inhabitants of those worlds, and how food and taste can allow select people to permeate established cosmic boundaries. Portions of these expectations can also be seen in other texts—such as the archangel Michael's anxiety about eating human food in Testament of Abraham or philosophical discussions about social bonding through

---

7. Alastair Fowler, *Kinds of Literature: An Introduction to the Theory of Genres and Modes* (Cambridge, MA: Harvard University Press, 1982), 22; Jacques Derrida, "The Law of Genre," in *Modern Genre Theory*, ed. David Duff (Harlow, UK: Longman, 2000), 230; Auken, "Genre and Interpretation," 165.

8. Auken, "Genre and Interpretation," 163.

shared food—but converge in hierophagy in a way that conveys meaning. These expectations are present across scholarly categories of analysis, occurring in Jewish, Christian, and other literature.

Because hierophagy happens across these imposed scholarly categories, it is important to remember the constructedness of these categories so as not to silo Christian texts from Jewish ones and Jewish and Christian ones from the broader ancient Mediterranean corpus that often falls into the discipline of classics rather than biblical studies. As scholars of antiquity, we need constantly to remind ourselves and our conversation partners of the fluidity of cultural exchange and to actively reflect it in our work.

Sensory Lens

This study has also demonstrated how important the nonvisual senses are to the analysis of ancient literature. Taste plays an explicit role in all but one of the texts examined here: Persephone's stories, Joseph and Asenath, Revelation, 4 Ezra, and the Passion of Perpetua and Felicitas, but not in Apuleius. In many cases, the sweet taste confirms the divine origins of the food. This is true with Perpetua's cheese, which leaves a sweet taste in her mouth after she wakes up, and with Aseneth's sweet heavenly honey. Revelation's use of honey is more complicated, since it turns bitter; this combined sensory experience points not only to the divine origins of the scroll but also to the efficacy and authority of the message John delivers due to its bitter taste. Persephone's honey-sweet pomegranate seeds mark them as special; they are not ordinary, acidic pomegranate seeds but possess transformative powers. This sweetness functions symbolically within a cultural framework; it makes use of expectations around what the divine tastes like to communicate meaning within each of these texts. As Korsmeyer articulates, our interpretation of ingestible objects relies on categories that each society creates. In the period and geography under discussion in this book, this sweet taste signals to the eater—and therefore to the reader—what might be about to happen. In 4 Ezra, where sweetness is not explicitly present, the progression of sensory experience makes clear that tasting yields a more intimate access to the divine realm than hearing and seeing.

Even if some texts are more explicit than others about describing the taste of the ingested item, the way in which taste transforms the foreign to something internal to the body should inform how we understand this kind of symbolic ingestion. Mouths are a gateway into the body; into them we insert items of food or communicate in the most intimate way. They mark a boundary point between what is inside and what is outside, what is part of us and what is external. The boundary point is breached in the ingestion and digestion of food, a process which makes internal that which had been external.[9] This binary of external and internal, which the mouth and its enzymes literally breaks down, is a mirror of the binary constructed between the earthly and heavenly realms. (Or rather, it is the mirror that allows hierophagy to be visible.) The heavenly realm, which many of the characters I discuss permeate through their hierophagy, is normally closed off to mortals, just as angelic beings must exercise caution in how they engage with the human world, that is, by avoiding human food. The intersection of these two sets of boundaries is at the hierophagic mouth: ingesting or tasting food from the other realm breaks down the dividing line between this realm and another realm as the food itself is broken down and made internal to the body.

Gender

Something that I have not mentioned yet is the question of gender. Observant readers might have noticed that women and men are equally represented in the hierophagic texts analyzed here. This is not intentional; these are the extant texts, as far as I know, that preserve this genre. Persephone, Aseneth, and Perpetua are women, and John, Ezra, and Lucius are men. In the case of Persephone, I suggested that the sexualized interpretation of the pomegranate is rendered less prominent when viewed in the context of hierophagy more generally. Other specific ramifications may well emerge from hierophagic analysis with gender explicitly in mind for other texts; since there is no part of social action that is untouched by constructions of gender, it seems necessary to comment more generally on this even split. What this split indicates is that access to other realms is not gender-restricted to only men; women also, under the same correct circumstances, can break down those cosmic boundaries.[10]

---

9. See Kilgour, *From Communion to Cannibalism*, 239.

10. Each of these texts has had gender analysis of its own; the issues are therefore far more complicated at the individual level. From a birds-eye view of hierophagic texts, however, it is remarkable and significant that women are represented so prominently. For discussion of gendered access to divine realm in the early Jesus movement,

Moving Forward

I began this conclusion with a reference to Alice and her adventures not to be quaint but to point towards the potential application of hierophagy to other texts and other fields. This book intentionally limited itself in chronology and scope; I only examined texts from the Hellenistic and Roman periods and from the area around the Mediterranean. As a genre, hierophagy might lend itself well to an analysis of how food can be transformative in a wider range of texts than this study identified. This is not to say that I propose hierophagy as some sort of universal pattern, or a monomyth, a construction of the previous century by mythologists such as Mircea Eliade and Joseph Campbell.[11] That is, I do not understand the genre of hierophagy as a preexistent myth acting upon human experience; rather I view it as the expression in literature of a human experience—ingesting and tasting foreign material—which then comes to have an effect on how the ancient authors of the Passion of Perpetua and Felicitas, Joseph and Aseneth, 4 Ezra, Revelation, and the two *Metamorphoses* constructed their understanding of the relationship between this world and another.[12] The meaning expressed by a hierophagic event in narrative is culturally bound. In other, much cleverer, words: "There is no experience that is not a way of thinking, and which cannot be analyzed from the point of view of the history of thought.... Thought has a historicity which is proper to it."[13] Indeed, I hope it is clear from this discussion that while three core elements of hierophagy can be identified in the above texts, the ramifications of the hierophagic experience for each character are situation specific—as a genre hierophagy has certain criteria, but texts from diverse religious, cultural, temporal, or geographical provenances might use the concept in very different ways. To avoid generalizing and presenting hierophagy as an archetype, I leave to other scholars in other disciplines the question of

---

see Sara Parks, *Spiritual Equals Women and the Feminine in the Q Gender Pairs* (Minneapolis: Fortress Academic, forthcoming).

11. See Robert S. Ellwood, *The Politics of Myth: A Study of C. G. Jung, Mircea Eliade, and Joseph Campbell* (Albany: SUNY Press, 1999) for the political underpinnings of monomythic analysis.

12. Glen Robert Gill, *Northrop Frye and the Phenomenology of Myth* (Toronto: University of Toronto Press, 2006), 106.

13. Michel Foucault, *The Foucault Reader*, ed. Paul Rabinow (New York: Pantheon Books, 1984), 335.

whether this genre that I have defined in a small sample of texts, limited by time and space, makes sense in other cases, and if so, then to observe the ways in which the genre shifts in meaning and changes shape in those other contexts.

Because I have found the work being done on genre as social action and as fictional action so useful in articulating the process of meaning-creation operating in the examples of hierophagy, it is my hope that this field of research makes its way into more biblical scholarship. Genre has been a key interpretive tool for biblical scholars for decades; engaging with new research that ties literary and fictional genres with social behaviors will allow us new insights into these ancient texts, in the same way that this kind of analysis has allowed me to identify and explore hierophagy here.

Bibliography

Ahearne-Kroll, Patricia D. "Joseph and Aseneth and Jewish Identity in Greco-Roman Egypt." PhD diss., University of Chicago, 2005.
Aitken, Ellen. " 'The Basileia of Jesus Is on the Wood': The Epistle of Barnabas and the Ideology of Rule." Pages 197–213 in *Conflicted Boundaries in Wisdom and Apocalypticism*. Edited by Benjamin G. Wright III and Lawrence M. Wills. SymS 35. Atlanta: Society of Biblical Literature, 2005.
Allegro, John Marco. *The Sacred Mushroom and the Cross: A Study of the Nature and Origins of Christianity within the Fertility Cults of the Ancient Near East*. Garden City, NY: Doubleday, 1970.
Allen, T. W., W. R. Halliday, and E. E. Sikes. *The Homeric Hymns*. Oxford: Clarendon, 1936.
Amat, Jacqueline. *Passion de Perpétue et de Félicité suivi des Actes*. SC 417. Paris: Editions du Cerf, 1996.
———. *Songes et Visions: L'au-delà dans la littérature latine tardive*. Paris: Études Augustiniennes, 1985.
Apuleius. *Cupid and Psyche*. Translated by Edward J. Kenney. Cambridge: Cambridge University Press, 1990.
———. *Books 7–11*. Vol. 2 of *Metamorphoses (The Golden Ass)*. Edited and translated by J. Arthur Hanson. LCL. Cambridge: Harvard University Press, 1989.
Artemidorius Daldianus. Oneirocritica: *Text, Translation, and Commentary*. Edited and translated by Daniel E. Harris-McCoy. Oxford: Oxford University Press, 2012.
Auken, Sune. "Genre and Interpretation." Pages 154–83 in *Genre and …* Edited by Sune Auken, Palle Schantz Lauridsen, and Anders Juhl Rasmussen. Copenhagen Studies in Genre 2. Copenhagen: Ekbatana, 2015.

———. "Genre as Fictional Action: On the Use of Rehtorical Genres in Fiction." *Nordisk Tidsskrift for Informationsvidenskab og Kulturformidling* 2.3 (2013): 19–28.

Aune, David. *Revelation 6–16*. WBC 52B. Dallas: Word Books, 1997.

Avrahami, Yael. *The Senses of Scripture: Sensory Perception in the Hebrew Bible*. New York: T&T Clark, 2012.

Barnard, L. W. "The Epistle of Barnabas in Its Contemporary Setting." *ANRW* 27.1:159–207.

Barnes, Timothy David. *Early Christian Hagiography and Roman History*. Tübingen: Mohr Siebeck, 2010.

Barrigón Fuentes, M. "Les dieux egyptiens dans l'*Onirocriticon* d'Artémidore." *Kernos* 7 (1994): 29–45.

Barton, Carlin A., and Daniel Boyarin. *Imagine No Religion: How Modern Abstractions Hide Ancient Realities*. New York: Fordham University Press, 2016.

Battistella, Edwin L. *Markedness: The Evaluative Superstructure of Language*. Albany, NY: State University of New York Press, 1990.

———. *The Logic of Markedness*. New York: Oxford University Press, 1996.

Bauckham, Richard. *The Climax of Prophecy: Studies in the Book of Revelation*. Edinburgh: Clark, 1993.

Baynes, Leslie. *The Heavenly Book Motif in Judeo-Christian Apocalypses 200 B.C.E.–200 C.E.* JSJSup 152. Leiden: Brill, 2014.

———. "Revelation 5:1 and 10:2a, 8–10 in the Earliest Greek Tradition: A Response to Richard Bauckham." *JBL* 129 (2010): 801–16.

Beebee, Thomas O. *The Ideology of Genre: A Comparative Study of Generic Instability*. University Park: Pennsylvania State University Press, 2004.

Belayche, Nicole. "Religious Actors in Daily Life: Practices and Related Beliefs." Pages 275–91 in *A Companion to Roman Religion*. Edited by Jörg Rüpke. Blackwell Companions to the Ancient World. London: Blackwell, 2007.

Boccaccini, Gabriele, and Carlos A. Segovia, eds. *Paul the Jew: Rereading the Apostle as a Figure of Second Temple Judaism*. Minneapolis: Ausberg Fortress, 2016.

Bogdanov, Stefan. *The Honey Book*. Bee Product Science, 2016. http://www.bee-hexagon.net/honey/

Bohak, Gideon. *Joseph and Aseneth and the Jewish Temple in Heliopolis*. EJL 10. Atlanta: Scholars Press, 1996.

Bonner, C. "Hades and the Pomegranate Seed (Hymn to Demeter 372–74)," *Classical Review* 53.3 (1939): 3–4.

Bowersock, Glen Warren. *Martyrdom and Rome.* Cambridge: Cambridge University Press, 1995.
Boyarin, Daniel. *Border Lines: The Partition of Judaeo-Christianity.* Divinations. Philadelphia: University of Pennsylvania Press, 2004.
———. *A Radical Jew: Paul and the Politics of Identity.* Contraversions 1. Berkeley: University of California Press, 1994.
Bradley, Keith. "Contending with Conversion: Reflections on the Reformation of Lucius the Ass." *Phoenix* 52 (1998): 315–34.
Bradley, Mark. "Introduction: Smell and the Ancient Senses." Pages 1–16 in *Smell and the Ancient Senses.* Edited by Mark Bradley. London: Routledge, 2015.
Brandenburger, Egon. *Die Verborgenheit Gottes im Weltgeschehen.* ATANT 68. Zurich: Theologischer Verlag, 1981.
Braun, René. *Approches de Tertullien.* Paris: Études Augustiniennes, 1992.
Bremmer, Jan N. "Perpetua and Her Diary: Authenticity, Family and Visions." Pages 77–120 in *Märtyrer und Märtyrerakten.* Edited by Walter Ameling. Altertumswissenschaftliches Kolloquium 6. Wiesbaden: Franz Steiner Verlag, 2002.
———. *The Rise and Fall of the Afterlife: The 1995 Read-Tuckwell Lectures at the University of Bristol.* London: Routledge, 2002.
———. "The Vision of Saturus in the *Passio Perpetuae*." Pages 55–73 in *Jerusalem, Alexandria, Rome: Studies in Ancient Cultural Interaction in Honour of A. Hilhorst.* Edited by Florentino García Martínez and Gerard P. Luttikhuizen. JSJSup 82. Leiden: Brill, 2003.
Bremmer, Jan N., and Marco Formisano. Introduction to *Perpetua's Passions: Multidisciplinary Approaches to the Passio Perpetuae et Felicitatis.* Edited by Jan N. Bremmer and Marco Formisano. Oxford: Oxford University Press, 2012.
Burchard, Christoph. *Joseph und Aseneth.* PVTG 5. Leiden: Brill, 2003.
———. "Joseph and Aseneth." *OTP* 2:177–247.
———. *Untersuchungen zu Joseph und Aseneth: Überlieferung—Ortsbestimmung.* WUNT 8. Tübingen: Mohr Siebeck, 1965.
Burkert, Walter. *Ancient Mystery Cults.* Cambridge: Harvard University Press, 1987.
Carr, David M. *Writing on the Tablet of the Heart: Origins of Scripture and Literature.* Oxford: Oxford University Press, 2005.
Carroll, Lewis. *Alice's Adventures in Wonderland.* New York: Gabriel Sons, 1916.

Castelli, Elizabeth. "'I Will Make Mary Male': Pieties of the Body and Gender Transformation of Christian Women in Late Antiquity." Pages 29–49 in *Body Guards: The Cultural Politics of Gender Ambiguity*. Edited by Julia Epstein and Kristina Straub. Routledge: London, 1991.

Chesnutt, Randall D. *From Death to Life: Conversion in Joseph and Aseneth*. JSPSup 16. Sheffield: Sheffield Academic, 1995.

Chouliara-Raïos, H. *L'abeille et le miel en Egypt d'après les payrus grecs*. Jannina, Greece: Université de Jannina, 1989.

Clements, Ashley. "Divine Scents and Presence." Pages 46–59 in *Smell and the Ancient Senses*. Edited by Mark Bradley. New York: Routledge, 2015.

Cohen, Shaye J. D. "Crossing the Boundary and Becoming a Jew." Pages 140–74 in *The Beginnings of Jewishness: Boundaries, Varieties, Uncertainties*. HCS 31. Berkeley: University of California Press, 1999.

Cohn, Naftali S. *The Memory of the Temple and the Making of the Rabbis*. Divinations. Pennsylvania: University of Pennsylvania Press, 2012.

Collins, Adela Yarbro. *The Combat Myth in the Book of Revelation*. Missoula: Scholars Press, 1976.

———. *Crisis and Catharsis: The Power of the Apocalypse*. Philadelphia: Westminster, 1984.

Collins, John J. *The Apocalyptic Imagination: An Introduction to Jewish Apocalyptic Literature*. Grand Rapids: Eerdmans, 1998.

———. *Between Athens and Jerusalem: Jewish Identity in the Hellenistic Diaspora*. Grand Rapids: Eerdmans, 2000.

———. "Introduction: Towards the Morphology of a Genre." *Semeia* 14 (1979): 1–20.

Columella, Lucius Junius Moderatus. *On Agriculture*. Translated by Harrison Boyd Ash, E. S. Forster, and Edward H. Heffner. LCL. Cambridge: Harvard University Press, 1941.

Conybeare, F. C., and St. George Stock. *Grammar of Septuagint Greek: With Selected Readings, Vocabularies, and Updated Indexes*. Peabody, MA: Hendrickson, 2007.

Cook, John Granger. Review of *The Cross before Constantine*, by Bruce W. Longenecker. *Int* 72 (2018): 88–89.

Crook, Zeba. *Reconceptualising Conversion: Patronage, Loyalty, and Conversion in the Religions of the Ancient Mediterranean*. BZAW 130. Berlin: de Gruyter, 2004.

D'Arms, John H. "The Culinary Reality of Roman Upper-Class Convivia: Integrating Texts and Images." *Comparative Studies in Society and History* 46 (2004): 428–50.

Davila, James R. *The Provenance of the Old Testament Pseudepigrapha: Jewish, Christian, or Other?* JSJSup 105. Leiden: Brill, 2005.

Derrida, Jacques. "The Law of Genre." Pages 219–31 in *Modern Genre Theory*. Edited by David Duff. Harlow, UK: Longman, 2000.

Desroche, Henri. *Jacob and the Angel*. Amherst: University of Massachusetts Press, 1973.

Dioscorides Pedanius. *The Greek Herbal of Dioscorides*. Translated by R. T. Gunther. London: Hafner Publishing, 1968.

Dodds, E. R. *Pagan and Christian in an Age of Anxiety*. Cambridge: Cambridge University Press, 1965.

Douglas, Mary. "Deciphering a Meal." *Daedalus* 101 (1972): 61–81.

Dozeman, Thomas B. *God on the Mountain*. SBLMS 37. Atlanta: Scholars Press, 1989.

Dozeman, Thomas B., and Konrad Schmid, eds. *A Farewell to the Yahwist? The Composition of the Pentateuch in Recent European Interpretation*. SymS 34. Atlanta: Society of Biblical Literature, 2006.

Dulaey, Martine. *Le Rêve dans la vie et la pensée de Saint Augustin*. Paris: Études Augustiniennes, 1973.

Ehrman, Bart, trans. *The Apostolic Fathers*. Vol. 2. LCL. Cambridge: Harvard University Press, 2003.

Ekroth, Gunnel. "Meat for the Gods." Pages 15–41 in *Nourrir les dieux? Sacrifice et représentation du divin*. Edited by Vinciane Pirenne Delforge and Francesca Rescendi. Kernos supplement 26. Liège: Centre International d'Étude de la Religion Grecque Antique, 2011.

Ellwood, Robert S. *The Politics of Myth: A Study of C. G. Jung, Mircea Eliade, and Joseph Campbell*. Albany: SUNY Press, 1999.

Fantham, Elaine. "The Growth of Literature and Criticism at Rome." Pages 220–44 in *The Cambridge History of Literary Criticism*. Edited by George A. Kennedy. Vol. 1. Cambridge: Cambridge University Press, 1989.

Faraone, C. "Aphrodite's ΚΕΣΤΟΣ and Apples for Atlanta: Aphrodisiacs in Early Greek Myth and Ritual." *Phoenix* 44 (1990): 219–43.

Farb, Peter, and George J. Armelagos. *Consuming Passions: The Anthropology of Eating*. Boston: Houghton Mifflin, 1980.

Farrell, Joseph, and Craig Williams. "The Passion of Saints Perpetua and Felicity." Pages 14–23 in *Perpetua's Passions: Multidisciplinary*

Approaches to the Passio Perpetuae et Felicitatis. Edited by Jan N. Bremmer and Marco Formisano. Oxford: Oxford University Press, 2012.

Flannery-Dailey, Frances. *Dreamers, Scribes, and Priests: Jewish Dreams in the Hellenistic and Roman Eras*. JSJSup 90. Leiden: Brill, 2004.

Foley, Helene P. *The Homeric Hymn to Demeter: Translation, Commentary, and Interpretive Essays*. Princeton: Princeton University Press, 1994.

Foucault, Michel. *The Foucault Reader*. Edited by Paul Rabinow. New York: Pantheon Books, 1984.

Fowler, Alastair. *Kinds of Literature: An Introduction to the Theory of Genres and Modes*. Cambridge: Harvard University Press, 1982.

Fox, Robin Lane. *Pagans and Christians*. London: Harmondsworth, 1986.

Frangoulidis, Stavros. *Witches, Isis, and Narrative: Approaches to Magic in Apuleius' Metamorphoses*. Berlin: de Gruyter, 2008.

Frayn, Joan M. *Sheep-Rearing and the Wool Trade in Italy during the Roman Period*. Liverpool: Cairns, 1984.

Fredriksen, Paula. *Paul: The Pagan's Apostle*. New Haven: Yale University Press, 2017.

Freeman, Jennifer Awes. "The Good Shepherd and the Enthroned Ruler: A Reconsideration of Imperial Iconography in the Early Church." Pages 159–195 in *The Art of Empire: Christian Art in Its Imperial Context*. Edited by Lee M. Jefferson and Robin M. Jensen. Minneapolis: Fortress, 2015.

Gaventa, Beverly R. *From Darkness to Light: Aspects of Conversion in the New Testament*. Philadelphia: Fortress, 1986.

Geronimi, Clyde, Wilfred Jackson, and Hamilton Luske, dirs. *Alice in Wonderland*. Walt Disney Productions, 1951.

Gill, Glen Robert. *Northrop Frye and the Phenomenology of Myth*. Toronto: University of Toronto Press, 2006.

Ginzberg, Louis. *Legends of the Jews*. Philadelphia: Jewish Publication Society, 2003.

Gollnick, James. *The Religious Dreamworld of Apuleius' Metamorphoses*. London, ON: Wilfrid Laurier Press, 1999.

Goodman, David. "Do Angels Eat?" *JJS* 37 (1986): 160–75.

Goodman, Martin. "Paradise, Gardens, and the Afterlife in the First Century CE." Pages 57–63 in *Paradise in Antiquity: Jewish and Christian Views*. Edited by Markus Bockmuehl and Guy G. Stroumsa. Cambridge: Cambridge University Press, 2010.

Gowers, Emily. "Tasting the Roman World." Pages 90–103 in *Taste and the Ancient Senses*. Edited by Kelli C. Rudolph. London: Routledge, 2017.

Graf, Fritz. "Ambrosia." *DNP* 1:581–82.

———. "The Bridge and the Ladder: Narrow Passages in Late Antique Visions." Pages 19–33 in *Heavenly Realms and Earthly Realities in Late Antique Religions.* Edited by Ra'anan Boustan and Annette Yoshiko Reed. Cambridge: Cambridge University Press, 2004.

Graverini, Luca. *Literature and Identity in the Golden Ass.* Translated by Benjamin Todd Lee. Columbus: Ohio State University Press, 2012.

———. "An Old Wife's Tale." Pages 86–110 in *Lectiones Scrupulosae: Essays on the Text and Interpretation of Apuleius' Metamorphoses in Honour of Maaike Zimmerman.* Edited by M. Zimmerman, Wytse Hette Keulen, Ruurd R. Nauta, and Stelios Panayotakis. Ancient Narrative Supplementum 6. Groningen: Barkhuis, 2006.

Green, Deborah A. *The Aroma of Righteousness: Scent and Seduction in Rabbinic Life and Literature.* University Park: Pennsylvania State University Press, 2011.

Griffiths, Alan H. "Ambrosia." *OCD*, 71.

Hall, Mark Seaborn. "The Hook Interlocking Structure of Revelation: The Most Important Verses in the Book and How They May Unify Its Structure." *NovT* 44 (2002): 277–96.

Harissis, Haralampos V., and Anastasios V. Harissis. *Apiculture in the Prehistoric Aegean: Minoan and Mycenaean Symbols Revisited.* BARIS 1958. Oxford: Hedges, 2009.

Harnisch, Wolfgang. *Verhängnis und Verheissung der Geschichte: Untersuchungen zum Zeit- und Geschichtsverständnis im 4.Buch Esra und in der syr. Baruch-apokalypse.* Göttingen: Vandenhoeck & Ruprecht, 1969.

Harris, J. Rendel, and Seth K. Gifford. *The Acts of the Martyrdom of Perpetua and Felicitas.* London: Clay & Sons, 1890.

Harrison, S. J. *Apuleius: A Latin Sophist.* Oxford: Oxford University Press, 2000.

———. "Apuleius' *Metamorphoses*." Pages 499–516 in *The Novel in the Ancient World.* Edited by Gareth Schmeling. Leiden: Brill, 2003.

Harvey, Susan Ashbrook. *Scenting Salvation: Ancient Christianity and the Olfactory Imagination.* Berkeley: University of California Press, 2006.

Heffernan, Thomas J. "Philology and Authorship in *The Passio Sanctarum Perpetuae et Felicitatis*." *Traditio* 50 (1995): 315–25.

———. *The Passion of Perpetua and Felicity.* New York: Oxford University Press, 2012.

Henshaw, John M. *A Tour of the Senses: How Your Brain Interprets the World.* Baltimore, MD: Johns Hopkins University Press, 2012.

Herzog Reinhart, and Peter L. Schmidt, eds. *Handbuch der Lateinischen Literatur der Antike*. Vol. 4. Munich: Beck, 1997.
Heyob, Sharon K. *The Cult of Isis among Women in the Graeco-Roman World*. Leiden: Brill, 1975.
Hicks-Keeton, Jill. *Arguing with Aseneth: Gentile Access to Israel's "Living God" in Jewish Antiquity*. Oxford: Oxford University Press, 2018.
Hinds, Stephen. *The Metamorphosis of Persephone: Ovid and the Self-Conscious Muse*. Cambridge: Cambridge University Press, 1987.
Hitch, Sarah. "Tastes of Greek Poetry: From Homer to Aristophanes." Pages 22–44 in *Taste and the Ancient Senses*. Edited by Kelli C. Rudolph. London: Routledge, 2017.
Hogan, Karina. "The Meanings of 'tôrâ' in '4 Ezra.'" *JSJ* 38 (2007]): 530–52.
———. *Theologies in Conflict in 4 Ezra: Wisdom, Debate, and Apocalyptic Solution*. JSJSup 130. Leiden: Brill, 2008.
Holwerda, David E. "The Church and the Little Scroll (Revelation 10, 11)." *Calvin Theological Journal* 34 (1999): 148–61.
Homer. *The Odyssey*. Translated by Emily Wilson. New York: Norton, 2018.
Horbury, William. "Jewish-Christian Relations in the Epistle of Barnabas and Justin Martyr." Pages 315–45 in *Jews and Christians: The Parting of the Ways A.D. 70 to 135*. Edited by James D. G. Dunn. WUNT 66. Tübingen: Mohr, 1992.
Horsley, Richard A. *Scribes, Visionaries, and the Politics of Second Temple Judea*. Louisville: Westminster John Knox, 2007.
Howes, David. *Sensual Relations: Engaging the Senses in Culture and Social Theory*. Ann Arbor: University of Michigan Press, 2003.
Hubbard, Moyer. "Honey for Aseneth: Interpreting a Religious Symbol." *JSP* 16 (1997): 97–110.
Irving, Thomas Ballantine, Khurshid Ahmad, and M. M. Ahsan, eds. *The Qur'ān*. Teheran: Suhrawardi Research & Publication Center, 1978.
Isambert, F. A. Review of *Religion and Society in Tension*, by Charles Y. Glock and Rodney Stark. *ASSR* 21 (1966): 183–84.
James, William. *The Varieties of Religious Experience*. New York: Penguin, 1984.
Jensen, Robin M. *The Cross: History, Art, and Controversy*. Cambridge: Harvard University Press, 2017.
Johnson, Mark. *The Body in the Mind: The Bodily Basis of Meaning, Imagination, and Reason*. Chicago: University of Chicago Press, 1987.
Julian. *Letters; Epigrams; Against the Galilaeans; Fragments*. Translated by Wilmer C. Wright. LCL. Cambridge: Harvard University Press, 1923.

Kilgour, Maggie. *From Communion to Cannibalism: An Anatomy of Metaphors of Incorporation*. Princeton: Princeton University Press, 1990.

Kindstedt, Paul. *Cheese and Culture: A History of Cheese and Its Place in Western Civilization*. White River Junction, VT: Chelsea Green, 2012.

Koester, Craig R. *Revelation: A New Translation with Introduction and Commentary*. AB 38A. New Haven: Yale University Press, 2014.

Korner, Ralph. "'And I Saw …': An apocalyptic Literary Convention for Structural Identification in the Apocalypse." *NovT* 42 (2000): 160–83.

Korsmeyer, Carolyn. *Making Sense of Taste: Food and Philosophy*. Ithaca, NY: Cornell University Press, 1999.

Kotrosits, Maia. *Rethinking Early Christian Identity: Affect, Violence, and Belonging*. Minneapolis: Fortress, 2015.

Kraemer, Ross S. "Aseneth as Wisdom." Pages 219–39 in *Wisdom and Psalms*. Edited by Athalya Brenner and Carole R. Fontaine. FCB 2nd series. Sheffield: Sheffield Academic, 1998.

———. "Jewish Tuna and Christian Fish: Identifying Religious Affiliation in Epigraphic Sources." *HTR* 84 (1991): 141–62.

———. *When Aseneth Met Joseph: A Late Antique Tale of the Biblical Patriarch and His Egyptian Wife, Reconsidered*. New York: Oxford University Press, 1998.

Lakoff, George, and Mark Johnson. *Metaphors We Live By*. Chicago: University of Chicago Press, 1980.

———. *Philosophy in the Flesh: The Embodied Mind and Its Challenge to Western Thought*. New York: Basic Books, 1999.

Lalonde, M. P. "Deciphering a Meal Again, or the Anthropology of Taste." *Social Science Information* 31 (1992): 69–86.

Landau, Brent. "The Star-Child and His Star-Food: Fragments of Visionary Experience in the Syriac *Revelation of the Magi*." Paper presented at the Second Century Seminar at Texas Christian University. Fort Worth, Texas, November 7, 2013.

Libby, Brigitte B. "Moons, Smoke, and Mirrors in Apuleius' Portrayal of Isis." *The American Journal of Philology* 132 (2011): 301–22.

LiDonnici, Lynn R. *Epidaurian Miracle Inscriptions*. SBLTT 36. Atlanta: Scholars Press, 1995.

Lieber, Andrea Beth. "I Set a Table before You: The Jewish Eschatological Character of Aseneth's Conversion Meal." *JSP* 14 (2004): 63–77.

———. "Jewish and Christian Heavenly Meal Traditions." Pages 313–39 in *Paradise Now: Essays on Early Jewish and Christian Mysticism*. Edited by April D. DeConick. SymS 11. Atlanta: Society of Biblical Literature, 2006.

Lipsett, Barbara Diane. *Desiring Conversion: Hermas, Thecla, Aseneth.* Oxford: Oxford University Press, 2011.

Longenecker, Bruce W. *The Cross before Constantine: The Early Life of a Christian Symbol.* Minneapolis: Fortress, 2015.

Maier, Harry O. *Apocalypse Recalled: The Book of Revelation after Christendom.* Minneapolis: Fortress, 2002.

Martin, Luther H. *Hellenistic Religions: An Introduction.* New York: Oxford University Press, 1987.

McDonald, Lee M. *The Formation of the Christian Biblical Canon.* Peabody, MA: Hendrickson, 1995.

McGaskil, Grant. "Paradise in the New Testament." Pages 64–81 in *Paradise in Antiquity: Jewish and Christian Views.* Edited by Markus Bockmuehl and Guy G. Stroumsa. Cambridge: Cambridge University Press, 2010.

McGowan, Andrew. *Ancient Christian Worship: Early Church Practices in Social, Historical, and Theological Perspective.* Grand Rapids: Baker, 2014.

———. *Ascetic Eucharists: Food and Drink in Early Christian Ritual Meals.* Oxford: Oxford University Press, 1999.

Meeks, Wayne A. *The First Urban Christians: The Social World of the Apostle Paul.* New Haven: Yale University Press, 1983.

Metzger, M. "The Fourth Book of Ezra." *OTP* 1:517–59.

Milik, J. T. "2 Enoch." *OTP* 1:91–213.

Miller, Carolyn R. "Genre as Social Action." *Quarterly Journal of Speech* 70 (1984): 151–67.

Miller, Patricia Cox. *Dreams in Late Antiquity: Studies in the Imagination of a Culture.* Princeton: Princeton University Press, 1994.

———. "A Dubious Twilight: Reflections on Dreams in Patristic Literature." *Church History* 55 (1986): 153–64.

Moo, Jonathan A. *Creation, Nature and Hope in 4 Ezra.* FRLANT 237. Göttingen: Vandenhoeck & Ruprecht, 2011.

Muir, Steven, and Frederick S. Tappenden. "Edible Media: The Confluence of Food and Learning in the Ancient Mediterranean." *LTQ* 47 (2017): 123–47.

Musurillo, Herbert Anthony. *Acts of the Christian Martyrs.* Oxford: Clarendon, 1979.

Myers, Jacob M. *I and II Esdras.* AB. Garden City, NY: Doubleday, 1974.

Myres, J. L. "Persephone and the Pomegranate (H. Dem 372–74)." *Classical Review* 52.2 (1938): 51–52.

Najman, Hindy. "Between Heaven and Earth: Liminal Visions in *4Ezra*." Pages 151–67 in *Other Worlds and Their Relation to This World: Early Jewish and Ancient Christian Traditions*. Edited by Tobias Nicklas, Joseph Verheyden, Erik M. M. Eynikel, and Florentino Garcia Martinez. JSJSup 143. Leiden, Brill: 2010.

Nasrallah, Laura. *An Ecstasy of Folly: Prophecy and Authority in Early Christianity*. Cambridge: Harvard University Press, 2003.

Neuman (Noy), Dov. *Motif-Index of Talmudic-Midrashic Literature*. PhD diss., Indiana University, 1954.

Nicklas, Tobias. "*Food of Angels* (Wis 16:20)." Pages 83–100 in *Studies in the Book of Wisdom*. Edited by Géza G. Xeravits and József Zsengellér. JSJSup 142. Leiden: Brill, 2010.

Nicklas, Tobias, Joseph Verheyden, Erik M. M. Eynikel, and Florentino Garcia Martinez, eds. *Other Worlds and Their Relation to This World: Early Jewish and Christian Traditions*. JSJSup 143. Leiden: Brill, 2010.

Nir, Rivka. *Joseph and Aseneth: A Christian Book*. HBM 42. Sheffield: Sheffield Phoenix, 2012.

Nock, Arthur Darby. *Conversion*. Oxford: Oxford University Press, 1933. Repr., 1969.

Nongbri, Brent. *Before Religion: A History of a Modern Concept*. New Haven: Yale University Press, 2013.

———. "Dislodging 'Embedded' Religion: A Brief Note on a Scholarly Trope." *Numen* 55 (2008): 440–60.

North, John A. "Novelty and Choice in Roman Religion." *JRS* 70 (1980): 186–91.

Oberhelman, Steven M. *Dreambooks in Byzantium: Six Oneirocritica in Translation, with Commentary and Introduction*. Farnham: Ashgate, 2008.

Oppenheim, A. Leo. *The Interpretation of Dreams in the Ancient Near East*. Piscataway: Gorgias, 1956. Repr., 2008.

Osmun, George F. "Roses of Antiquity." *The Classical Outlook* 52.10 (1975): 114–16.

Ovid. *Fasti*. Translated by A. Wiseman and P. Wiseman. Oxford: Oxford University Press, 2011.

———. *Fasti*. Translated by George Patrick Goold and James George Frazer. LCL. Cambridge: Harvard University Press, 2003.

———. *Metamorphoses V–VIII*. Edited and translated by D. E. Hill. Warminster, UK: Aris & Philips, 1992.

Paget, James Carleton. *The Epistle of Barnabas: Outlook and Background*. WUNT 2/64. Tübingen: Mohr, 1994.

Parks, Sara. *Spiritual Equals Women and the Feminine in the Q Gender Pairs*. Minneapolis: Fortress Academic, forthcoming.

Perkins, Judith. "The Rhetoric of the Maternal Body in the *Passion of Perpetua*." Pages 313–32 in *Mapping Gender in Ancient Religious Discourses*. Edited by Todd Penner and Caroline Vander Stichele. BibInt 84. Leiden: Brill, 2007.

Pfister, Oskar. *Christianity and Fear: A Study in History and in the Psychology and Hygiene of Religion*. Translated by W. H. Johnston. London: Allen & Unwin, 1948.

Philonenko, Marc. *Joseph et Aséneth: Introduction, texte critique, traduction et notes*. SVTP 13. Leiden: Brill, 1968.

Plutarch. *Table-Talk, Books 1–6*. Vol. 8 of *Moralia*. Translated by P. A. Clement, H. B. Hoffleit. LCL. Cambridge: Harvard University Press, 1969.

Poirier, John C. "Apicultural Keys to *Joseph and Aseneth*: An Argument for the Priority of the Shorter Text." Paper presented at the Annual Meeting of the Society of Biblical Literature, 19 November 2017.

Portier-Young, Anathea E. "Sweet Mercy Metropolis: Interpreting Aseneth's Honeycomb." *JSP* 14 (2005): 133–57.

Potter, David. "The Social Life of the Senses: Feasts and Funerals." Pages 23–44 in *A Cultural History of the Senses in Antiquity*. Edited by Jerry Toner. London: Bloomsbury 2014.

Potts, Charlotte R. "The Art of Piety and Profit at Pompeii: A New Interpretation of the Painted Shop Façade at IX.7.1–2." *Greece and Rome* 56 (2009): 55–70.

Putthoff, Tyson L. "Aseneth's Gastronomical Vision: Mystical Theophagy and New Creation in *Joseph and Aseneth*." *JSP* 24 (2014): 96–117.

Rabens, Volker. *The Holy Spirit and Ethics in Paul: Transformation and Empowering for Religious-Ethical Life*. WUNT 2/283. Tübingen: Mohr Siebeck, 2010.

Radermacher, Ludwig. *Die Erzählungen der Odyssee*. Sitzungsberichte der Kaiserlichen Akademie der Wissenschaften in Wien, Philosophisch-Historische Classe 178. Wien: A. Hölder, 1915.

Rajak, Tessa. "Jews and Christians as Groups in a Pagan World." Pages 355–72 in *The Jewish Dialogue with Greece and Rome: Studies in Cultural and Social Interaction*. AGJU 48. Leiden: Brill, 2001.

Relihan, Joel C., ed. and trans. *The Golden Ass: Or, A Book of Changes*. Indianapolis: Hackett Publishing, 2007.

Reynolds, Benjamin E. "The Otherworldly Mediators in *4 Ezra* and *2 Baruch*: A Comparison with Angelic Mediators in Ascent Apocalypses and in Daniel, Ezekiel, and Zechariah." Pages 176–93 in *Fourth Ezra and Second Baruch: Reconstruction after the Fall*. Edited by Matthias Henze and Gabriele Boccaccini. JSJSup 164. Leiden: Brill, 2013.

Richards, Ivor A. *The Philosophy of Rhetoric*. Oxford: Oxford University Press, 1936.

Richardson, Nicholas J. *The Homeric Hymn to Demeter*. Oxford: Clarendon, 1974.

Richardson, Peter, and Martin B. Shukster. "Barnabas, Nerva, and the Yavnean Rabbis." *JTS* 2/34 (1983): 31–55.

Robert, L. "Une Vision de Perpétue Martyre à Carthage en 203." *CRAI* (1982): 228–76.

Roddy, Nicolae. "Fill Your Stomach with It: Hierophagy as Religious Experience." Paper presented at the Annual Meeting of the Society of Biblical Literature, San Diego, CA, 20 November 2007.

———. "'Taste and See...': Hierophagy as Religious Experience." Paper presented at the Trends of Ancient Jewish and Christian Mysticism Seminar (TAJCM), University of Dayton, 7 March 2008.

Rohde, Erwin. "Zu Apuleius." *Reinisches Museum* 40 (1885): 66–95.

Roshcer, W. H. *Nektar und Ambrosia*. Leipzig: Teubner, 1883.

Ruck, Carl A. P., Blaise D. Staples, and Clark Heinrich. *The Apples of Apollo: Pagan and Christian Mysteries of the Eucharist*. Durham, NC: Carolina Academic Press, 2001.

Rudolph, Kelli C. "Introduction: On the Tip of the Tongue; Making Sense of Ancient Taste." Pages 1–21 in *Taste and the Ancient Senses*. Edited by Kelli C. Rudolph. The Senses in Antiquity. London: Routledge, 2017.

———, ed. *Taste and the Ancient Senses*. The Senses in Antiquity. London: Routledge, 2017.

Rüpke, Jörg. Introduction to *Rituals in Ink: A Conference on Religion and Literary Production in Ancient Rome Held at Stanford University in February 2002*. Edited by Alessandro Barchiesi, Jörg Rüpke, and Susan A. Stephens. Postdamer altertumswissenschaftliche beiträge 10. Stuttgart: Steiner, 2004.

Sanders, E. P. "Testament of Abraham." *OTP* 1:871–902.
Sanders, Gabriel. *Licht en duisternis in de Christelijke grafschriften*. 2 vols. Brussels: Paleis der Academiën, 1965.
Scheinberg, Susan. "The Bee Maidens of the Homeric *Hymn to Hermes*." *HSCP* 83 (1979): 1–28.
Schlam, Carl C. *The* Metamorphoses *of Apuleius: On Making an Ass of Oneself*. Chapel Hill: University of North Carolina, 1992.
Sulzbach, Carla. "When Going on a Heavenly Journey, Travel Light and Dress Appropriately." *JSP* 19 (2010): 163–93.
Scullion, S. "Olympian and Chthonian." *Classical Antiquity* 13 (1994): 75–119.
Segal, Alan F. *Paul the Convert: The Apostolate and Apostasy of Saul the Pharisee*. New Haven: Yale University Press, 1990.
Sheinfeld, Shayna. "From Nomos to Logos: Torah Observance in First Century Judaism." In *Paul within Judaism: New Perspectives*. Edited by Mgr. František Ábel. Lexington Books/Fortress Academic, forthcoming.
Shumate, Nancy. *Crisis and Conversion in Apuleius' Metamorphoses*. Ann Arbor: University of Michigan Press, 1996.
Smit, Peter-Ben. "Reaching for the Tree of Life: The Role of Eating, Drinking, Fasting, and Symbolic Foodstuffs in *4 Ezra*." *JSJ* 45 (2014): 1–22.
Smith, Christopher R. "The Structure of the Book of Revelation in Light of Apocalyptic Literary Conventions." *NovT* 36 (1994): 373–93.
Smith, Dennis E. *From Symposium to Eucharist: The Banquet in the Early Christian World*. Minneapolis: Fortress, 2003.
Smith, Jonathan Z. *Drudgery Divine: On the Comparison of Early Christianities and the Religions of Late Antiquity*. Chicago: University of Chicago Press, 1990.
Smith, Mark M. *Sensing the Past: Seeing, Hearing, Smelling, Tasting, and Touching in History*. Berkeley: University of California Press, 2007.
Smyth, Herbert Weir. *Greek Grammar*. Cambridge: Harvard University Press, 1984.
Solmsen, Friedrich. *Isis among the Greeks and Romans*. London: Harvard University Press, 1979.
Speiser, E. A. 1964. *Genesis*. AB. Garden City, NY: Doubleday.
Standhartinger, Angela. "Recent Scholarship on *Joseph and Aseneth* (1988–2013)." *CurBR* 12 (2014): 353–406.
Steinsaltz, Adin. *Koren Talmud Bavli*. Noé ed. 42 vols. Jerusalem: Shefa Foundation; Jerusalem: Koren Publishers, 2015.

Stone, Michael. *Fourth Ezra: A Commentary on the Book of Fourth Ezra.* Minneapolis: Fortress, 1990.

———. "A Reconsideration of Apocalyptic Visions." *HTR* 96 (2003): 167–80.

———. "Seeing and Understanding in *4 Ezra*." Pages 122–37 in *Revealed Wisdom: Studies in Apocalyptic in Honour of Christopher Rowland.* Edited by John Ashton. AJEC 88. Leiden: Brill, 2014.

Stover, Ed, and Eric W. Mercure. "The Pomegranate: A New Look at the Fruit of Paradise." *HortScience* 42 (2007): 1088–92.

Stuckenbruck, Loren T. "Ezra's Vision of the Lady: Form and Function of a Turning Point." Pages 137–50 in *Fourth Ezra and Second Baruch: Reconstruction after the Fall.* Edited by Matthias Henze and Gabriele Boccaccini. JSJSup 164. Leiden, Brill, 2013.

Summers, Richard G. "Apuleius' *Juridicus*." *Historia* 21 (1972): 120–26.

Suter, A. *The Narcissus and the Pomegranate: An Archaeology of the Homeric Hymn to Demeter.* Ann Arbor: University of Michigan Press, 2002.

Sutton, R. "The Interaction between Men and Women Portrayed on Attic Red-Figure Pottery." PhD dissertation. University of North Carolina, Chapel Hill, 1981.

Tilford, Nicole L. *Sensing World, Sensing Wisdom: The Cognitive Foundation of Biblical Metaphors.* AIL 31. Atlanta: SBL Press, 2017.

Tilg, Stefan. *Apuleius' Metamorphoses: A Study in Roman Fiction.* Oxford: Oxford University Press, 2014.

Tilley, Maureen A. "The Passion of Perpetua and Felicity." Pages 829–58 in *A Feminist Commentary.* Vol. 2 of *Searching the Scriptures.* Edited by Elisabeth Schussler Fiorenza. New York: Crossroad, 1994.

Toner, Jerry. *A Cultural History of the Senses in Antiquity.* Vol. 1. London: Bloomsbury, 2014.

Totelin, Laurence. "Tastes in Botany, Medicine and Science in Antiquity: Bitter Herbs and Sweet Honey." Pages 60–71 in *Taste and the Ancient Senses.* Edited by Kelli C. Rudolph. London: Routledge, 2017.

Touna, Vaia. *Fabrications of the Greek Past: Religion, Tradition, and the Making of Modern Identities.* Leiden: Brill, 2017.

Van Lieshout, R. G. A. *Greeks on Dreams.* Utrecht: HES, 1980.

Veenker, Ronald A. "Forbidden Fruit: Ancient Near Eastern Sexual Metaphors." *HUCA* 70–71 (1999–2000): 57–73.

Vielhaur, P. "Paulinisms of Acts." Pages 35–50 in *Studies in Luke-Acts.* Edited by Leander E. Keck and J. Louis Martyn. Nashville: Abingdon, 1966.

Von Albrecht, Michael. *Masters of Roman Prose: From Cato to Apuleius—Interpretive Studies*. Translated by Neil Adkin. Leeds: Francis Cairns Publications, 1989.

Vuong, Lily C. *Gender and Purity in the Protevangelium of James*. Tübingen: Mohr Siebeck, 2013.

Waldner, Katharina. "Visions, Prophecy, and Authority in the *Passio Perpetuae*." Pages 201–19 in *Perpetua's Passions: Multidisiplinary Approaches to the Passio Perpetuae et Felicitatis*. Edited by Jan N. Bremmer and Marco Formisano. Oxford: Oxford University Press, 2012.

Walsh, P. *The Roman Novel: The "Satyricon" of Petronius and the "Metamorphoses" of Apuleius*. Cambridge: Cambridge University Press, 1970.

Warren, Meredith J. C. "Like Dew from Heaven: Honeycomb, Religious Identity and Transformation in *Joseph and Aseneth*." MA Thesis, McGill, 2006.

———. *My Flesh Is Meat Indeed: A Nonsacramental Reading of John 6:51–58*. Minneapolis: Fortress, 2015.

———. "My Heart Poured Forth Understanding: *4 Ezra*'s Fiery Cup as Hierophagic Consumption." *SR* 44 (2015): 320–33.

———. "A Robe Like Lightning: Clothing Changes and Identification in *Joseph and Aseneth*." Pages 137–53 in *Dressing Judeans and Christians in Antiquity*. Edited by Kristi Upson-Saia, Carly Daniel-Hughs, and Alicia J. Batten. Farnham: Ashgate, 2014.

———. "Tastes from Beyond: Persephone's Pomegranate and Otherworldly Consumption in Antiquity." Pages 104–19 in *Taste and the Ancient Senses*. Edited by Kelli C. Rudolph. London: Routledge, 2017.

———. "Tasting the Little Scroll: A Sensory Analysis of Divine Interaction in Revelation 10:8–10." *JSNT* 40 (2017): 101–19.

Waszink, J. H., ed. *Quinti Septimi Florentis Tertuliani: De Anima*. Amsterdam: Meulenhoff, 1947.

Waugh, L. R. "Marked and Unmarked: A Choice between Unequals in Semiotic Structure." *Semiotica* 38 (1982): 299–318.

Weichart, G., and P. van Eeuwijk. "Preface." *Anthropology of Food* S3 (2007): 1–14.

Wernicke, K. "Ambrosia." Pages 1809–11 in vol. 1 of *Paulys Real-Encyclopädie der Classischen Altertums-wissenschaft*. Stuttgart: Calwer 1894.

Winkler, John J. *Auctor and Actor: A Narratological Reading of Apuleius' Golden Ass*. Berkeley: University of California Press, 1985.

Yarbrough, Oliver Larry. "The Shadow of an Ass: On Reading the Alexamenos Graffito." Pages 239–54 in *Text, Image, and Christians in the Graeco-Roman World*. Edited by Aliou Cissé Niang and Carolyn Osiek. Eugene, OR: Pickwick, 2012.

Yoshiko Reed, Annette. "Partitioning 'Religion' and Its Prehistories: Reflections on Categories, Narratives, and the Practice of Religious Studies." Paper presented at the annual meeting of the North American Association for the Study of Religion. 17 November 2017. Available at https://tinyurl.com/SBL4211b.

Zurawski, Jason. "Ezra Begins: *4 Ezra* as Prequel and the Making of a Superhero." Pages 289–304 in *Old Testament Pseudepigrapha and the Scriptures*. Edited by Eibert Tigchelaar. BETL. Leuven: Peeters, 2014.

Index of Ancient Texts

Hebrew Bible

Genesis 33, 35
  2:8 91
  2:15 91
  2:16–18 14
  3 33
  3:1–7 14
  3:5 34 n. 44
  3:6–7 34
  3:22 34
  3:22–23 34
  3:22–24 34, 91
  18:1–8 10 n. 23
  22:11 53
  28:10–22 135

Exodus
  3:4 53
  33:1–3 90
  34:28 10

Leviticus
  20:4 90

Deuteronomy
  6:18 90

1 Samuel
  3:10 53

Psalms
  19:10 14, 71
  34:9 14
  119:103 71

Proverbs
  2:6 91
  16:24 71
  24:13–14 71
  25:16 88

Ezekiel 3–4, 12, 38, 69, 72, 131
  2:8–3:4 68
  9:4 64 n. 12

Daniel
  7 50
  7:9 136
  10:2–3 10

Zechariah 38

Deuterocanonical Books

Sirach
  24.19 91

Wisdom of Solomon
  19:21 11, 71

Pseudepigrapha

2 Baruch
  5.7 10
  9.1 10
  12.5 10
  20.5–21.1 10
  43.3 10
  47.1 10
  86.1 10

3 Baruch		9.28	52
4:10	41	9.38–10.4	45
		9.38–10.28	52
1 Enoch		9.39	46
14.20	136	10.5	46
24.4	41	10.5–6	47
46.1	136 n. 32	10.12–14	47 n. 33
62.15–16	136	10.15–17	47 n. 33
71.10	136 n. 32	10.25–28	45
106.2–6	136 n. 32	10.28	45
		10.30–37	49
2 Enoch		10.32	52
1–22	86 n. 35	10.55	45
8.1–12	135	10.55–56	46
8.2	41	10.58	46
		11.1–12.51	42
4 Ezra 3, 15, 16, 36–58, 60, 69, 72, 99,		11.2–3	52
110, 115–16, 127, 129, 131–32, 153–		11.5	52
54, 156		11.7	52
3.1–5.20	42	11.10	52
4.1–2	43	11.37	50
4.9–12	43	12.1–39	50
4.23	43	12.3–9	50
5.13	43	12.4–5	48
5.18–19	43 n. 22	12.6	48
5.20	10	12.7–9	50
5.20–21	43	12.23	51
5.21–30	44	12.30	51
5.21–6.34	42	12.32	51
5.46–55	44	12.34	50
5.51–53	47 n. 33	12.37	51
5.54–55	47 n. 33	12.51	42 n. 21, 46, 51
6.30–31	44	13.1–58	42, 52
6.35	10	13.3	52
6.35–9.25	42	13.5	52
6.38–9.25	44	13.8	52
6.55–59	44	13.14–15	52
7.1–9	44	13.15	51
7.10	44	13.51	51
7.11–8.3	44	14	28, 40, 57
8.4	54	14.1–48	42
9.24	46	14.9	56
9.25	44	14.24–26	53
9.26	49	14.25	53
9.26–10.59	42	14.38–41	53–54, 69

14.39–40	40	16.8/14	17, 77, 87, 91, 95, 96 n. 64
14.40–42	152	16.8–9	77
14.41	52, 54	16.9/16	80, 90, 96
14.42	54	16.10–11/17	92, 96
14.45–48	51	16.12–14	77, 95
14.49–50	54 n. 54	16.14–16	41
14.50	54, 56 n. 62, 57, 152	16.15–16	71 n. 27, 96
		16.15–17/20–22	96

Apocalypse of Abraham
11.2	136 n. 32

17.1	96, 152
17.1–2	17, 79, 94
17.2	94

Apocalypse of Adam
7.21	41

17.6/7–10	97
18.3/5	97
18.3–4	97

Epistle of Barnabas 89
6.8–7.2	90
6.11–12	90
6.17	90

18.3–6/5–7	97, 152
18.7–9	17, 79
18.9	3
18.11	3
21.3–8	83

History of the Rechabites
7.2	11, 71, 87
11.4	11, 71, 87
12.5	11, 71, 87

Passion of Perpetua and Felicitas 3, 12–13, 15, 18, 22 n. 9, 55, 87, 115, 118, 129–50, 153–54, 156

3	148

Joseph and Aseneth 3, 12, 17, 22 n. 9, 55, 60, 75–100, 115, 117, 119, 127, 129, 154, 156

3.8	138
4.1	147
4.1–2	133, 144

3.6	98
8	78
8.5	98–99
10.13–14	94
11–13	94
14.1–2	86
14.7–15	95
14.9	86
15–17	94
15.3/4	94
15.4/5	88, 94
15.6/7	83, 90, 94
15.14	94
16	77–78, 81, 99
16–18	17
16.2–3	87
16.4/8	95
16.6/9	95

4.3	134
4.6	134
4.7	134
4.8	136
4.8–10	18, 71 n. 27, 132–33, 137
4.9	137
4.10	18, 146–47, 152
5.1	148
5.5	148
5.6	148
6.5	148
6.6–8	148, 152
8.3–5	144
9.7	131
11.5–7	136 n. 29
14	130
14	130
16–12	130

Passion of Perpetua and Felicitas (cont.)
20.2 — 138

Protoevangelium of James
8.2 — 11

Testament of Abraham — 9
4 — 10, 87

ANCIENT JEWISH WRITERS

Josephus, *Contra Apionem*
1.38 — 54 n. 53

Philo of Alexandria, *On Flight and Finding*
138 — 88

NEW TESTAMENT

Matthew
4:4 — 14
17:2 — 136

Luke
23:43 — 135

John
20:12 — 136

Acts — 111
1:10 — 136

1 Corinthians
2:6–3:3 — 14
10:17 — 32, 70
10:20 — 32, 70

2 Corinthians
12:4 — 135

Revelation — 3, 12–13, 17, 22 n. 9, 38, 55, 59–74, 99, 110, 115, 129, 131, 154, 156
1:1 — 65 n. 15
1:14 — 136 n. 32
2:7 — 135–36
4:2 — 65
4:8 — 66
5 — 63–65
5:1 — 62, 67
5:2 — 66 n. 18
5:2–3 — 62
5:3 — 63
5:12 — 66
6:1–4 — 65
6:10 — 63
6:11 — 63
6:11–14 — 66
7:3 — 64
7:9 — 136
8:2–3 — 66
8:5 — 66
9:1 — 65
9:4 — 64 n. 11
10 — 60, 62–66, 68–69, 71
10:2 — 67
10:5 — 67
10:6–7 — 63
10:8 — 63
10:8–10 — 17, 60–61, 68–69, 73
10:9 — 59, 67
10:10–11 — 152
10:11 — 61, 68, 152
11:1–13 — 63
12:14 — 63
12:16 — 63
13 — 50
13:5 — 63
13:16–17 — 64 n. 13
14:1 — 64 n. 12
14:9 — 64 n. 13
16:2 — 64 n. 13
18:21 — 66 n. 18
22:1–5 — 135
22:4 — 64 n. 12

RABBINIC WORKS

b. Hagigah
14b — 88

Index of Ancient Texts

b. Kerithot		11.5	112
9a	81 n. 22	11.5–6	17
b. Yevamot		11.6	119–20
47a–b	81 n. 22	11.7	119, 123
		11.9	120 n. 68
m. Gerim		11.9–10	124
2:4	81 n. 22	11.12	119
		11.13	106, 120, 124, 126, 152
Sifre Numbers		11.14	124
108	81 n. 22	11.15	105, 152
		11.15–16	125
		11.16	125

Greco-Roman Literature

		11.19	106
		11.23	126
Aelius Aristides, *Orations*		11.24	31, 126
48.30	136 n. 30	11.27	102

Apollodorus, *Bibliotheca*		Argonautica Orphica	
1.5.1–3	21 n. 6	1191–1996	21 n. 6

Apollonius of Rhodes, *Argonautica*		Aristophanes, *Pax*	
4.869–872	12 n. 31	869	22 n. 11

Apuleius, *Hermagoras*	102	Aristotle, *De anima*	
		421a25	15

Apuleius, *Metamorphoses* 3, 16, 17, 20 n. 3, 60, 101–27, 153, 156

		Aristotle, *De sensu et sensibilibus*	
1–10	103, 125	437a9–10	15
3–10	121	438b21	15
3.25	112, 121		
3.27	120 n. 70, 121	Aristotle, *Historia animalium*	
3.29	121	5.22.29–30	85 n. 33
4	121		
4.27	122	Artemidorus, *Oneirocriticon*	134, 140
4.28–6.24	122	1.72	140 n. 44
6.19	123	1.77	120
6.20	123	2.123	118
6.23–24	123	4.81	121
9.14	113		
10.29	122 n. 75	Augustine, *Heresies*	
11	101–2, 104, 109, 114, 117, 122–23	28	141 n. 50
11.1	112, 117–18		
11.2	109, 116, 118	Augustine, *The Soul and Its Origin*	
11.3–4	117	1.10.12	130
11.4	123		

182   Food and Transformation in Ancient Mediterranean Literature

Callimachos, *Hymn to Ceres*	21 n. 6	Germanus, *Oneirocriticon*	
		T.228–229	140
Cato, *Agriculture*			
76	139 n. 41	Herodotus, *Histories*	
150	139	6.69	137 n. 34
Celsus, *De medicina*		Hesiod, *Theogonia*	
4.16.1.8	146 n. 62	9.14	21 n. 6
Cicero, *In Verrem*		Homer, *Iliad*	
2.4	21 n. 6	5.342	11 n. 27
		16.670	12
Claudian *On the Rape of Proserpina*	21	16.689	12
n. 6		19.37–39	12
		19.352–354	12
Columella, *Agriculture*		24.642	25 n. 18
7.8	139		
7.8.6	140	Homer, *Odyssey*	
		1.105–149	23
Daniel, *Oneirocriticon*		5.135	11 n. 27
T.449	140	5.194	11 n. 27
		5.195–199	35
Diodorus Siculus, *Bibliotheca historica*		5.197–199	12
5.3–5	21 n. 6	8	23 n. 13
Dioscorides, *De Materia Medica*		Homeric Hymn to Demeter	4, 16, 19,
2.82.1	72	21–2, 29, 33, 35–36	
		5–14	22 n. 8
Ephrem the Syrian, *Hymni Contra*		43–44	28
Haereses		50	25 n. 21
47.6	142	78–79	22
		302–313	22
Epiphanius of Salamis, *Panarion*		334–349	22
49.1.1	141	360–369	22, 71 n. 27
		371–374	25
Euripides, *Helena*		373	22
1301–1368	21 n. 6	390–400	24, 26, 152
		398	24
Euripides, *Orestes*		398–400	29
10	12 n. 29	411–413	25
		446–448	25
Filastrius of Brescia, *Diversarum Haeresium Liber*		463–466	26
		Homeric Hymn to Hermes	
74	141	559–562	12

Index of Ancient Texts

Isocrates, *Panegyricus (Or. 4)*
   28–29 — 21 n. 6

Lactantius Placidus, *In Statius Thebais commentum*
   5.347 — 21 n. 6

Lucan, *Pharsalia*
   6.698–700 — 21 n. 6
   6.739–742 — 21 n. 6

Lucius of Patras, *The Ass* — 103

Nicander, *Alexipharmaca*
   129–132 — 21 n. 6

Nicander, *Theriaca*
   483–487 — 21 n. 6

Nonnos, *Dionysiaca*
   6.1–168 — 21 n. 6

Orphic Hymn to Persephone — 21 n. 6

Orphic Hymn to Pluto — 21 n. 6

Orphic Hymn to the Ceralian Mother — 21 n. 6

Orphic Hymn to the Seasons — 21 n. 6

Ovid, *Fasti* — 19–20, 22, 28, 30, 32–33, 36, 60, 153
   1 — 89
   4.445–446 — 28
   4.569–576 — 28
   4.584 — 29
   4.601–604 — 29
   4.607–608 — 26 n. 25, 29
   4.610–614 — 29
   4.614 — 27 n. 25

Ovid, *Metamorphoses* — 19–20, 26, 28, 30, 32–33, 36, 60, 99, 153, 156
   5.530–533 — 27, 28
   5.534–537 — 26, 71 n. 27
   5.537 — 79
   5.434 — 28
   5.438–459 — 28
   5.462–463 — 28
   5.492 — 29
   5.501–508 — 29
   5.564–567 — 27, 152
   5.568–571 — 28
   5.572 — 28 n. 28
   8.616–724 — 23, 29
   8.621–96 — 23 n. 13
   15 — 89

P.Oxy
   471.101 — 136 n. 30

Pamphos, *Hymn to Demeter* — 21 n. 6

Pausanias, *Graeciae descriptio*
   1.38.3 — 21 n. 6
   8.37.9 — 21 n. 6
   9.31.9 — 21 n. 6

Pindar, *Olympionikai*
   1.26–27 — 23 n. 13
   1.95 — 12 n. 29
   13.61–80 — 137 n. 34

Plato, *Laws*
   956a — 136 n. 30

Pliny the Elder, *Natural History*
   11.7 — 85 n. 33
   11.23 — 89

Plutarch, *Amatoriae narrations*
   1 (77d) — 136 n. 30

Plutarch, *Solon*
   89C — 22 n. 11

Pluarch, *Table-Talk*
660b ... 32

Porphyry, *De antro nympharum*
8 ... 89
15–19 ... 12

Praedestinatus, *Praedestinatorum haeresis*
1.28 ... 141 n. 50

Pseudo-Jerome, *Indiculus de Daeresibus*
20 ... 142

Pseudo-Julian, *Letter to Sarapion*
391A-B ... 72

Second Vatican Mythographer
94–100 ... 21 n. 6

Statius, *Achilleid*
1.122–223 ... 12 n. 31
1.169–270 ... 12 n. 31
1.480–481 ... 12 n. 31

Suetonius, *Divus Augustus*
91 ... 137 n. 34

Suetonius, *Galba*
4 ... 137 n. 34

Tertullian, *Against Marcion*
1.14.3 ... 143

Tertullian, *Modesty*
10.12 ... 136 n. 32

Tertullian, *The Crown*
3.3 ... 139, 143

Tertullian, *The Soul*
47.2 ... 133

Vergil, *Aeneid*
6.617–618 ... 123
8.27–68 ... 137

Vergil, *Georgica*
1.39 ... 21 n. 6
4 ... 89

QUR'AN

Hud
11:69–70 ... 10 n. 23

Adh-Dhariyat
51:24–37 ... 10 n. 23

Index of Modern Authors

Ahearne-Kroll, Patricia D.	85, 87	Clements, Ashley	12, 23, 30
Aitken, Ellen	89	Cohen, Shaye J.	83–84
Allegro, John Marco	6	Cohn, Naftali S.	82
Amat, Jacqueline	130, 133, 139	Collins, Adela Yarbro	59, 62, 67–68, 73
Armelagos, George J.	32, 70	Collins, John J.	8, 38–39, 90, 131
Auken, Sune	4–8, 152–53	Crook, Zeba	108–9, 113–15
Aune, David	67–68, 70	D'Arms, John H.	139
Avrahami, Yael	61	Davila, James R.	76, 82
Barnard, L. W.	90	Derrida, Jacques	153
Barnes, Timothy David	131	Desroche, Henri	2
Barrigón Fuentes, M.	118	Dodds, E. R.	104
Barton, Carlin A.	83	Douglas, Mary	32, 70
Battistella, Edwin L.	24	Dulaey, Martine	133–34
Bauckham, Richard	62–63	Ekroth, Gunnel	23
Baynes, Leslie	62	Ellwood, Robert S.	156
Beebee, Thomas O.	39	Fantham, Elaine	26
Belayche, Nicole	120	Faraone, C.	20
Boccaccini, Gabriele	111	Farb, Peter	32, 70
Bohak, Gideon	80	Flannery-Dailey, Frances	9, 42, 46, 137–38
Bonner, C.	20, 23		
Bowersock, Glen Warren	130	Foley, Helene P.	19, 22–25
Boyarin, Daniel	83–84, 111	Formisano, Marco	129–31, 133
Bradley, Keith	102–3, 110, 112–13, 119	Foucault, Michel	156
Bradley, Mark	12	Fowler, Alastair	153
Brandenburger, Egon	46	Fox, Robin Lane	130–31
Bremmer, Jan N.	129–31, 133–35, 137, 146	Frangoulidis, Stavros	103, 106
		Frayn, Joan M.	139
Burchard, Christoph	76–77, 79, 87, 94, 96–97	Fredriksen, Paula	108
		Freeman, Jennifer Awes	136
Burkert, Walter	104, 109	Gaventa, Beverly R.	110–13
Carr, David M.	21, 33	Gill, Glen Robert	156
Carroll, Lewis	151	Ginzberg, Louis	140
Castelli, Elizabeth	132, 148–49	Gollnick, James	104, 106–7, 118
Chesnutt, Randall D.	80, 83, 99	Goodman, David	9, 19
Chouliara-Raïos, H.	85	Goodman, Martin	135

Gowers, Emily	11, 27, 79	McDonald, Lee M.	54
Graf, Fritz	11, 134–35, 165	McGaskil, Grant	135
Graverini, Luca	103, 122	McGowan, Andrew	47, 141–45
Green, Deborah A.	61	Meeks, Wayne A.	84
Hall, Mark Seaborn	62	Metzger, M.	44
Harrison, S. J.	102–3	Milik, J. T.	135
Harvey, Susan Ashbrook	61	Miller, Carolyn R.	4–5, 7, 152
Heffernan, Thomas J.	130, 140, 143	Miller, Patricia Cox	133, 136, 139
Heinrich, Clark	6	Moo, Jonathan A.	40–41
Henshaw, John M.	14	Muir, Steven	14, 71, 85–86
Heyob, Sharon K.	104	Musurillo, Herbert Anthony	138–39, 144
Hicks-Keeton, Jill	84–85, 91		
Hinds, Stephen	22, 26–27	Myers, Jacob M.	36, 39, 56
Hitch, Sarah	11, 24–25, 30–31, 34	Myres, J. L.	20, 23
Hogan, Karina	37–38, 45–50, 53, 55	Najman, Hindy	39, 43, 45, 55, 57
Holwerda, David E.	70	Nasrallah, Laura	149
Horbury, William	89	Neuman (Noy), Dov	156
Horsley, Richard A.	21	Nicklas, Tobias	11, 19, 39
Howes, David	60	Nir, Rivka	76, 81–82, 84, 92
Hubbard, Moyer	89–90	Nock, Arthur Darby	107–10, 112–13
Isambert, F. A.	2	Nongbri, Brent	83
James, William	107–9, 112	North, John A.	121
Jensen, Robin M.	93, 136	Oberhelman, Steven M.	120, 140
Johnson, Mark	86	Oppenheim, A. Leo	137
Johnson, Mark	86	Osmun, George F.	120
Kilgour, Maggie	124, 155	Paget, James Carleton	90
Kindstedt, Paul	153	Parks, Sara	156
Koester, Craig R.	59, 62–64, 68, 70, 72, 74	Perkins, Judith	132, 138, 141
		Pfister, Oskar	2
Korner, Ralph	65	Philonenko, Marc	76–78, 88, 91–92, 97
Korsmeyer, Carolyn	13–16, 31, 55, 70, 154	Poirier, John C.	76, 78–79, 93
		Portier-Young, Anathea E.	85, 89, 91
Kotrosits, Maia	83	Potter, David	23, 31
Kraemer, Ross S.	12, 76–78, 83, 88–94, 96–97	Potts, Charlotte R.	120
		Putthoff, Tyson L.	82, 86–88
Lakoff, George	86	Rabens, Volker	42
Lalonde, M. P.	31, 70	Rajak, Tessa	82
Landau, Brent	41	Reynolds, Benjamin E.	40
Libby, Brigitte B.	121	Richards, Ivor A.	14
Lidonnici, Lynn R.	137	Richardson, Nicholas J.	19, 21, 23, 33–35
Lieber, Andrea Beth	15, 46, 55, 86, 98		
Lipsett, Barbara Diane	99	Richardson, Peter	89
Longenecker, Bruce W.	93	Robert, L.	130
Maier, Harry O.	63	Roddy, Nicolae	1–2
Martin, Luther B.	104	Ruck, Carl A. P.	6

Rudolph, Kelli C.	1, 30, 61
Rüpke, Jörg	6–7
Sanders, Gabriel	136
Scheinberg, Susan	12
Schlam, Carl C.	104
Segal, Alan F.	110–11, 113
Segovia, Carlos A.	111
Sheinfeld, Shayna	53
Shukster, Martin B.	89
Shumate, Nancy	109–10
Smit, Peter-Ben	41, 42, 55
Smith, Christopher R.	62–64
Smith, Dennis E.	31, 70
Smith, Jonathan Z.	83
Smith, Mark M.	19
Solmsen, Friedrich	114–15
Speiser, E. A.	33
Standhartinger, Angela	76–77
Staples, Blaise D.	6
Stone, Michael	37–38, 42, 45–55
Stuckenbruck, Loren T.	40, 45, 49
Sulzbach, Carla	10, 19, 39, 68
Summers, Richard G.	104
Suter, A.	20, 22, 25
Sutton, R.	22
Tappenden, Frederick S.	14, 71, 85–86
Tilford, Nicole L.	61
Tilg, Stefan	103
Tilley, Maureen A.	147, 149
Toner, Jerry	19, 31
Totelin, Laurence	24, 72
Touna, Vaia	83
Van Lieshout, R. G. A.	137
Veenker, Ronald A.	33
Von Albrecht, Michael	122
Vuong, Lily C.	11
Waldner, Katharina	133, 143
Walsh, P.	102
Warren, Meredith J. C.	1, 19, 37, 59, 86, 95, 97–98
Waugh, L. R.	24
Winkler, John J.	117–18, 121, 124–26
Yarbrough, Oliver Larry	93
Yoshiko Reed, Annette	83–84, 135
Zurawski, Jason	54, 56

Index of Terms

Adam and Eve, 32–35, 43, 91–92
ambrosia, 11–14, 23, 25, 35, 87, 123
angels, 9–11, 17, 37, 40, 43–44, 50–51, 56, 59–68, 70, 73–75, 77–79, 83, 94–96, 116, 135–37, 143, 153, 155
    food of, 9–11, 19, 70, 85, 87, 96
apocalypses, 8, 15–16, 37–40, 55–56, 60, 65–66, 71, 73, 131, 153
banquets, 23, 29, 121, 123, 126
baptismal meals, 18, 80–81, 139, 142–46
bees, 3, 77, 78–80, 85, 87–89, 91, 96–97, 99
blood, 63, 79–81, 85, 92, 141–42.
boundaries
    cosmic, 2, 4, 9, 19–21, 33–5, 39, 57, 67–8, 73, 86–7, 129, 152–3, 155
    religious, 18, 84, 146, 153
bread, 29, 70, 77–78, 80–81, 87–88
cheese, 3, 7, 18, 23, 110, 129, 132, 134, 137–49, 154
conversion, 17, 30, 47–48, 51, 75, 80–82, 93, 99–101, 106–15
dreams, 8–9, 15, 42, 46, 49–52, 57, 105, 116, 118–121, 133–140, 146. *See also* visions
    tokens in, 119, 137–38
drinking, 3, 9–10, 12, 25, 34, 41, 44, 53–54, 56, 69, 94–5, 98–9, 120, 123, 139, 142, 144, 151
drunkenness. *See* intoxication
dating. *See* ingestion
Eden, 33–34, 41, 91–92, 136. *See also* paradise
Eucharist, 18, 81–82, 88, 92, 94, 141–45
flavor   1, 13, 70–72, 88, 125, 151

bitter, 1, 13, 17, 59, 64, 67, 69–72, 154
sour, 24
sweet, 1, 11–14, 17–18, 20, 22, 25, 32, 36, 59, 64, 67–72, 79, 87–88, 96, 123, 132, 135, 137, 146, 149, 154
flowers, 17, 41–42, 44–46, 49, 51–52, 57, 91, 101, 103, 105, 107, 115–16, 119–24, 126, 135–37
fruit, 135
    of the tree of knowledge, 33–34, 91
    of the tree of life, 34, 136
    pomegranate, 23, 26–7, 34
garden, 26–27, 33, 79, 91, 121, 132, 135–36, 140–41, 149. *See also* Eden
genre, 3–8, 13–16, 18, 20, 35, 37–39, 56–57, 59, 67, 69, 71, 73, 91, 99–103, 110, 115, 119, 123–27, 131, 145, 152–53, 155–57
Hades (place), 3, 16, 20–22, 24–29, 30–32, 35–6, 60, 99, 123, 129
Hades (god), 20–26, 28, 30–31, 35–36, 79
heaven, 2–3, 6, 8–11, 17–19, 27–30, 34–37, 39–41, 43–50, 54–58, 60–63, 65–71, 74–75, 77, 79–80, 85–88, 90–92, 95–99, 116, 127, 132, 134–38, 141, 145–47, 149, 154–55. *See also* paradise
hierophagy, 1–4, 6–11, 13–22, 29, 31–39, 48, 52–54, 56–61, 65, 67–69, 71–75, 77, 82, 85–86, 91–93, 98–101, 104–7, 110, 115–18, 121–27, 129, 131–37, 145, 147, 149, 151–57
honey, 3, 7, 11–13, 17, 22, 24–25, 32, 59, 68, 72, 75–82, 85–100, 110, 116, 142–43, 145, 154

Index of Terms

initiation, 3, 17, 31, 80, 83, 101, 104–7, 110–13, 116–18, 126, 146. *See also* baptism
ingestion (consumption, eat), 1–4, 6, 8–17, 19–28, 30–43, 45–46, 49, 51–52, 54–65, 67–75, 79–80, 82, 85–88, 90–96, 98, 101, 105, 107, 110, 115–16, 120–26, 129, 132, 138–39, 144–47, 151–52, 154–56
intoxication, 54
Isis, 3, 17, 101–7, 109–10, 112–24, 126–27
knowledge, transmission of, 3, 14, 16–18, 33–35, 37, 46, 48, 55–57, 59–61, 64, 67, 69, 71–74, 75–76, 84–86, 88, 90, 100, 107, 125, 127, 129, 133–34, 138, 147–49, 152
life, the universe, and everything, 117
lips, 27, 30, 79
milk, 90, 132, 137–46, 148
mortals, 2, 9–12, 14, 17, 19, 21, 23, 34–36, 39, 45–46, 49, 52, 55–58, 65, 67–69, 70–71, 73, 86–87, 101, 116, 118–19, 123, 133–34, 153, 155
mouth, 1, 10, 12–13, 18, 25–27, 30, 52–53, 55, 59, 68–69, 71–72, 78–80, 91, 95–96, 124, 132, 137, 139, 146–47, 154–55
nectar, 11–12, 14, 25, 87, 89
paradise, 33, 35, 41, 77, 91–92, 95, 135–36
Persephone/Proserpina, 3, 16–18, 19–37, 60, 70–71, 73, 99, 110, 116, 129, 147, 152, 154–56
scent, 30, 66, 87, 120, 123–24, 135
scroll, 3, 7, 12, 13, 17, 59–65, 67–74, 120, 154
senses and sensory analysis, 11–16, 30–32, 36, 41, 46, 52, 55, 57, 60–61, 65–66, 70–73, 123–26, 154–55
sex, 20–22, 27, 29, 31–33, 155
sight, 15–16, 31, 52, 55
soul, 49, 51, 89, 108, 133, 146–47
stomach, 17, 32, 59, 64, 67–68, 71
synaesthesia, 34
taste, 1, 6, 11–20, 22, 24–25, 27, 29–33, 34–36, 44, 55, 57, 59, 61, 64, 67, 70–75, 79, 88, 96, 124–26, 130, 132, 137, 143, 146–47, 149, 151, 153–54
toast, hot buttered, 151
tongue, 27, 30, 67, 79, 125
torah, 3, 15, 53
transformation, 1–4, 7–8, 10, 14, 17–18, 23, 26, 28, 30–31, 34, 36–38, 45–52, 56–57, 60–61, 67, 69–70, 73–75, 77, 79–81, 84–86, 88–91, 97–101, 104–13, 115–27, 129, 132, 144–47, 149–50, 153–54, 156
tree of knowledge, 14, 33–34
tree of life, 33–34, 136
underworld. *See* Hades (place)
visions, 3, 8–10, 12–13, 15, 18, 42, 45–52, 56–58, 61–62, 64–65, 68, 71–74, 105, 118–20, 131–38, 140–41, 143–49. *See also* dreams
wisdom, 14, 17, 37, 39, 41, 48, 51–54, 56, 69, 85–86, 88, 91. *See also* knowledge

www.ingramcontent.com/pod-product-compliance
Lightning Source LLC
Chambersburg PA
CBHW021857230426
43671CB00006B/423